A Fearsome Heritage

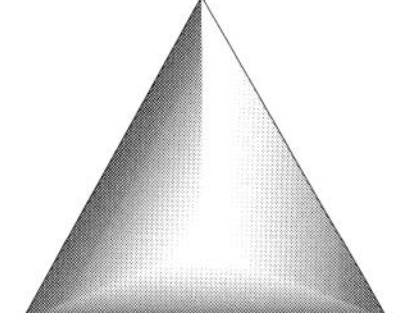

One World Archaeology Series

Sponsored by the World Archaeological Congress

Series Editors: Joan Gero, Mark Leone, and Robin Torrence

One World Archaeology volumes contain carefully edited selections of the exemplary papers presented at the World Archaeology Congress (WAC), held every four years, and intercongress meetings. The subject matter of this series is wide-ranging, reflecting the diverse interests of WAC. WAC gives place to considerations of power and politics in framing archaeological questions and results. The organization also gives place and privilege to minorities who have often been silenced or regarded as beyond capable of making main line contributions to the field. All royalties from the series are used to help the wider work of WAC, including providing the means for less advantaged colleagues to attend WAC conferences, thereby enabling them to contribute to the development of the academic debate surrounding the study of the past. Beginning with volume 48, the One World Archaeology series will be published by Left Coast Press, Inc.

51 Rethinking Agriculture, Timothy P. Denham, José Iriarte, Luc Vrydaghs (eds.)
50 A Fearsome Heritage, John Schofield and Wayne Cocroft (eds.)
49 Archaeology to Delight and Instruct, Heather Burke and Claire Smith (eds.)
48 African Re-Genesis, Jay B. Haviser and Kevin C. MacDonald (eds.)

Previous volumes in this series, available from Routledge:

47 Indigenous Archaeologies
46 Archaeologies of the British
45 Natural Disasters and Cultural Change
44 Matériel Culture
43 The Dead and Their Possessions
42 Illicit Antiquities
41 Destruction and Conservation of Cultural Property
40 Madness, Disability & Social Exclusion
39 The Archaeology of Dry Lands
38 The Archaeology of Difference
37 Time and Archaeology
36 The Constructed Past
35 Archaeology and Language IV
34 Archaeology and Language III
33 Cultural Resource Management in Contemporary Society
32 Prehistory of Food
31 Historical Archaeology
30 The Archaeology and Anthropology of Landscape
29 Archaeology and Language II
28 Early Human Behaviour in the Global Context
27 Archaeology and Language I
26 Time, Process and Structured Transformation in Archaeology
25 The Presented Past
24 Social Construction of the Past
23 Sacred Sites, Sacred Places
22 Tropical Archaeobotany
21 Archaeology and the Information Age
20 The Archaeology of Africa
19 Origins of Human Behaviour
18 From the Baltic to the Black Sea
17 The Excluded Past
16 Signifying Animals
15 Hunters of the Recent Past
14 What's New?
13 Foraging and Farming
12 The Politics of the Past
11 Centre and Periphery
10 Archaeological Approaches to Cultural Identity
9 Archaeological Heritage Management in the Modern World
8 Conflict in the Archaeology of Living Traditions
7 Animals into Art
6 The Meaning of Things
5 Who Needs the Past?
4 State and Society
3 Domination and Resistance
2 The Walking Larder
1 What is an Animal?

A Fearsome Heritage

Diverse Legacies of The Cold War

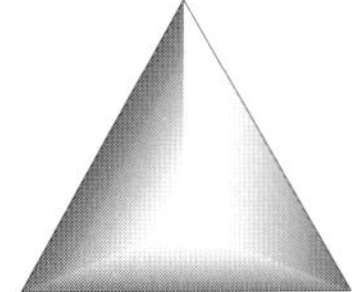

John Schofield
Wayne Cocroft
editors

Walnut Creek, California

LEFT COAST PRESS, INC.
1630 North Main Street, #400
Walnut Creek, CA 94596
http://www.LCoastPress.com

Library of Congress Cataloging-in-Publication Data

Schofield, A. J.
A fearsome heritage : diverse legacies of the Cold War / edited by John Schofield and Wayne Cocroft.
p. cm. — (Publications of the Institute of Archaeology , University College London)
Includes bibliographical references and index.
ISBN-13: 978-1-59874-258-9 (hbk. : alk. paper)
Cold War. 2. Cultural property. 3. Historic preservation. 4. Civilization, Modern—1950- I. Cocroft, Wayne . II. Title.
D843.S327 2007
909.82'5—dc22

2007002304

Editoral Production: Last Word Editorial Services
Typesetting: ibid, northwest

Printed in the United States of America

The paper used in this publication meets the minimum requirements of American National Standard for Information Sciences—Permanence of Paper for Printed Library Materials, ANSI/NISO Z39.48–1992.

07 08 09 5 4 3 2 1

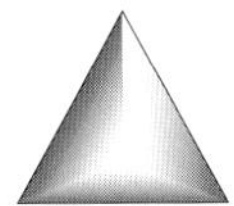

CONTENTS

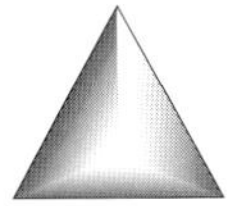

ILLUSTRATIONS

FIGURES

Front cover Photo of a nuclear missile detonated over the Pacific Ocean in the 1962 Frigate Bird test, taken through a periscope.

TABLES

Introduction: Cold War, diversity and contemporary archaeology

JOHN SCHOFIELD and WAYNE COCROFT

This book provides a critical assessment of the places, events, people and things that together constitute the contemporary archaeology of the Cold War era. This was a period – roughly 1946–89 – materially represented by unprecedented developments in weapons technology accompanied by a massive military construction effort. Geopolitical tensions were a defining characteristic, and the Cold War stand-off imposed an apparently permanent global division between communism and capitalism. This is exclusively northern-hemisphere heritage in a way, even though the influence of the Cold War was transglobal, as seen for example in trade networks and the participation in (or boycott of) cultural events – the less tangible legacies of the Cold War era, but a significant dimension nevertheless and one this volume also seeks to address. Here the archaeological record is thus unfiltered by time, or the biases of preservation and social intervention; the archaeological record is essentially complete and wholly representative of the historic era now known as the Cold War.

This collection of essays and images has a wider point to make about the archaeological record, and about heritage in general: that we don't simply inherit from the past, but rather actively engage with it – creating new archaeological sites and assemblages, altering those that existed previously and reinterpreting the whole in new and previously unforeseen ways. The work of contemporary artists is therefore included in this collection, being themselves interpretations of Cold War material culture, but also (now, after the event) archaeological sites or interventions in their own right (Schofield 2006). These artistic works include film, video and music, as well as recognising archaeological field survey as performance. But is this archaeology? Colin Renfrew believes so. He explains:

> The world of the visual arts today is made up of tens of thousands of individuals, most of them doing their own thing. Among them are creative thinkers and workers who are nibbling away all the time at what we think we know about the world, at our assumptions, at our preconceptions. Moreover, the insights that [artists] offer are not in the form of words, of long and heavy texts. They come to us through the eyes, and sometimes the other senses, offering us direct perceptions from which we may sometimes come to share their insights. The visual explorations ... offer a fundamental resource for anyone who wants to make ... sense of the world. ... It is not that this resource offers new answers, or that it will directly tell us how we should understand the world. On the contrary, it offers us new, often paradoxical experiences, which show us how we have understood, or only imperfectly mastered, what we think we know. (2003, 7–8)

It is hard to be certain now, but the idea for this book probably has its origin in meetings and discussions between us and two of these artists – Louise K Wilson and Angus Boulton – separately, some time after the millennium. In these discussions it first became obvious to us that Cold War material culture was of interest in many ways to a wide and diverse group, from archaeologists to artists, and from historians and sociologists to politicians. We were all interested in it for different reasons, but ultimately for the same reason – that these material remains tell us about the world we know, and that by understanding its material remains we can begin to question the familiar world around us. From the point that we realised this, and began to seek out further studies of Cold War material culture, the conference session from which this book derives became inevitable. Graham Fairclough's chapter refers to the political context surrounding the World Archaeological Congress (WAC) at Washington DC, in summer 2003, causing some participants to withdraw in opposition to the USA's involvement in Iraq. The fact that our session was in Washington at this time (and that we then organised a Cold War round table in St Petersburg later the same year) seemed fitting. All of the participants made their own decisions on whether or not to attend WAC, and for us at least, the decision to attend and debate military heritage and material culture at a time of political unease and uncertainty was preferred. War and heritage in fact became a major theme of the congress, with other sessions and contributions. But ours was perhaps the most diverse and the least archaeological – in the conventional sense – of them all. Our session 'briefing' made this point, and part of it is repeated here:

> Following the end of World War II came the Cold War, in which the conflicting ideologies of East and West led to escalations in the

> arms race, and increased militarisation around the globe. In the years 1946–89 this was a world in which the three minute warning was a constant threat and the shadow of the mushroom cloud an enduring image.
>
> At WAC4 in 1999 a session on modern military remains described some of this legacy [now published as Schofield et al. 2002]: nuclear test sites in the Nevada Desert and giant radar installations in Alaska. But the legacies of the Cold War went far beyond military installations, embracing or influencing many aspects of popular culture, science and technology, architecture, landscape and people's perceptions of the world; of their locality (where they lived close to military installations) and of the future. Many of course believed there would be no future, a belief that grew at times of international crisis.

The conference session, and now the book, sought to document and deconstruct these diverse interests, taking material culture in its broadest sense, and exploring the ownership and relevance of the past to a range of communities and interest groups. The biologist EO Wilson has made a strong case for the unity of intellectual disciplines in his book *Consilience* (1998), and we concur with this vision for the academy. Like the session before it, this book crosses many borders (intellectual, ideological and geographical), including for example: peoples displaced by the location of nuclear testing grounds (described in the chapters by Smith and by Beck, Drollinger and Schofield); the difficulty of treating Cold War sites as cultural heritage (Beazley), the inspiration for artists and musicians of the events or architecture of the Cold War (Boulton, Wilson, Kyriakides, Watson); the role of museum curators (Vining, Hacker) and those charged with finding a new use for what are often massive and functional remains (Fiorato); and finally the role of archaeologists (Gorman and O'Leary, Cocroft), anthropologists (Buchli), conservation bodies (Feversham and Schmidt) and cultural historians (Steingrover) in documenting and interpreting the Cold War's material remains. And these material remains are extraordinary in their diversity: domestic appliances, satellites, films and photographs, missiles and their shelters, parts of nuclear submarines, military uniforms and the subtle traces of the Berlin Wall, being the 'first generation' material record – objects *of* the Cold War; a 'second generation' being those artistic projects and installations influenced by the Cold War but which postdate its closure.

The point of film is worth elaborating upon here, as it reflects the wider point of the volume, not as a conventional archaeology of an historic period, but one that draws out the wider influences of a range of practitioners who share the ambition of documenting and interpreting – and in some cases deconstructing and reassembling – past events. Reinhild

Steingröver documents East German filmmaking at the time of the Change, c.1989–90. While her contribution stands in part as literary critique it also provides an unique contribution to this volume, emphasising how the contemporary past can be studied in a multitude of different ways, given the diversity of sources and material cultures available for research. The films are archives, documents – even artefacts – and we as archaeologists can examine these, just as we can early photographs, paintings and representations. But in constructing an archaeology of the contemporary past we also recognise that specific pieces of research are best conducted by those most familiar with the materials and the methodologies best suited to their examination. Hence the inclusion of Steingrover's contribution alongside those of artists and composers.

After Graham Fairclough's introduction, the book explores this diversity through examples that are indicative of a wide field of research, being projects known to us prior to or immediately after WAC 2003. The book is strongly visual, deliberately so to emphasise the strength and symbolism of the visual image. In Wilson's, and particularly Boulton's and Watson's chapters, the focus is the photographic essays each has provided. In the case of Kyriakides' contribution, musical compositions are described, with links to a specially commissioned web page where these sounds of the Cold War can be heard. Heritage management is a recurring theme: Cocroft and Fiorato, for example, discuss the approach taken to managing Cold War sites in England, while Beazley, Gorman and O'Leary, and Feversham and Schmidt all raise issues concerning World Heritage Site status.

A Fearsome Heritage examines what archaeology can contribute to understanding the Cold War and all that it entailed. By exploring diversity in this way we use archaeology in its broadest sense to demonstrate the strong influence of the Cold War on modern culture and on perceptions of the world in which we live – a kind of critique on modern life at a time when a return to arms looks increasingly likely.

+++

We are grateful to all of our participants and contributors for their enthusiasm for this project, and for their support in helping us bring it to publication. It has been a particular pleasure to work with those from other disciplines less familiar to us, and whose rather different take on the subject has been both stimulating and refreshing. We are grateful also to staff at Left Coast Press, and in particular to Jennifer Collier and Ginny Hoffman, for their assistance and support, and to English Heritage for supporting this project and our participation in the conference from which this book derives. English Heritage also provided a financial contribution to Left Coast Press, allowing the inclusion of more colour imagery than would otherwise have been possible. Finally, we are indebted to Mark Leone and another anonymous referee for their advice and assistance in producing the final manuscript. Other acknowledgements are included in the individual chapters of the book.

REFERENCES

Renfrew, C (2003) *Figuring It Out: The Parallel Visions of Artists and Archaeologists*, London: Thames and Hudson

Schofield, J (2006) *Constructing Place: When Artists and Archaeologists Meet*, eBook published at http://diffusion.org.uk/#SERIES

Schofield, J, Beck, CM and Johnson, WG (eds) (2002) *Matériel Culture: The Archaeology of Twentieth Century Conflict*, London: Routledge

Wilson, EO (1998) *Consilience: The Unity of Knowledge*, London: Little, Brown and Company

The Cold War in context: Archaeological explorations of private, public and political complexity

GRAHAM FAIRCLOUGH

INTRODUCTION: A NEW CONTEXT FOR ARCHAEOLOGY

Not behind us – past in the present

Archaeology is a discipline that invites, and perhaps requires, constant critical review. In particular, review is needed of the assumptions that we make about our relationship with the past and how we use material remains to create present-day perceptions and understanding. This is relatively widely accepted for the study of prehistoric periods and of indigenous cultures, but it is equally true when dealing with apparently familiar and thus seemingly straightforward topics such as the Cold War. Many of the issues raised in this chapter are not exclusive to the Cold War, and are applicable to our contact with any periods of the past, yet they can be argued to be particularly relevant to the archaeology of the Cold War (and other recent conflicts). The Cold War provides a particularly valuable and relevant arena for reflexive analysis. This is partly because its study so readily transcends the disciplinary barriers between archaeologists, historians, anthropologists, artists and writers (among others), but mainly because it is such a recent past.

This chapter, therefore, preceding the more detailed sections of the book, looks critically at some of the assumptions and presumptions that can arise when considering Cold War material remains from a heritage perspective. It began as the outline for a paper that was intended to be delivered at World Archaeological Congress 2003 in Washington DC, but which was not delivered because of a personal decision not to attend so soon after the invasion of Iraq. A modified version was subsequently presented at European Archaeological Association 2003 in St Petersburg, the 'northern capital' of a country whose own military conflicts are concealed beneath a cloak of silence. The paper's 'prehistory' is mentioned here simply to show how events in the world even during its preparation seem to have underlined its central thesis: that the closeness of the Cold War to current politics makes this a very problematic area to deal with. The problems can be compounded if too innocent a view is taken of the Cold War legacy, material or otherwise.

Going back further, the stimulus for this chapter came from a peripheral involvement in the Cold War research that English Heritage carried out during the 1990s, leaving this author with anxieties that he could not fully define (and still cannot). The early 1990s had seen a great deal of work on the material legacy of the Second World War, and extending this work into the postwar period was an unproblematic, obvious, natural and necessary step. Both programmes of research took over approaches and methods that had been developed for studying and managing the legacy of more distant periods with their different problems and attributes, a normal process that was seen throughout the 20th century as archaeology moved into new periods (compare with medieval, postmedieval and 'industrial' archaeology). For a very recent period still in living memory, still undigested so to speak, such methodological borrowings seem to call for more conscious analysis to reflect some of the period's unique characteristics: the apparent obviousness of the material remains that seem to need no interpretation, the more than usually extensive survival of ephemeral and transient structures, the scale of survival (and level of condition) generally, the close proximity of the period (with all that implies for detachment or engagement) or the multiplicity of both traditional and new sources of 'evidence'.

As an introduction to the rest of the book, therefore, this chapter reminds us that while we may think we know all about this recent and still well-remembered period, its interpretation is not so clear-cut. It is far more complex, more questionable and more unknown than we sometimes care to admit. The 'knowledge' we think we have can be a minefield for those encountering it, trapping the unwary into simplified or unwarranted interpretation. The things that the botanist Oliver Rackham has called 'factoids' – well-accepted assumptions that do not stand many tests but which are often comforting – come to mind, along with his contention that (in his case, within the field of landscape studies) everything is 'always older than you think' which is equivalent to acknowledging that material culture is always more complex than we think (just as the fabric of any building of any age will have a more complex story to tell than may be imagined). In the same way, everything in heritage is always more debatable and arguable than you think, and this applies most dramatically to recent, still very freshly contested heritage. The very recent past and its legacy is not merely the latest 'layer' but is also the still-forming transition from the past to the future; it differs in kind as well as degree simply by being so recent – it is the 'contemporary past', and it is still forming our future by guiding our thoughts about the world. So it is an important study to 'get right'. Much of what this chapter says may seem self-evident to readers, but it is always worth turning over a few stones to reflect on our starting point.

Coming to terms with a remembered past

The archaeological study of recent periods is worthy of pursuit for its own sake. Archaeology knows no chronological boundaries (although there is a certain unease in moving into this most recent period, since archaeology tends to focus first on military, or at least monumental, hardware). It may also know no geographical boundaries, but there is debate here about intellectual imperialism and whether archaeology is principally a 'western' way of looking at the past. This also makes the Cold War a good laboratory because it is often claimed to be one of the few truly global topics. As well as needing study for its own sake, our work on the Cold War has the added advantage of encouraging and facilitating a reflexive approach to the discipline's principles and methods, and to its 'taken-for-granteds'. The Cold War raises very strong issues of source criticism, of the relationships between material culture, contemporary documents and living memory (for example), and of accommodating multiple voices. It also acutely raises issues of how far a single past is knowable, or whether we should merely define conflicting views and perspectives. There are difficulties inherent (because of its recent-ness) in doing so, but should we attribute heritage value now rather than in 30 years' time; and if so, how? Do we choose to privilege some 'monuments' over others for passing on to our successors? We like to think that we have inherited a 'natural' selection from distant periods of prehistory or the middle ages, whereas we inherit only those sites that are naturally durable (that is, are nonephemeral on some time scale), or those whose value (mundane or spiritual) has continued and ensured survival, or those that were overlooked in marginal, unused areas. The Cold War (and all late 20th-century heritage, a position recently put forward in a manifesto about historic landscape character of the period 1950–2000 called 'Change and Creation' – www.changeandcreation.org) opens new lines of questioning, but these can be applied to earlier periods, too: can we choose to be conscious agents of the process of selection and survival? Has past selection been less natural than we think?

A further consideration is that the wealth of data and its proximity to living memory can mislead us into thinking that everything is known, and this trap for the unwary is a major theme of this short essay. It is often said that theory is what archaeologists do when faced with a lack of data; yet theory – the unpacking of assumptions and the transformation of innocence into wisdom, the critical approach to data whether documentary, oral or material – is even more essential in recent periods of archaeology with their surfeit of evidence.

Part of the attraction of the archaeological study of the recent and contemporary past is that it can act as a laboratory for methodological and conceptual testing, especially in the field of archaeological resource (or heritage) management, whose results can be of wider applicability in more distant periods as well. The proximity of the Cold War period, which brings clarity and access to unparalleled data of various types, also brings a more visible and tangible sense of multilocality and of conflicting interpretation; working in such conditions can force us to test assumptions about data and its use that would in earlier periods be taken uncritically as givens. The stakes are higher, too, because the contemporary past often matters more in terms of current views of identity, being and motivation.

The Cold War's significance and interpretation continues to change with every passing year. New official records are found or released, and in the United Kingdom (UK), for example, the new Freedom of Information Act may lead to more new evidence. More fundamentally, the importance that people attach to the Cold War continually changes. As it starts to be perceived as being more distant, a more finished (and closed) episode of history, the seemingly instinctive human desire to find interpretative closure begins to take effect. Should archaeology facilitate that closure or challenge it?

At the same time, still-unfolding world events cause people to reexamine interpretations; in other words, memory is modified by hindsight. Responses to the Cold War, as any recent still-relevant events, are constantly recalibrated in light of what has happened since. This is perhaps nothing more than the result of the period's close proximity to us, but it is nevertheless an important aspect. Writing an essay like this so soon after the events it considers means that the ideas in it can change even between first thoughts and final draft. Have events in New York, Afghanistan or Iraq given us a new perspective on the national and international politics behind the Cold War?

The way that people are starting to change their views about only slightly less recent events surely encourages us to reflect on how long our certainties about the Cold War will last – the Second World War, for example, is from a United Kingdom perspective seen as spanning the years 1939–45, but perhaps 1936 and 1949 are also valid starting and ending dates for the interlocking conflicts. The final version of this essay was being written, for example, in the weeks after the Indian Ocean tsunami and the Iraqi elections, a period which invites us to revise some of the assumptions we have about the global interaction between countries and polities, and thus to a degree some of the ways we thought these global patterns had formed during the Cold War. As other events occur, however (the so-called 'War on Terrorism', for example), their relationship to the 'Cold War' may oblige us to review what we 'know' about recent history and to question the neatness of our categories.

THE MINEFIELDS OF KNOWING

The Cold War appears to be extraordinarily well documented. A subset of the documentary evidence (mainly about politics) might still be sealed in state archives, but it is there waiting. The material remains of the period's military aspects (and there is a temptation to see the Cold War almost purely in military terms, so these remains can loom large) also seem to survive completely. They don't of course; most are shells or skeletons devoid of the people, activities, equipment, hardware, software and so forth that made them function. But they have a real presence and seem to tell their story with little interrogation, almost symbolically. Such simple concrete structures seem to invite simple concrete explanation; we normally reject now purely military technological interpretation of medieval castles, so why be less sophisticated when we explain 20th-century missile silos? One interpretation of the Greenham cruise missile shelters is that they were intended to make the missiles visible. They could have been hidden, or kept in submarines: their physical display was a conscious political decision, their visibility intended to win supporters and to frighten enemies; one consequence seems to have been to prompt the USSR to maintain ruinous levels of expenditure.

The English Heritage ARM-linked archaeological study of the Cold War decades was a step into new territory, especially as it involved dealing with structures as recent as the 1980s, or even the 1990s. In some respects, the period presents itself to us almost as prehistoric periods do, or more accurately, perhaps, as a period with many ahistoric characteristics. Despite being so thoroughly documented, it is still a period that requires us to 'hear' the material culture as well as (and sometimes instead of) reading what people chose to write at the time. Not everything that happened in the period was recorded in writing, and much of the documentation shows little neutrality of record.

While documents of any period require careful source criticism when used to write history, it must be especially true of a period that is almost characterised by duplicity. Obfuscation, disinformation and propaganda were the hallmarks of the Cold War in many eyes; despite the heaps of newspapers and the reports of lengthy government inquiries, recent events surrounding decisions about the Iraq invasion remind us of this. Not all documentary evidence from the Cold War is yet fully available for security reasons. Even if it were all available, it would provide a very specific perspective. Not all aspects of the Cold War were documented as fully as its military aspects. 'Public' documents tend to be political and military. They more rarely cover social, personal or other perspectives. Their motivation has to be questioned. What they do not say needs to be considered as much as what they do say. The Cold War was not only 'cold' but secret or at least veiled – most documents, especially those in the media, can (not wholly inaccurately) be portrayed as propaganda. This does not render them useless – far from it, but the use to which they are put needs to be adjusted accordingly. Source criticism becomes even more essential. Furthermore, the situation may be different if it is not seen from a comfortable armchair in the UK. The Cold War was global, but not all its participants were willing, and not all involved governments have the same approach to openness and democracy: the extent to which the Cold War is documented worldwide varies enormously.

What the Cold War means to a military historian is likely to be very different from what it means to a social historian, or to a conformist citizen or a nonconformist peace protester. The Cold War as an episode never enjoyed a single narrative, and some of its narrative strands do not have a 'history' in the sense of history drawn from studying documents; many of them, however, stories of other sorts, can be approached through disciplines such as archaeology, anthropology and sociology, and through the media of the visual and performing arts.

Multivocality, of course, applies to analysis of all periods of the past, but it is simply more obvious and more unavoidable in recent periods. For a subject such as the Cold War, where the character of its remains – military, technological, 'hard' – can easily without care and conscious correction or calibration lead to simplistic and deterministic interpretations. The simultaneous existence of evidence that is ahistorical (through material culture, memory and oral traditions) and historic (through documents) is not new; they have coexisted, in Britain alone, to varying degrees for the past 2,000 years. These are not new problems that arise from the Cold War, but they arise far more prominently, more consistently, more fundamentally and more challengingly (that is, more unavoidably and yet seemingly avoided) in such a recent and problematic period. Their visibility in this period, however, is a useful reminder to look for them in studying more distant periods, when they may not attract our attention as readily.

People know about or even remember the period because they lived through it or their parents told them about it, or they have seen TV programmes about it. It therefore has a strong (if partly false) solidity and vividness for people. We have the newspapers in our archives to tell us quite clearly what happened. If it's in the newspaper it must be true. What else can archaeology add? This is no more than the familiar conundrum of any period of historical archaeology, but it is writ large in the Cold War, and its repudiation is not complicated.

A couple of more fundamental but simple points can also be mentioned. There is the issue of 'contemporary distance'. How much people knew at the time (and about what and through what mediation), affects both oral and documentary history, and affects the survival and treatment of material culture from the period. The secrecy, propaganda, filters and omissions that were characteristic of the Cold War on all sides influenced the manner of reporting and documenting at the time (and its material equivalence, the closure to study, until recently, of military sites). Further, there is the question of 'subsequent readjustment', the revising of personal history, the changes to memory, but more important the way that memory is continually contextualised and explained in light of new knowledge and different perspectives, referring here as much to oral memory as to the interpretations of historians or archaeologists. New events – the 'War on Terror' – create new perspectives, themselves mediated in perhaps unrecognised ways.

A further repudiation of the suggestion that we know all about the Cold War is the diversity of situations across the world. The relationships between the United States of America (USA) and its clients, and that between the Union of Soviet Socialist Republics (USSR) and its clients were very different. Different levels of trust, cooperation and openness, for example, are evident, both across the East/West divide and also within the blocs. The material evidence gives some examples, such as how the control and storage of nuclear warheads in East Germany and in the UK and West Germany were different – under separate Soviet control in the east, even though the delivery vehicles (planes or missiles) were maintained by the East German armed forces, but delegated with varying degrees of completeness to 'home' forces in the UK and West Germany (as Wayne Cocroft's comparisons show us in Chapter 7). These different levels of trust and collaboration also affect documentary evidence. A study of the Cold War drawing on, for example, French archives would present another very different view, as would the archives of Warsaw Pact countries, for whom, for example, it may be that their subservience to the USSR weighs larger in interpretation than the Cold War against the West.

The simple dichotomy of East and West itself calls out for more sophisticated challenge and this is unlikely to happen through documentary history, since by and large the documentary evidence is produced by the leaders of the two blocs and by internal conformity. It is the archaeological interpretation of material culture that can open new interpretations. Cold War material culture was not only very different between the western and eastern parts of Germany, but it must also have been very different between eastern Germany and Poland or the Czech Republic, just as the experiences of living through it were very different. Even at the local level there are differences, for example between the regions of the UK which contained USA bases and those that did not. There is also another important aspect of Cold War material culture, albeit with the difficulty that all negative evidence presents: what things were not built, made or created because so much state expenditure went to military uses? Furthermore, nonaligned countries have material remains of the period that directly or indirectly refer to the Cold War paradigm: the concrete defences/monitoring posts along the Swedish Baltic coast, for example, or Switzerland's domestic nuclear bunkers, some now used to house the washing machines. To understand the Cold War, it needs to be contextualised into a wider social and political framework which also has its material culture, even if little has yet been studied by archaeologists.

SHELTERING AGAINST COMPLEXITY?

Is there a case to argue against seeking interpretative closure as a deliberate strategy? Archaeologists and historians traditionally pursue some ever-more-correct truth about what happened in the past. It should be salutary that even for, say, the two World Wars, let alone for the 19th century (British imperialism, for example), history is never finished. There are always revisions and readjustments, made as often in the light of contemporary perspectives of the world as of new documentary evidence. The twists and turns throughout the 20th century in how British archaeologists interpreted their country's Roman centuries is a good lesson from an earlier period. Why should we think we can assume that we know all about the Cold War?

For very recent periods such as this, it is certainly too soon to seek any final interpretation because of proximity and lack of objective distance; perhaps not desirable because the memory and lessons, not to mention the consequences, of the Cold War are still changing; and perhaps not possible because we cannot distil its complexity. The Cold War was by definition highly controversial in the past, and its particular past is still all too present. It is perhaps better to avoid interpretative closure even if it appears possible. Uncertainty and conflict are characteristic of the Cold War, and perhaps these should be the traits of its archaeology, being a filter through which we view and use this contemporary past. There is a real risk that closure will oversimplify and in the process understanding will be lost along with complexity.

There is another area of risk for Cold War studies, deriving partly from their origin in military archaeology and history, and partly from the sheer 'presence', character and legibility of its material remains, which is such a strong incitement to simple interpretation. This is the risk that the technicalities of the subject – the typology of rocketry and nuclear shelters, the classification of concrete, for example – can divert us from wider meaning and symbolism. Focussing on the hardened shelters of USAF Upper Heyford (Oxfordshire), or the hangars at RAF Scampton (Lincolnshire), could prevent us seeing the whole base; more importantly, focus on the air base will disguise the impact of the base on the wider landscape, material and cultural, in which it sits. The seductive interest of concrete should not hide wider significances; what it tells us about the Cold War cannot be assumed to be obvious or unarguable.

By landscape in this context we should mean a wide range of different things – a landscape of culture, such as the diffusion into the surrounding villages and towns of East Anglia (UK) of US lifestyles, from cars to fast food and beyond; a landscape of politics, of acceptance and conformity as much as of protest and dissidence; a landscape of vision, sound and experience, such as when aircraft roar in and out; a landscape of psychology, whether fear or security (there are children in Hatfield, UK, who remember their teachers anxiously rushing them indoors when Second World War vintage aircraft flew overhead on the way to bomb the film set for *Saving Private Ryan*, long after the Cold War's end), and, beyond that, how the massive bases made people think of distant landscapes, cultures and people at whom they were aimed.

Again, this is a UK perspective; one assumes that the equivalent Polish (for example) social and cultural response to Soviet bases was sometimes different, whilst nonaligned countries offer still other insights. A colleague from Finland, for example, on visiting a small town in post-Soviet Latvia, recognised the place name from TV news in the 70s and 80s: 'So this is what it looks like, where the missiles aimed at my home were kept'. Thus, a new geography of foreign places emerges. There are landscapes of identity, too. How far (and for whom) was being 'British' (or Belgian, or Hungarian) in the 1980s shaped by the existence of 'British' nuclear capacity and the 'special relationship' with the US? This takes physical form in a wider interpretation of the term 'Cold War heritage', an area that largely requires archaeologists and anthropologists to handle it.

Taking a look, for example, at Greenham Common (see Chapter 8) and its material culture and memories can illuminate some of these issues, drawing attention to the complexity of the situation and to some of its many actors and participants, not all of whom have equal (or any) presence in the documentary record. The Greenham protests were not a simple standoff between the state (the military) and the peace movement. The 'state' was multiple – army, police, politicians – and (especially the latter) divided; it also represented two polities, the USA and the UK.

The Greenham peace movement included both those on the ground and those supporting; the peace camps ultimately became women-only, but this was not at first inevitable. Having taken that route, not only the rhetoric but the material culture of the camps was altered. But even amongst the peace women, there were shades of politics, policy and practice which are by no means all captured in the books written after the event by a few of the women; some women were more or less permanent residents, while others were just visitors – visitors from all regions of the UK and from most social groups. Each gate's colour-coded camps had a distinct agenda. They didn't always agree. Just as there were tabloid scare stories (or jokes – who could tell?) that the Greenham women included undercover *spesnatz* forces (Soviet special forces), so some women accused others of being CIA plants. Complexity abounded. Greenham for many was not only about peace, but about the wider antinuclear campaign, and for many to various degrees it was a feminist, antipatriarchal campaign – the slogans 'take the toys from the boys' and 'no to nuclear' had a second, family-linked meaning.

Residents of Greenham Common often sided with the authorities, not necessarily in support of military policy but because they objected to the presence and goals of the peace camp inhabitants on a range of political grounds, from gender to political outlook to lifestyle, that were not necessarily connected at all to Cruise missiles. After all, they had lived next to the base, in its successive incarnations, all their lives. Opposition to the peace camp among this group did not necessarily mean that they supported the government's nuclear policies, of course: the mixture of motives and opinions was far more complex. Some of the conflict continued after the base was abandoned, and carried on, transmuted, into the debate about the site's future – housing, industrial park, monument, nature reserve. It still remained a contested place after Cruise left. Greenham – at its widest – might have been the perfect place for an anthropological deconstruction of tribalism and ethnicity among the English, notorious as they are becoming for their lack of defined self-identity. To contain all this within simply a military view of the Cold War would seem to be misguided.

History, it is said, is written by the victors. Perhaps so, but archaeology need not be so directed. Who, anyway, were the victors? There is a political and economic elite in Russia now who wouldn't have power and wealth without the 'defeat' of the 1980s. Judged by the shift of, for instance, the USA's foreign policy attention since 1991 towards countries that weren't involved in the Cold War, maybe such countries were beneficiaries of the Cold War (which balanced USA power with that of the USSR, achieving a stasis for a time: the MAD thesis, now apparently deemed obsolete), but were these same countries also losers once the Cold War ended? It has been noticed that the success of more left-wing parties in most of the recent elections in South America might be a reflection of Washington's foreign policy preoccupation with the Middle East oil countries. Here would be another arena for interrogating material culture of all types.

The Cold War has also been called the third chapter in the 20th-century European Civil War. Some military material culture shows the seamless transitions from war to war (such as anti-aircraft technology from the Second World War into the Cold War, and the use of Spain as a technological rehearsal for the Second World War and an ideological rehearsal for both the Second World War and the Cold War). Since all three 'chapters' in Europe were brought to their conclusion ('won', I could say, being born in the UK) by USA investment of people and resources, the question of where the two Gulf wars and Afghanistan fit must come to the fore. Is the War on Terrorism in part the next stage of an episodic conflict (Cold War II, in the language of Hollywood sequels), a long-term conflict reflecting the need of governments (and societies) to ensure national and social coherence through the creation of strongly defined enemies? It has been noticed by many journalists that the current White House seems to use the word *battle* not *war* to describe the invasion of Iraq. What is the material culture of such global events? The distribution of US bases in a growing number of countries, including ex-Soviet republics, and their impact on surrounding material culture? Global distribution maps, decade by decade, showing the spread of landmines and the other remains of war? The empty niches of the Buddhas in Afghanistan (or the 21st-century replicas that might replace them soon)? This is scarcely a new idea, of course, but there have been few studies of how this is reflected in the material culture.

It is also easy to interpret the Cold War not only in military terms but more restrictively as being solely nuclear. It had a massive conventional military dimension, too, and one which may leave a larger material legacy. In short, an archaeology of the Cold War (and understandings forged by other disciplines) needs to look beyond all of the simple assumptions. At best, studying the Cold War gives an opening to the archaeology of all aspects of the 20th century; it opens the way for almost global analysis, and it leads to recognition of the vast complexity of human social activity.

FALLOUT FROM THE COLD WAR: CONCLUSIONS

Questions rather than answers have been offered in this chapter. The aim is to suggest that a much higher level of uncertainty and caution in the study of the Cold War's material legacy is unavoidable. It is not only to be grudgingly accepted but ideally it should be actively sought as something valuable in its own right and appropriate for a period that still lives so strongly in the present, and whose memory is still so much invoked to justify actions. In part this is a plea for archaeological study of the Cold War not to stop at recording structures. Like all archaeology, that of the Cold War should seek to challenge or enrich existing interpretations of the past, to create new interpretations, and to put Cold War remains into a multitude of wider contexts.

There are two particularly important scales: the context of the wider contemporary world (social as well as military, personal as well as social, views from both sides of the wall, and views from beyond the conflict, diversity and views within the 'blocs'), and (more importantly, because of its recentness, complexity and still baleful influence on attitudes) the contextualisation of present-day world views, to which it is still so close and relevant. The past is never over, never finished, but continues to live in the present, and it usually has a much stronger life when it is so recent and remains the subject of heated political and moral debate. It is also forever changing: being marginalised (belittled) or expropriated (brought centre stage for some reason), being contested. This reinforces rather than reduces its importance to the present. It is critical that they as archaeologists, historians, anthropologists or members of other disciplines, or just interested students, be highly conscious of how they study the Cold War, and how we use it. It cannot comfortably be studied simply as a set of facts, tempting though this is given the apparent fullness of the historical record.

This general essay has looked at some of the reasons why the Cold War is a particularly sensitive subject for research and heritage management; the rest of the book will offer many more examples. The Cold War is a subject whose technicalities can divert us from wider meanings and symbolism, a tendency that is often countered by use of artistic and literary interpretation. It is, of course, a period very close to us in time and many of us may be tempted to think that we understand it naturally, without the usual expected critical gaze, because we lived through it (and in various ways participated in it). Shifting layers of memory overlying ill-understood complexity and deliberate obfuscation by governments and others, however, do not seem a very firm basis for understanding. The greatest fear about this fearsome heritage is that we should accept a too 'clean' interpretation that leaves too little room for conflicting memory and re-interpretation; closure is perhaps best avoided for the moment, even if it were possible. One theme of the Cold War itself was disinformation – of 'enemies', both foreign and within – and archaeologies of the Cold War ought not to emulate this.

The main thrust of this chapter has been that archaeologists and others could begin to ask different questions of the Cold War's material remains. Trying to imagine the many different ways that archaeologists in the future (even only 50 years ahead, for example, and especially from many different countries or cultures) might interpret the Cold War can be a start by giving us an idea of the distance that we ourselves cannot have. The Cold War may in the future appear to have been merely one episode in a much more long-term western-led violent trend towards globalisation, and there will be material culture that can be adduced to support this view. The way in which the Cold War is commonly defined as a 'conflict between capitalism and communism' might need to be revisited at some future date. Even if seen in such simple terms now (and surely it rarely was), it should not be condensed to slogans just when we might begin to have a broader perspective from passing time and can see what happened next.

Concepts that we take for granted – such as that we have lived through a postcolonial period – might be open to challenge in the future from the archaeological record. Concepts of victors and losers might not change, but the concepts of right and wrong, good and bad might appear different, and if so archaeologists (not always from the West) will approach their evidence with different assumptions and questions.

Will emerging or future overviews of Cold War archaeology – for example, in the European Union – take us down the paths of celebration as 'victors' and of forgetting as 'losers', a distinction that is even less sound for this war than for others? There is a temptation to believe in the inevitability of the result, and to treat the 'Cold War' as a single conflict with beginning and end, whereas it can also be seen as being embedded seamlessly in preceding and succeeding conflicts.

We may start to assume that there was a single, straightforward agenda to the 'War'. Even where we notice that this was not true (at Greenham, for example, where the material culture highlights for us the existences of many agendas, belonging to the military garrison, the peace women, the police buffer between them and local residents), we have to fight hard to avoid oversimplifying, and to make sure we recall that 'residents' stood on both sides, that there were sympathies inside the fence for the peace 'cause', that for some of the peace women the gender conflict took precedence over the nuclear. In this, Greenham could be said to be a microcosm of the world of nation-states that were caught up in the Cold War: some as aggressors, others as victims, some protagonists, others willing allies; some unwilling combatants, others threatened, many affected indirectly, for example by the nuclear fallout of various kinds from Bikini atoll testing to the Chernobyl 'Zone' (the connections of the nuclear energy industry to military uses being so complex that Chernobyl cannot easily be seen as separate from the Cold War).

At this point, the Cold War as a topic moves from complexity to universality, and this starts to suggest that warfare and conflict (on a scale unlike any other century) actually characterise the 20th century (or at least peoples' current perceptions of it) and penetrate its material culture very substantially. More than that, it has shaped whole swathes of existence and culture: literature and film in particular showed throughout the 20th century an obsession with war and its immediate and long-term social and economic effects. In what other century (and what other continent than Europe) has the term *postwar* been stretched to cover a period of at least 40 if not more years, despite being demonstrably grossly inaccurate for most of that period (even in the UK: Malaya, Suez, and Kenya, for instance)? There is a question of whether the Cold War is best seen as a symptom or a cause of how the 20th century turned out: it is not desirable to study the Cold War in military historical isolation, but neither perhaps should we label a whole period by one of its attributes.

Finally, the Cold War was as much as anything the manifestation of the idea of Us and Them. *1984* is still the key insight. In the UK, interestingly, Big Brother (that is, the one who 'is watching', not the reality TV voiceover) seems finally to have displaced the famous Kitchener poster from cartoonists' imagery. Orwell's doublespeak survives and thrives in reports of the Iraq and Chechnya wars. Archaeologists studying the Cold War need to transcend this. We cannot afford to see it in such a simplistic or partisan way as winners and losers; in truth, perhaps there were no victors. The point goes further, however. Cold War studies need to be global, capturing the experience and material cultures of all countries and societies and all subgroups within them. They also need to be thoroughly interdisciplinary. This essay does not noticeably escape from my archaeologists' starting point, but that is a failing. An archaeological reading of material culture is essential (even in this most recent and therefore supposedly wholly historical of periods) to lay alongside the results of historians' labours, but neither alone nor taken together is likely to prove to be adequate. As other chapters in this book suggest, we need to join archaeology with other perspectives such as anthropology, art, sociology and politics if we are not to see Cold War heritage being used to set orthodoxy into concrete.

A paradox of peace: The Hiroshima Peace Memorial (Genbaku Dome) as world heritage

OLWEN BEAZLEY

> The Hiroshima Peace Memorial, Genbaku Dome, is a stark and powerful symbol of the achievement of world peace for more than half a century following the unleashing of the most destructive force ever created by humankind.
>
> (ICOMOS 1996)

INTRODUCTION

At 8.15 am on 6 August 1945, the nuclear bomb *Little Boy* was dropped from the United States (US) aeroplane the *Enola Gay*. It obliterated the city of Hiroshima, Japan. This event brought a conclusive end to World War II and initiated the nuclear arms race of the Cold War (1945–1989/91).

The purpose of this chapter is to focus on the cultural heritage legacies of this nuclear annihilation, and how this event is commemorated through the United Nations Educational and Scientific Committee's (UNESCO) World Heritage Committee, by the inclusion of the Hiroshima Peace Memorial (Genbaku Dome) on the World Heritage List.

In 1996, fifty-one years after dropping the Atom Bomb on the city of Hiroshima, the US administration, through its delegation to UNESCO's World Heritage Committee, attempted to prevent this symbol of the first use of the atomic bomb against humanity, the Hiroshima Peace Memorial, receiving international recognition through inscription on UNESCO's World Heritage List. This chapter will narrate the events that surrounded the nomination and inscription of this locus of contested memory and contested values. It will illustrate how world and domestic politics are played out in the World Heritage arena.

Far away from Japan, in the old colonial city of Merida, Mexico, an American delegate to UNESCO's 1996 World Heritage Committee meeting read the following statement:

> The United States is disassociating itself from today's decision to inscribe the Hiroshima Peace Memorial on the World Heritage List. The United States and Japan are close friends and allies. We cooperate on security, diplomatic, international and economic affairs around the world. Our two countries are tied by deep personal friendships between many Americans and Japanese. Even so, the United States cannot support its friend in this inscription.
>
> The United States is concerned about the lack of historical perspective in the nomination of the Hiroshima Peace Memorial. The events antecedent to the United States' use of atomic weapons to end World War II are key to understanding the tragedy of Hiroshima. Any examination of the period leading up to 1945 should be placed in the appropriate historical context.
>
> The United States believes the inscription of war sites [is] outside the scope of the Convention. We urge the Committee to address the question of the suitability of war sites for the World Heritage List. (UNESCO 1996)

This was the meeting that considered whether the Hiroshima Peace Memorial (Genbaku Dome), the pre-eminent symbol of the first use of nuclear weapons on a civilian population, should be included on the World Heritage List for its 'outstanding universal value'. Was it to be inscribed as a symbol of peace, as Japan and ICOMOS constructed it, or

Figure 3.1. The Hiroshima Peace Memorial (Genbaku Dome) World Heritage Site April 2003. © O Beazley

as a symbol of war as the US Administration viewed it? Was Hiroshima's role in the history of the Cold War, and indeed the history of the world, to be marked in any defining way?

The consideration of the Dome nomination by the World Heritage Committee was the culmination of events that witnessed a series of contested narratives and contested memories about that place. The name on the nomination document, Hiroshima Peace Memorial (Genbaku Dome) mirrors this contestation, and also reflects the antithetical nature of the heritage legacy of the place. Hiroshima Peace Memorial articulates peace; Genbaku Dome – translated from the Japanese to mean Atom Bomb Dome – articulates war.

The Hiroshima Peace Memorial (Genbaku Dome) is located on the banks of the Motoyasu River; it is the renamed ruin of the former Hiroshima Prefectural Industrial Promotions Hall, a building that was constructed in 1915 to promote industrial production in the Prefecture. The memorial dome takes its name from the five-storey rotunda that is topped by the iron frame of the architectural dome.

THE PLACE

Hiroshima, April 2003; it is a hot spring day. I wander through an urban riverside park under a cloudless, blue Japanese sky. Voices of men, women and children fill the air, laughing and talking as they picnic beneath trees festooned with candyfloss-pink cherry blossom. This, however, is no normal park. Fifty-eight years earlier the park did not exist. Early on that summer morning, 6 August 1945, the voices here, of people bustling through the streets on their way to work and to school, were silenced forever. This is where the first atomic bomb was dropped as a weapon of mass destruction. The tranquil park I walk through today, in the centre of this vibrant Japanese city, is the Hiroshima Peace Memorial Park.

The Peace Park was designed by Tange Kenzo in 1949 and built between 1950 and 1964 (Japan Agency for Cultural Affairs 1995). It commemorates those who lost their lives in the Hiroshima bombing and contains the Dome and the Cenotaph for the Atomic Bomb Victims, together with many other memorials. The focus of the park is the Dome: the ruined Promotions Hall building that is a surviving testimony to the events that occurred early on that August morning.

The Promotions Hall was located 150 metres northwest of the hypocentre of the atomic blast. It survived because the atomic blast occurred directly above the building (Japan Agency for Cultural Affairs 1995). Today, when one visits the site, one is struck by the size of the ghostly building. Compared with the high-rise buildings of the once-again thriving city of Hiroshima that form a backdrop to the Dome on its

Figure 3.2. The Hiroshima Peace Memorial Park April 2003. © O Beazley

eastern side, the Dome appears diminutive. When viewed from the city, looking across the river to the west, the ruined building is silhouetted against the sky (Figure 3.1). This desolate image provides a haunting mnemonic for the events that allowed the building's survival but caused the total destruction of an entire city and the loss of 140,000 lives.

The area identified for inscription on the World Heritage List to commemorate such a shattering event is very small. The Dome is set on a piece of grassy ground that is surrounded by a black, iron railing fence. This fence circumscribes the boundary of both the plot on which the Dome stands and also the World Heritage area itself. The Peace Park is not included in the World Heritage area because at the time the Dome was nominated, the Park was less than 50 years old. Under Japanese legislation, this meant that it could not be designated as an historic site and consequently could not be considered as part of the World Heritage nomination (Inaba 2003).

Every year on 6 August, the Peace Park is the location of an annual Peace Festival. The first such festival, *The Peace Restoration Festival*, was in 1946, and 'amidst tears, the surviving citizens of the city prayed for the peace of the souls of the A-bomb victims and pledged themselves to the restoration of world peace' (Kosakai 1990:20). The first peace festivals were closely monitored by the occupying Allied forces in Tokyo

(Kosakai 1990). Nevertheless, the festivals endured and achieved the first steps in securing the social construction of Hiroshima as a 'Mecca of World Peace' (Kosakai 1990). The peace festivals also probably helped secure the inscription of the Genbaku Dome on the World Heritage List as a symbol of hope for lasting peace, not only for the people of Japan, but for the entire world.

The Peace Park is a paradox. It is a place that commemorates the first use of the atomic bomb on a live target. It also commemorates the birth of the nuclear age and the Cold War 'peace'. It is a memorial to the thousands of people who lost their lives as a result of the bomb and it is a focus for antinuclear peace protests. For the Japanese people, it is an icon of peace. In the postwar period the promotion of peace became the main objective for the city of Hiroshima. In 1949 the Hiroshima Peace Memorial City Construction Law (Peace City Law), Article 1, stated: 'This law aims at the construction of Hiroshima as a Peace Memorial City, a symbol of the ideal of making lasting peace a reality' (quoted in Kosakai 1990:23). It was under this law that the land for the Peace Park was designated. The US government supported the idea of transforming Hiroshima into 'an international showcase that would link the atomic bomb with post war peace' (Yoneyama 2002:1) on the basis that it would help create Hiroshima as a 'Mecca' of peace and commemorate the birth of the atomic age (Yoneyama 1999). This, in fact, never occurred and there are no monuments that specifically commemorate the beginning of the atomic age – only those that commemorate the tragic loss of life at Hiroshima in 1945 near the end of World War II.

The rationale behind the US Administration's support for transforming Hiroshima into a symbol of peace was political. It wanted to illustrate that through the use of the atomic bomb, world peace – or at least an end to World War II – had been achieved, and that it could be maintained by ensuring US atomic superiority, particularly its superiority to the Soviets. The rationale ultimately accommodated the American build-up of nuclear arms in the name of peace (Yoneyama 2002). The Hiroshima Peace Memorial and the Peace Memorial Park became the physical manifestation of that rationale, and 'observed the universal ideals of world peace while embracing the specific concern of defending the free world against the threat of communism' (Yoneyama 1999:24). Thus, its heritage legacies became not only a monument to commemorate the dead of Hiroshima, but also an unwitting marker for the beginning of the Cold War.

The official message of peace from Hiroshima did not end with the Peace Law of 1949. The mayors of both Hiroshima and Nagasaki played a continuing role in spreading the message of peace and antinuclear proliferation. In 1975 the municipal assemblies of both Hiroshima and Nagasaki signed the *Agreement on Hiroshima and Nagasaki Partnership*

Figure 3.3. Cenotaph for the A-Bomb Victims, The Hiroshima Peace Memorial Park April 2003. © O Beazley

for Peace Culture Cities, which stated the cities' commitment to world peace (Tachibana 1996). The peace declarations from the two bombed cities continued, and by 1993 the mayors of Hiroshima and Nagasaki had called for 'an international agreement for the complete abolition of nuclear weapons to be concluded' (Tachibana 1996:183).

THE WORLD HERITAGE NOMINATION

The stories relating to the nomination and inscription of the Dome to the World Heritage List began in 1993 and they are as varied as they are intriguing. In 1993 it is purported that the US Administration had informally suggested that the Dome should be part of a joint nomination with the Trinity Site in New Mexico, the site where an atomic bomb was first tested, on 16 July 1945, as part of the Manhattan Project (Domicelj 1994). Yet, at the time the Dome was nominated to the World Heritage List in 1995, there was no collaboration between the state party delegations of Japan and the US over the nomination; in fact, quite the reverse.

Japan's perspective

In 1993, a conversation reportedly took place between a member of the Japanese delegation to UNESCO's World Heritage Committee,

Mr Masuda, and Dr Henry Cleere, the then ICOMOS International World Heritage Convenor (Cleere 2002). The conversation focussed on how the Japanese State Party to the World Heritage Convention could progress the nomination of the Dome following the US State Party's purported withdrawal from a joint nomination of the Dome with the Trinity Site. Joan Domicelj, a member of the ICOMOS delegation to Japan in 1993, has also supported the suggestion that there had, at one time, been a proposal for a joint nomination. She reported that, whilst in Japan as part of the ICOMOS delegation, a Japanese World Heritage professional had told her that he had recently received, from the State Department in Washington, a letter suggesting the joint nomination of the Dome and the Trinity Site (Domicelj 1994). Representatives of delegations from Japan and America have not been willing to corroborate these events.

Whilst it is possible that discussions at the nongovernmental organization (NGO) level may have taken place, four members of the former US Delegation to UNESCO's World Heritage Committee, interviewed on this subject, have refuted that any such discussions took place with Japan at a State Party level (Reynolds 2002; Charlton 2004; Milne 2003b). Mr Masuda, a member of the Japanese Delegation in 1993, also confirms that no discussions were held at the State Party level, but that there may have been NGO-level discussion at the World Heritage Committee meeting in Santa Fe in 1992.

Whatever the facts of the matter – some of which, perhaps as a result of State Party secrets, may have eluded this research – the Japanese State Party proceeded on its own with the Dome nomination with the following justification:

> Firstly the Hiroshima Peace Memorial, Genbaku Dome, stands as a permanent witness to the terrible disaster that occurred when the atomic bomb was used as a weapon for the first time in the history of mankind. Secondly, the Dome itself is the only building in existence that can convey directly a physical image of the tragic situation immediately after the bombing. Thirdly, the Dome has become a universal monument for all mankind, symbolizing the hope for perpetual peace and the ultimate elimination of all nuclear weapons on earth. (Japan Agency for Cultural Affairs 1995:10)

Ironically, Japan's independent submission of the Dome nomination did not end the US Administration's involvement. In fact, the US became very active in its attempts to control and change the way the Dome was presented to the World through the World Heritage Nomination process.

The USA's perspective

Sites associated with war are 'not a priority for the Convention' (Charlton 2004).Through its delegation to UNESCO's World Heritage Committee, this was the US Administration's position in relation to the nomination of the Dome to the World Heritage List in 1996. It had also been its position on the inscription of Auschwitz-Birkenau, Poland, in 1978 (Charlton 2004). The US did not think such places as Auschwitz-Birkenau should be included on the World Heritage List because they did not reflect the great achievements of man which, the US believed strongly, was the purpose of the List (Milne 2003a). But unlike the case of Auschwitz-Birkenau, there was more to the US Delegation's objection to the Dome inscription than pure heritage philosophy and the inclusion of war sites on the List.

In 1996, in the days leading up to the World Heritage Committee meeting in Merida, the US delegation spoke out against the inclusion of war sites on the List and petitioned against it occurring (Charlton 2004). This may, however, have been little more than an agenda to prevent the particular inscription of the Dome on the World Heritage List. In an attempt to prevent the Dome nomination proceeding, the US Administration undertook strong lobbying tactics. The following excerpts of an interview with Henry Cleere clearly illustrate this:

> Oh they [the Americans] were lobbying … oh well they saw it [the nomination] as an affront to the Americans, they saw it as an insult to the Americans. (Cleere 2002)

He reflected that the nomination of Hiroshima was opposed by the US Administration and seen as anti-American:

> because 140,000 people died as a result … Well it [the nomination] was certainly being interpreted that way in Washington … I am not talking about officials, I am not talking about people in the State Department, I am talking about Congressmen, people in Congress, this is where the problem was coming from … there was a lot of pressure and I think Newt Gingrich was the top honcho on the Hill [Capitol Hill, Washington] at that time and he was very, very vehement about it, Jesse Helms too, Jesse Helms … there was all sorts of stuff that came to us in the form of press cuttings around that time. It was very unpleasant. (Interview, 14 August 2002, Dr H Cleere)[1]

When it became clear that the US delegation was not going to be able to derail the Dome nomination, through lobbying tactics or by convincing ICOMOS of the unsuitability of war-related sites on the World

Heritage List, the US government began to consider other ways in which it might be able to influence the format of the Dome nomination.

Ironically, these considerations in the US State Department (once more) raised the possibility of a joint nomination with a site in the US. Robert Milne, former member of the US Delegation working for the World Heritage Centre at the time of the nomination, stated:

> there was even a counter discussion of the possibility of calling for a joint nomination with the US for both Hiroshima and either the Fermi laboratory at U[niversity] of Chicago, or White Sands N[ew]M[exico] as an 'Alpha to Omega' site. However, despite the highest level of US involvement in W[orld] H[eritage] matters from our Dept of State in dealing directly with the Japanese, the Japanese would not find any compromise and hardened up their 'peace rationale'. (Milne 2003a)

Realising there was little scope for manoeuvre on the question of the suitability of war sites, or on the possibility of a joint nomination, members of the US Delegation then raised concerns regarding the historical integrity of the Dome nomination document. This concern is reflected in the opening statement to this chapter, which was made by the US Delegation at the Merida Committee meeting in 1996.

The US suggested to ICOMOS that the nomination should be altered to reflect the context of the events that led to the bombing of Hiroshima, that is, as a response to the continuing Japanese aggression in the Pacific. The US had even made representations, informally, through US/ICOMOS to make it clear that they thought 'ICOMOS as a learned society ... as the formal review body, was not upholding what we [the US] considered to be appropriate canons of historical analysis and writing' (Charlton 2004). The US delegation was particularly concerned that if the nomination was going to proceed, there should be an historical context for the inscription.

Nevertheless, these efforts by the US delegation did not achieve any change in the ICOMOS support of the Dome nomination or in its recommendations to the Committee. Neither were attempts by the US to influence the Japanese State Party to change their approach in the nomination document, putting Hiroshima in historical context in relation to the events of the entire war, successful.

In spite of efforts by the US Administration, through its delegation, to change the content of the Dome nomination, by the time of the World Heritage Committee meeting in Merida in 1996, the US delegation members were, apparently, in favour of the nomination. For domestic political reasons, however, the US delegation was not able to openly support it. In fact, it was required by the US State Department to make a statement against the nomination at the meeting in Merida (Reynolds 2003).

US delegation support for the nomination is substantiated by information John Reynolds gave me regarding a meeting in Washington DC between the State Department and the National Park Service in 1996, both of which represented the US State Party at the World Heritage Committee meetings. The meeting was held in preparation for the World Heritage Committee meeting in order to discuss the way the consideration of the nomination of the Dome was to be tackled by them. Reynolds said:

> everybody was sitting around trying to decide what to do and we knew that the Administration was pretty worried about the reaction from the American public, particularly ... the Veterans of the Second World War because they had just gone through the *Enola Gay* controversy over here ... and everyone was looking dower because nobody in the meeting was really a representative of the Administration and everybody in the meeting ... thought that in one way or another, that Hiroshima ought to go on the list and ought to be recognised. I said ... before we figure out the politics of this thing, let's agree on what the right thing to do is, where do we want to get if we weren't limited. And so then we quickly agreed that it should be on the List. ... Then we started to evolve a way in which we could represent ourselves as positively as possible without getting the Administration in trouble ... we wanted to be able to represent ourselves as powerfully as possible given the political environment. (Reynolds 2003)

Reynolds confirmed that the Administration was not against the nomination per se, but was just trying to protect political interests at home in relation to pacifying the veterans groups, who would not approve of the tone of Japan's nomination document: 'They [the Administration] didn't want to do anything that would create a backlash from the military or from the war veterans'[2] (Reynolds 2003).

> This approach by the US Administration would accord with it having previously supported a Hiroshima nomination (in conjunction with the Trinity Site, New Mexico) until the events of the *Enola Gay* exhibition occurred. For the sake of domestic politics, the Administration then perhaps had to distance itself from the nomination as far as possible, without causing an international incident.
>
> According to Reynolds, the US delegation had received instructions from the US Administration via the State Department that they must not appear to be openly supporting the Dome nomination but there was never a directive to block the nomination. In fact, Reynolds said, 'we had been instructed to go to the meeting to do all we could to get it put on the list but we would not be able to vote yes'. (Reynolds 2003)

DISCUSSION

In the case of both Auschwitz-Birkenau in 1978 and the Dome in 1996, the US delegation was opposed to inscription on the World Heritage List because these were sites associated with war. In spite of the US delegation's apparent opposition to the inscription of the Dome on the List, it would not vote against it, it would not 'break with consensus' (Commonwealth of Australia Permanent Delegation to UNESCO Paris 1996).

If the Dome was initiated as a symbol of peace by the Japanese, and its construction immediately following the war had been supported by the US Administration, why was the US so opposed to its World Heritage List inscription in 1996? The answer perhaps lies in the way both nations have constructed Hiroshima in their national histories and memories. It can be suggested that the US considers the dropping of the atom bombs on Hiroshima and Nagasaki as the defining acts ending World War II (Hogan 1996). Accordingly, it is apparent that they will only consider Hiroshima synonymous with the end of World War II and the provision of peace in this context. The defeated Japanese, conversely, reconstructed themselves and their values in the early postwar years as a nation looking towards peace and reconstruction, both political and physical (Dower 1996). To them, the Dome could be the focus of this new ideology, leaving the politics of World War II behind them but at the same time paying homage to their dead. It was also a way to enable them to create an identity for Japan as a victim of the war (Yoneyama 1999). Harrison (1995) would describe this struggle over the representation of the Dome on the World Heritage List as a 'proprietary contest', where there is a struggle for the monopoly over a cultural symbol – that is, the Dome – or at the very least as a valuation contest where there is a struggle over the most valid memory at the site. As Yoneyama says: 'Hiroshima as the memory site of the nuclear holocaust is almost always composed of the discourses of collective entities, particularly of nation states' (Yoneyama 1992).

The fact that Japan did not propose a joint nomination of Hiroshima and Nagasaki illustrates that perhaps the object of the memorial was not a war-related nomination, but a commemoration of the dropping of the atomic bomb on Hiroshima and the subsequent peace movement that grew in Japan. Dower (1996:123), however, states that 'Hiroshima and Nagasaki became icons of Japanese suffering – perverse national treasures'. It was, nevertheless, the peace rationale that was to be the overt message of the Hiroshima Peace Memorial (Genbaku Dome) nomination.

By the Cold War's end (1989–1991) it can be suggested that the US Administration had realised that the glorification of a place that symbolised its nuclear supremacy was no longer viable or desirable. This may be the reason the US Administration changed its view on the advantages of the continuum of the symbolism of the Dome. It may be why they were so set against Japan's 'peace rationale' and the inscription of the Dome on the List. Whilst the Japanese have never explicitly charged the US with any crime against humanity, the US Administration may also have continued to fear such a prospect (Yoneyama 1999). The inscription of the Dome would, perhaps, only add prominence to the event that could be linked to such charges.

The apparent opposition from the US Administration to the Dome was foreshadowed by the events that took place surrounding the proposed *Enola Gay* exhibit at the National Air and Space Museum, Washington DC, in 1993. At this time, museum officials had planned an exhibition entitled *The Crossroads: The End of World War II, the Atomic Bomb, and the Origins of the Cold War* and had met with Japanese officials and museum professionals to discuss their display proposals. The exhibition was to display the aeroplane the *Enola Gay* and to provide an historical context to the atomic bomb drops on Japan (Harwit 1995).

The exhibition of the *Enola Gay* had been designed to commemorate the 50th anniversary of the end of World War II. Its approach to the display of the aircraft that dropped the atomic bomb on Hiroshima, however, was seen by many Americans to be unpatriotic because it portrayed the event in an objective historical context. Amongst other aspects, the exhibition illustrated the terrible effects of the atomic explosion and its aftermath at ground zero. The proposed exhibition displayed exhibits such as the 'shadow pictures', images of silhouettes of human forms that were created on stonework where people were sitting or standing when they were vaporised in the blast. By 1994, the proposed exhibition had caused a huge domestic political uproar (Harwit 1995). In September 1994, resolutions were passed in the American Senate stating that:

> any exhibit displayed by the National Air and Space Museum with respect to the *Enola Gay* should reflect appropriate sensitivity toward the men and women who faithfully and selflessly served the United States during World War II and should avoid impugning the memory of those who gave their lives for freedom. (Senate Resolution United States of America 1994)

The proposed exhibition was interpreted by many, including veterans, as a revisionist history of the era and one that cast Americans as racist war criminals (Harwit 1995, Wallace 1995). According to Harwit, director of the museum, much of this criticism was the result of display texts being read by critics without the accompanying graphics, which would have provided balance in the exhibition's message (Harwit 1995).

Because of the events surrounding the *Enola Gay* exhibition, the US Administration's approach to the Dome nomination had to be one that would protect political interests at home. Until the backlash to the *Enola Gay* exhibition in 1993, the US Administration had appeared to support the Dome inscription.

As a result of this policy decision by the US Administration, in the way it responded to the Dome nomination, a number of US World Heritage professionals were put in a compromising position during the World Heritage meeting that considered the nomination. The professionals had to maintain their professional integrity whilst appearing to oppose the Dome nomination.

> I even recollected during the time I ... was mostly focused on ... how I could get away with the least show of opposition and the greatest amount of signalling that the United States in fact ... was anxious for this to be inscribed, without ever saying so. (Reynolds 2003)

Further, James Charlton (2004) explains that the US Administration, through its delegation, made very concerted efforts in its consideration of the Dome nomination to avoid a diplomatic incident with the Japanese:

> We really wanted ... to continue to find ways to cooperate, we didn't want to cause unnecessary irritation or by the actions we took inflame the situation. And I am convinced that if we had simply gone in [to the World Heritage Committee meeting] and voted no, it would have made the papers, of the world. (Charlton 2004)

The conflicting approach by the US Administration towards the Dome nomination is not one that can easily be explained. There may have been other more complex reasons, apart from the clear domestic ones, why the US was opposed to the Dome inscription on the World Heritage List. These reasons could relate to the broader political motivations that were behind the bombing in 1945. Contemporary wartime accounts have revealed that the major motivation for dropping the bomb was to send a sign to Stalin and the Soviet Union by showing the US's atomic power. It was intended that this would prevent the Soviet Union's aspirations for gaining a power share in the division of postwar Eastern Europe and the Far East. President Truman wanted to 'roll back' the Potsdam Agreement that agreed to the Soviet Union holding a portion of postwar power if they entered the war against Japan. Truman used the US's atomic capability and the results of its use as a warning to the Soviet Union (Burchett 1983; Sherwin 1995). Another reason probably had to do with the politics of the Cold War and how these politics in the early to mid-1990s still heavily influenced the way the US thought about World War II as a 'just' and 'good' war and the way they wished it to be represented to the world (Sherwin 1995). It is probable that it is also for these historical reasons that the US Administration did not desire the Dome inscribed on the World Heritage List without its historical context. The US may have also feared that the inscription would provide an indelible anti-American focus on the historical use of the atomic bomb, the start of the Cold War and the broader proliferation of weapons of mass destruction.

CONCLUSION

The evidence I have presented in this chapter suggests that some politicians in the US Administration were opposed to the memories and values of Hiroshima being framed by the Japanese nomination to the World Heritage List. For the US, such a nomination could potentially mark Hiroshima as, primarily, a victim of US aggression in World War II.

There were politicians in the US who did not wish the Dome inscription to detract from their nationally constructed memory, that is, a memory of the dropping of the atomic bomb being a justifiable and good thing, an act that ended World War II and saved American lives. Further, they did not wish to support the peace rationale that they had held immediately postwar, which used the Dome as a symbol of nuclear supremacy against the Soviet Union and the promise of a long-term, nuclear peace. As Sherwin states in his article 'Hiroshima as politics and history', 'even in the post-Cold War United States, history remains a hostage to politics, past and present' (Sherwin 1995: 22). As a result of these agendas, the US Administration attempted to prevent the Dome nomination being considered for inscription on the basis of it being a war-related site – something the US had been opposed to since the consideration of Auschwitz-Birkenau in 1978. The US Administration then attempted to have the nomination modified, in order to illustrate the historical context of the dropping of the bomb on Hiroshima as a response to the continuing Japanese aggression in the Pacific. Finally, it even proposed what it considered to be a more balanced, joint nomination with Japan on the basis of scientific achievement. None of these attempts by the US Administration to influence the content of the Dome nomination succeeded and, in 1996, the nomination proceeded to the World Heritage Committee for consideration.

The US Administration had attempted to find reasons to block or change the nomination in order to protect the American war veterans' memory of the end of World War II and with it, perhaps, the politically

---

Figure 3.4. The Hiroshima Peace Memorial (Genbaku Dome) April 2003. © O Beazley

constructed memory of the Administration itself. In this way it hoped to avoid a political backlash such as the one it experienced during the proposed exhibition of the *Enola Gay*, the plane that dropped the bomb on Hiroshima on 6 August 1945.

As with the *Enola Gay* exhibition, American veterans groups, and the shadow of their political influence, affected the treatment of the Hiroshima nomination by the US delegation. The veterans, and fear of the disapproval they would stir at home, influenced the way the US State Party to UNESCO represented itself in the international arena in relation to the Dome inscription. The US delegation was instructed by the US State Department to read out a statement at the World Heritage Committee meeting opposing the nomination. This occurred in spite of the fact that, for philosophical and heritage reasons, the delegation members were actually in favour of its inclusion on the List. These events underline Huyssen's observation that 'memory and amnesia always exist side by side and remain part of the political struggle' (Huyssen 2003:95).

Today, we have the *Hiroshima Peace Memorial (Genbaku Dome)* inscribed on UNESCO's World Heritage List for its 'outstanding universal value'. As identified in the ICOMOS quotation at the start of this chapter, it has been a 'stark and powerful symbol of the achievement of world peace for more than half a century' (ICOMOS 1996). It is a symbol of nuclear annihilation and the birth of the nuclear age – the end of World War II and the beginning of the Cold War. The paradox of the *Hiroshima Peace Memorial (Genbaku Dome)* is that as a mnemonic of nuclear war, it has become a symbol of nuclear peace, especially for the people of Japan.

NOTES

1. Newt Gingrich became Speaker of the House of Representatives in the USA in 1995 and was defacto leader of the Republican Party. Jesse Helms was a Republican senator from North Carolina.

2. The author thanks the anonymous reviewer for comments concerning the veterans' position in these events. Further detail of the veterans' role is not within the scope of this chapter but provides another avenue of history to be explored.

REFERENCES

Burchett, W (1983) *Shadows of Hiroshima,* Norfolk: The Thetford Press

Charlton, J (2004) 'The inscription of the Hiroshima Peace Memorial on the World Heritage List', unpublished telephone interview transcript, 7 May, Canberra, Australia

Cleere, H (2002) 'Hiroshima and the global strategy', unpublished interview transcript, 14 August, Paris

Commonwealth of Australia Permanent Delegation to UNESCO Paris (1996) 'Inward Cablegram: UNESCO: World Heritage Bureau and Committee Meetings, Merida, Mexico 2–7 December 1996', unpublished Australian and World Heritage Group Department of Environment, Sport and the Territories, Canberra, Australia

Domicelj, J (1994) 'Diverse cultural values and conservation principles', in D Marshall (ed), *Diversity, Place and the Ethics of Conservation*, Canberra: Australian Heritage Commission

Domicelj, J (2002) 'The inscription of the Hiroshima Peace Memorial on the World Heritage List, Criterion (vi) and the Global Strategy', 27 July, Leura, Australia

Dower, JW (1996) 'The Bombed: Hiroshimas and Nagasakis in Japanese memory', in MJ Hogan (ed), *Hiroshima in History and Memory*, Cambridge: Cambridge University Press

Harrison, S (1995) 'Four types of symbolic conflict' *The Journal of the Royal Anthropological Institute* 1, 255–272

Harwit, M (1995) 'Academic freedom in the 'Last Act'' 82(3) *The Journal of American History* 1064–83

Hogan, MJ (ed) (1996), *Hiroshima in History and Memory*, Cambridge: Cambridge University Press

Huyssen, A (2003) *Present Pasts, Urban Palimpsests and the Politics of Memory*, Stanford, Calif.: Stanford University Press

ICOMOS (1996) 'Hiroshima Peace Memorial Genbaku Dome, Japan 775', unpublished Evaluation Report, Paris

Inaba, N (2003) 'The inscription of Hiroshima on the World Heritage List', unpublished interview transcript, 5 April, Kyoto, Japan

Japan Agency for Cultural Affairs (1995) 'Hiroshima Peace Memorial Genbaku Dome World Heritage Nomination', unpublished World Heritage Nomination 775

Kosakai, Y (1990) *Hiroshima Peace Reader*, Twelfth edition, Hiroshima: Hiroshima Peace Culture Foundation

Masuda, K (2003a) 'Discussions for a joint nomination, Hiroshima and the Trinity Site', unpublished personal communication, 8 May

Masuda, K (2003b) 'The inscription of Hiroshima Peace Memorial on the World Heritage List', unpublished personal communication, 8 May

Milne, R (2003a) 'Inscription of Auschwitz and Hiroshima on the World Heritage List', unpublished personal communication, 24 February

Milne, R (2003b) 'Inscription of Auschwitz and Hiroshima on the World Heritage List', unpublished telephone interview transcript, 28 February, Canberra, Australia

Reynolds, J (2003) 'Inscription of the Hiroshima Peace Memorial on the World Heritage List in 1996', unpublished telephone interview transcript, 19 August, Canberra, Australia

Senate Resolution United States of America (1994) Senate Resolution 257 – Relating to the 'Enola Gay' Exhibit (Senate–September 19, 1994), 82(3) *The Journal of American History* 1136.

Sherwin, MJ (1995) 'Hiroshima as politics and history', 82(3) *The Journal of American History* 1085–93

Tachibana, S (1996) 'The quest for peace culture: the A Bomb survivors' log, struggle and the new movement for redressing foreign victims of Japan's war', in MJ Hogan (ed), *Hiroshima in History and Memory*, Cambridge: Cambridge University Press

UNESCO (1996) 'Report of the Rapporteur on the Twentieth Session of the World Heritage Committee, Merida, Mexico, 2–7 December 1996', unpublished World Heritage Committee paper WHC-96/CONF.201/21 ANNEX V, Paris

Wallace, M (1995) 'The battle for the Enola Gay', 6062 *Museum News* (July–Aug) 40–45

Yoneyama, L (1992) *Hiroshima Narratives and the Politics of Memory*, Stanford University

Yoneyama, L (1999) *Hiroshima Traces: Time, Space, and the Dialectics of Memory*, Berkeley: University of California Press

Yoneyama, L (2002) 'Remembering and imagining the nuclear annihilation in Hiroshima' *The Getty Conservation Institute Newsletter* 17(2) (on-line)

Colonialism and the bomb in the Pacific

ANITA SMITH

> Here we are, fifty years after Bravo, and the people forcibly removed from their homes for the atomic tests, with the exception of Utrik, have yet to return home. The question of exposure as it affects other atolls of the Marshalls has yet to be fully addressed. Many claims are still being prepared. ... Bravo is not over. The people of Kwajalein, who sacrificed their home and society for America's nuclear ambitions, still live in squalid conditions on Ebeye, unable to live in peace and comfort in their own homeland. ... For our people, for the Marshall Islands, March 1, 1954 is the defining moment in world history. That is the Fourth of July, the Assassination of President Lincoln and Kennedy, Pearl Harbor and 9/11 all wrapped into one.
>
> That is the day the world stood still and also changed forever. That is the day we went from being an occupied nation to becoming a dependent nation. That is the day we went from being survivors of the World War to victims of the Cold War. (Rongelap Mayor James Matayoshi, Bravo Day, 1 March 2004, Marshall Islands www.bikiniatoll.com/history.html)

Castle Bravo was the largest atomic bomb detonated in the atmosphere by the United States. It was equal to a force nearly a thousand times that of the Hiroshima bomb and created a fireball four miles wide that vaporized the entire test island and parts of two others. Its fallout covered an estimated 7,000 square miles and there was no prior warning of the test for the people in the region (Weingartner 1991:11). Bravo was one of 23 atomic and hydrogen bombs tested by the United States at Bikini Atoll in the Marshall Islands, Micronesia, between 1946 and 1958.

INTRODUCTION

The Marshall Islands are one of several island groups in the Pacific Ocean to be used as nuclear test sites during and after the Cold War. Between

1946 and 1996, Great Britain, the United States and France all tested nuclear devices in the region. Along with the obvious environmental damage resulting from these tests, ongoing health and social problems for people directly and indirectly involved in the testing constitute a Cold War legacy little known outside the region. Although in Western thought the Cold War may now be recognised, analysed and theorised as an historic era, for Pacific Island nations such reflection is not yet possible. For many the processes of colonialism that enabled small and remote islands to be used as testing grounds or strategic military sites in the second half of the twentieth century continue. In some, missile testing ranges have replaced the nuclear test bases; in others the atomic test sites have been closed and concreted over but the threat and reality of radioactive contamination continues alongside the dominance of the colonial regimes that appropriated scarce land and resources in the Pacific for the 'greater good of world peace' (Niedenthal 2001).

A pattern of militarisation, environmental devastation and the displacement of Indigenous or local peoples is visible in the landscapes of many Cold War test sites, island and continental. However, in the Pacific Islands where all human behaviour is informed by the oceanic environment of fragile islands amid vast tracts of water, the archaeological expression of nuclear testing is unlike that found elsewhere. The tiny, remote islands affected by nuclear testing represent a large proportion and in some cases the entire land surface on which particular peoples have lived or regularly visited for at least a millennium. Some of these archaeological landscapes are readily characterised by material remains – military hardware, bunkers, concrete domes, shipwrecks, airstrips. More insidiously, some are recognisable only in the illnesses of those who have dwelt in these landscapes while others now exist only in the memories of those who once lived there.

This chapter attempts to make these landscapes visible for others. It provides a context in which the archaeological evidence – the material remains – of nuclear testing in the Pacific have regional as well as global meaning. The chapter discusses the colonial histories that enabled the United States, United Kingdom and France to test nuclear devices at specific Pacific locations during and following the Cold War; the legacies of those tests for Pacific peoples; and the role of the nuclear-free Pacific movement in claims for self-determination and the building of Pan-Pacific identity.

It goes without saying that the cultural geography of twentieth century international conflict cannot be understood in isolation from analyses of Western colonialism, yet most analyses of the Cold War focus on the major protagonists in Western and Eastern Europe and the United States, even though Western economic domination in the second half of the twentieth century was underpinned by nineteenth- and early twentieth-century colonialism. As such, they tend to overlook roles played by the periphery and the remote and as a consequence the legacies of these conflicts in regions outside Europe and North America. It is precisely because of pre-World War II European and United States territorial expansion in the Pacific that tiny pieces of land and their indigenous populations could be subjected to environmentally and socially catastrophic atomic testing in the decades following World War II. The Cold War testing of nuclear devices in the Pacific is but one, albeit significant, expression of a larger and longer history of Western imperialism in the region.

Given this, the commonly cited dates or chronologies of the era have only limited relevance for history and experiences of people in the Pacific Islands in the mid- to late twentieth century. From a social and political perspective, it is more relevant to investigate the Cold War in the Pacific within a framework of 'colonial' and 'post-colonial' histories in the region. It was during the latter half of the twentieth century, as many of the Pacific Island nations gained independence, that a united political voice emerged in the Pacific in protest at the continued use of the region for nuclear testing and the transport and dumping of radioactive waste. Specifically, in regard to the impacts of the testing programme on the health and environment of Pacific Islanders, it may be more relevant to speak of the Cold War era in the Pacific in two distinct phases of the testing programmes. The first, involving atmospheric and surface tests, began with the detonation of the atomic bomb over Hiroshima in August 1945 and continued until the signing of the Partial Test Ban Treaty in 1963 by the United States, United Kingdom and Soviet Union – but, notably, not France – that ended atmospheric testing by these powers. The second phase is principally associated with French testing in French Polynesia in which atmospheric tests were conducted from 1966 to 1975 followed by underground tests until 1996, long after Cold War hostilities had subsided. Such a chronology is useful as a framework for looking at specific impacts of the nuclear age in the Pacific, but it is limited in providing a framework for investigating why it was possible for particular nations to test weapons in particular locations, and over such a long period. It also does not recognise that the processes of militarisation in the Pacific region that commenced early in the twentieth century have continued to expand throughout two World Wars, the Cold War and into present.

MICRONESIA 'SETTING THE SCENE': 1898–1946

Micronesia stretches over a vast distance of the Western Pacific, east of the Philippines to the dateline in the Central Pacific, at and immediately north of the Equator (Figure 4.1). As the name suggests, Micronesia is made up of thousands of small islands and atolls, in far-flung groups, separated by huge tracts of water. Despite the seeming isolation of the islands and island groups, Indigenous Micronesians and more recently Europeans and Americans have navigated within and between the island groups, exploiting the resources of land and sea. The Spanish were the first Europeans to explore the region, establishing colonies in Guam and the Mariana Islands in the seventeenth century. Since then, the Micronesian people have been subjected to a mosaic of European, American and Asian colonial regimes.

It was at a United States Air Force base on the island of Tinian in the Northern Mariana Islands in Western Micronesia, that the atomic bomb bound for Hiroshima was loaded onto the *Enola Gay* in August 1945. The base had been reconstructed by the United States following their regaining control of the island from the Japanese in 1944. From 1943 to 1945 the United States progressively 'liberated' the Micronesian islands, bringing to an end 25 years of Japanese colonial rule over much of the region. This had begun after World War I when the newly established League of Nations mandated the Micronesian territories annexed by the German Empire in the 1880s to Japan as Trust Territories. Although under the mandate Japan was forbidden to build any defensive sites or military bases in the territories, from the early 1930s as the Japanese Empire grew and strengthened on the Asian mainland, the Japanese Trust Territories in Micronesia were increasingly fortified and militarised. When Japan withdrew from the League of Nations in 1935, the territories were incorporated into the Japanese Empire and increasingly closed to foreign scrutiny.

Japan was not the only foreign nation to have a military presence in Micronesia in the first half of the twentieth century. When the Japanese launched their 1941 attack on Pearl Harbour from their bases in Micronesia, they simultaneously attacked the islands of Guam and the northern Marianas that had been controlled by the United States for more than 40 years. The 1898 Treaty of Paris that formally ended hostilities of the Spanish American War delivered these Spanish colonies to the United States along with the Philippines and Puerto Rico. Alongside its Micronesian territories, the United States had also annexed the Hawai'ian Islands in 1898 and the islands of American Samoa in 1899. Several other small, uninhabited islands including Palmyra and the Midway Islands, Wake and Johnston Atolls also gradually came under United States territorial control. By 1941 these island territories gave the United States a string of military bases stretching from Hawai'i across the Pacific to East Asia.

Within a few months of the attack on Pearl Harbour, the Japanese controlled all Micronesia, including the British colonies of the Gilbert

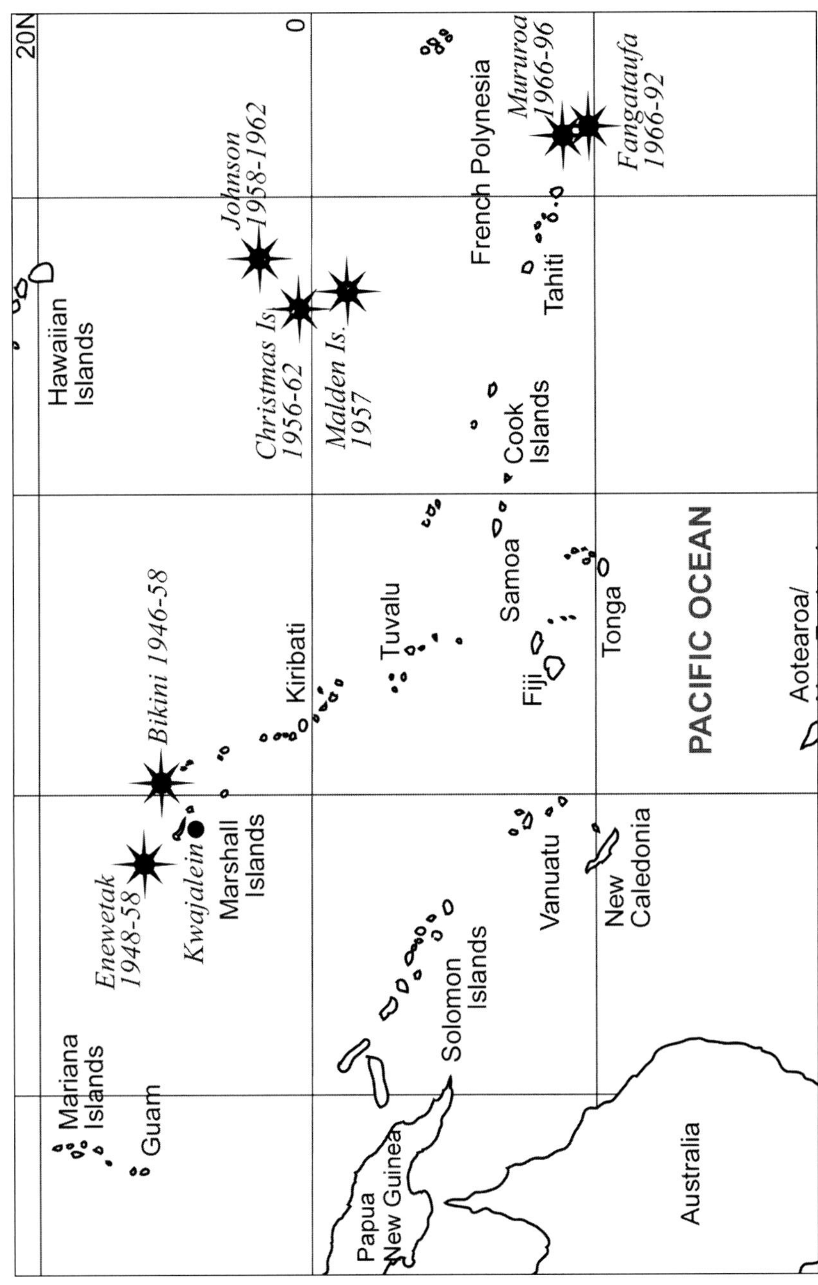

Figure 4.1. Pacific nuclear test sites as discussed in the text.

Islands (Kiribati) and Nauru. By late 1943 the United States and allies had begun to push back the Japanese forces in Micronesia. The United States 'liberation' of Japanese-occupied islands involved a strategy of persistent and consistent bombing of the islands from sea and air, often for months, prior to the deployment of soldiers transforming 'the once verdant physical environments of many Micronesian Islands into ravaged, potted desolate landscapes' (Hanlon 1998:23). On landing, infrastructure systematically destroyed by the United States bombardment was reconstructed as strategic bases, harbours and landing fields from which to launch the westward offensive against the retreating Japanese.

Just how many Micronesian people died during World War II through battle, forced labour and starvation is unknown. What is clear is that images of the ravaged islands and the need for postwar social and economic rebuilding of Micronesia provided a justification for continued United States control of the islands following cessation of hostilities in 1945 (Hanlon 1998:23). By promoting the process of development, military and later civilian leaders were able to address certain humanitarian concerns about progress and betterment while at the same time ensuring that Micronesia would be remade in ways that served the strategic interests of the larger American state (Hanlon 1998:10).

In 1947 the United States, as the occupying power, entered into a 'security trusteeship' with the United Nations Security Council to administer Micronesia, including the Marshall Islands, as the Trust Territory of the Pacific Islands. As early as 1942 the United States began planning for military bases in the Pacific and arguing for a 'forward defence strategy' (Weingartner 1991:13) that would, in a nuclear world, draw firepower away from the United States mainland. By 1945, 15 of the United States Navy's 18 major bases were in the Pacific (Weingartner 1991:14). In the postwar era Micronesia became an 'American Lake' (Hayes *et al.* 1986). Along with the existing United States territories in the Pacific, this effectively allowed the Unites States military control of a vast area of the Pacific Ocean. By the 1980s the United States had created in the Pacific the most heavily armed region of the world outside Eastern Europe.

For the United States, control of the Islands of Micronesia was the strategic equivalent to the Soviet Union's control over Eastern Europe. In the Second World War, Japan attacked the United States from bases in Micronesia just as Germany attacked the USSR through Eastern Europe. After the war both sought to control these territories in the name of national security. Both maintained that never again would these places be used as a platform for aggression. Both saw the wishes of the inhabitants as far outweighed by security consideration and denied political self-determination and independence to the captured lands (Smith 1991:3).

THE MICRONESIAN TESTS, RADIATION AND THE CREATION OF 'NUCLEAR NOMADS': 1946–1958

The United States nuclear testing programme in the Pacific commenced as 'Operation Crossroads' at Bikini Atoll in the northern Marshall Islands in 1946, prior to the formal agreement with the United Nations on the status of the territories. Between 1946 and 1958, the United States carried out 66 nuclear tests in the Marshall Islands on Bikini Atoll (1946–1948, 1954–1958) and neighbouring Enewetak Atoll (1948–1958). The surface or atmospheric tests were conducted in or over the Bikini Atoll lagoon dispersing radiation over all the islands of the atoll (Stegnar 1998:15). The Enewetak tests obliterated two of the islands in the atoll.

At the same time Americans embraced the fantasy tropical paradise as the favoured backdrop for musical romance (the musical *South Pacific* opened on Broadway in 1949 and ran for five years), the nuclear test programme in Micronesia was demanding the removal of Marshallese peoples from their traditional lands on Bikini, Enewetak, Rongelap and Wotho Atolls, Kwajalein and Roi Namur Islands, Lib Island and the Mid-Atoll Corridor Islands to permit continued testing (Niedenthal 2001; Hanlon 1998; Smith 1991; Hayes *et al.* 1986). For those who were relocated, the consequences were varied. Some returned to their traditional homes within a few years; others remain 'nuclear nomads', unable to return due to dangerously high levels of radioactivity. Overall the relocation of people meant the loss of self-determination, traditional resources and for many a radical change in social and economic circumstances.

Best known of the displaced peoples are the Bikini Islanders whose traditional home was the principal United States test site and continues to be uninhabitable due to radioactive contamination. In 1946 the atoll's entire population was removed to Rongerik Atoll, 200 km to the west, then in 1948 to Kwajalein Atoll and later that year to Kili, in the southern Marshall Islands. Kili remains home to most Bikinians, but life there remains difficult. Kili is a single island, while Bikini Atoll has 23 islands and a 243-square-mile lagoon. Kili has no sheltered fishing grounds, rendering useless traditional Bikini skills for exploiting lagoon resources. In 1972, following a clean-up operation by the United States in 1968, 130 Bikini Islanders returned to the atoll. Subsequent tests found these people to have dangerously high levels of radiation. They were again moved to Kili Island in 1977 and Bikini was deemed unfit for habitation (Stegnar 1998).

The people of Enewetak Atoll in the northwest Marshall Islands were moved south to Ujelang Atoll in December 1947 in preparation for the first series of nuclear tests at the site. When testing ceased in Micronesia in 1958, the United States had conducted 42 tests on the atoll. Enewetak

Atoll continued to be used for defence programmes until 1977 when the United States began a clean up and rehabilitation programme. The people of Enewetak remained on Ujelang Atoll until 1980 when resettlement of Enewetak Island began. Only the southern half of the atoll is habitable, due to high radiation levels in the northern half.

The most significant contaminating event of the Micronesian tests was the aforementioned Bravo test at Bikini Atoll in 1954. Bravo was an experimental thermonuclear device, the largest ever tested. Widespread fallout from the blast contaminated the inhabited islands of Rongelap and Utrik Atolls to the east of Bikini. The United States Navy arrived three days after the blast to evacuate the population of 64, all of whom were ill having received significant exposure to radioactive fallout. They were evacuated to Kwajalein Atoll for medical treatment and then spent the next three years living on Majuro Atoll, also in the Marshall Islands, before returning home to Rongelap in 1957.

Nuclear testing ceased in Micronesia in 1958 at least partly in response to increasing international concerns over atmospheric testing, and in particular its effect on Pacific Islanders (Smith 1991:20). In 1961 the United States recommenced its atmospheric testing programme on uninhabited islands of the Central Pacific.

THE CENTRAL PACIFIC TEST SITES: 1956–1963

Unlike many other parts of the world, the end of World War II in Europe did not herald decolonisation of the European territories in the Pacific. It was not until the beginning of the 1980s that the majority of Pacific nations had gained their independence. The exceptions were much of Micronesia and other United States Pacific territories, French Polynesia and (French) New Caledonia.

In 1979 the tiny island nation of Kiribati in Eastern Micronesia (formerly the Gilbert Islands) gained independence from the United Kingdom. Included in this string of far-flung islands in the Central Pacific was the tiny and relatively remote Christmas Island (Kirimati). Christmas Island was formally annexed by Great Britain in 1919, the last in a series of such island annexations in Micronesia and northern Polynesia (McDonald 1982). At that time Christmas Island had no permanent inhabitants, but copra plantations had been established on the island and a small population of Gilbertese (I-Kiribati) plantation workers were still resident on the island in the early-1950s when Christmas Island along with the uninhabited Malden Island, also British territory approximately 500 miles to the southwest, came under the gaze of Britain's Atomic Energy Commission. Like other nations looking to test their newly developed atomic weapons, the British turned their attention to locations remote and underpopulated – to their distant colonial territories. Britain began its nuclear testing programme in the Pacific region in 1956 on Christmas Island where a total of 25 nuclear devices were tested between 1956 and 1958.

In 1956 Malden Island was selected as the instrumentation site for Britain's first series of nuclear weapons tests at Christmas Island. Subsequently, in 1957, Malden also became a test site with three nuclear devices being detonated at high altitude a short distance offshore of the island. By the late 1950s, increasing international attention on accidents during testing in Micronesia led the United States to request use of Christmas Island from the British for its atmospheric tests, 25 of which were carried out in 1962 (Danielsson and Danielsson 1977:45).

The United States also carried out 12 atmospheric nuclear tests at the uninhabited Johnston Atoll in the Central Pacific between 1958 and 1962. Both the United States and the Kingdom of Hawai'i annexed Johnston Atoll in 1858, but it was the United States that mined the guano deposits there until the late 1880s. The atoll was designated a wildlife refuge in 1926, but in 1934 the United States Navy took over the atoll followed by the United States Air Force which assumed control in 1948.

The atmospheric testing of nuclear devices by the British, United States and Soviet Union ceased in 1963 with their signing of the Treaty Banning Nuclear Weapon Tests in the Atmosphere, Outer Space and Under Water, known as the 'Partial Test Ban Treaty' that entered into force 10 October 1963. As mentioned, the only 'nuclear' nation not to sign was France.

THE PACIFIC MISSILE RANGE, THE PACIFIC SLUM AND MARSHALLESE INDEPENDENCE: 1958–PRESENT

The cessation of nuclear testing in Micronesia in 1958 did not herald any reduction in United States militarisation of the region. Almost immediately upon ceasing the testing programme, the nuclear test operations base on Kwajalein Island in the central Marshall Islands became the United States Air Force missile test facility. From 1959 the United States concentrated on testing delivery systems for missiles over the 'Pacific Missile Range' that stretched from the Californian coast to Kwajalein Atoll. In this capacity, the Kwajalein base contributed more to the nuclear arms race than any other single site (Smith 1991:21). Here the United States tested Intercontinental Ballistic Missiles, submarine-launched ballistic missiles, sea-launched cruise missiles and radar defence systems (Weingartner 1991:15). The site was central to Ronald Reagan's 'Star Wars' Strategic Defense Initiative during the mid-1980s.

The Kwajalein base is on Kwajalein Island, one of a number of islands in the atoll of the same name. In 1944 the United States military had moved most of the surviving Indigenous population from Kwajalein Island, which had previously been a Japanese naval base, to the neighbouring tiny island of Ebeye to make way for the reconstruction of the base. This meant overcrowded living conditions on Ebeye, a situation that worsened when the Kwajalein labour camp, comprising Islanders from all over the Marshall Islands brought to work on reconstruction of the Kwajalein base, was also moved to Ebeye in the late 1940s. The opportunities for waged work on the Kwajalein base continued to draw Marshallese to Ebeye. By 1951, 1,200 Marshallese labourers and dependents were living on the island which had become a slum with associated poor sanitation and outbreaks of epidemic diseases on the island during the 1960s (Hanlon 1998:193).

Ebeye, often likened to a small urban ghetto, by the early 1960s served as a convenient site for the placement of all of the unexpected, barely imaginable, and little cared-about problems that testing in Kwajalein caused (Hanlon 1998:187).

In the early 1980s the Micronesian Trust Territories began to move toward political independence, although economic independence from the United States is still to be achieved. The Northern Mariana Islands became a commonwealth in political union with the United States in 1986. Palau (1994), the Federated States of Micronesia (1986) and the Republic of the Marshall Islands (1986) each entered a Compact of Free Association with the United States in 1994. Under the terms of the Compact of Free Association with the Republic of the Marshall Islands, the United States military continues to have rights over Kwajalein Island and parts of Ebeye. Since the 1980s, the Kwajalein base, now renamed the ‘Reagan Test Site’, has continued to play a central role in United States defence strategies and missile testing.

The US Army’s Reagan Test Site (RTS) is a premiere asset within the Department of Defence Major Range and Test Facility Base. The unquestioned value of RTS is based upon its strategic geographical location, unique instrumentation, and unsurpassed capability to support ballistic missile testing and space operations. With nearly 40 years of successful support, RTS provides a vital role in the research, development, test and evaluation effort of America’s missile defence and space programs (www.smdc.army.mil/RTS.html).

Nearly 10,000 Marshallese now reside on Ebeye, many of whom are economically dependent on work at the Reagan Test Site (www.yokwe.net/downloads/EbeyePart1.pdf).

THE 'FRENCH LAKE' IN THE EASTERN PACIFIC: 1842–1996

In 1962 the French colonial presence in the Pacific coalesced with its aspirations as a nuclear nation. Between 1960 and 1962 France had carried out 17 atomic tests in the Sahara Desert in Algeria but in 1962 the African colony gained independence, ending French access to the territory as a nuclear testing ground. In search of a suitable alternative, France looked to its other colonies and found the remote and isolated islands of French Polynesia an appropriate replacement. In early 1963 French President Charles de Gaulle announced that Mururoa and subsequently Fangataufa Atolls would become France's new nuclear test sites. Algeria's independence following a decade of resistance to French authority effectively led to the creation of French Polynesia as a 'nuclear vassal' (Fischer 2002:223), entrenching French colonial rule through social and economic changes brought by the establishment of two test sites to the south of Tahiti.

French Polynesia consists of 118 islands stretching over five archipelagos. France annexed Tahiti and the Society Islands in September 1842, creating a French protectorate that, along with the Marquesas Islands in Eastern Polynesia, became a colony in 1880. During the nineteenth century the islands were considered of little economic importance, although they played a key role in supplying ships en route from Europe to the Pacific via Cape Horn until completion of the Panama Canal in the early twentieth century. The colony, known initially as French Oceania and subsequently French Polynesia, became an Overseas Territory of France in 1946 and recently was given a new status as an 'Overseas Country of France'. French Polynesia has its own locally elected Territorial Assembly but the French State maintains control over crucial areas of government including foreign policy, law and order, and defence. The French nuclear test programme in the Pacific was a matter for defence and therefore any decision on the continuation of the testing programme was outside the Territorial Assembly's jurisdiction.

The colonial reshuffle of many Pacific territories during and following World War I and the armed conflict of World War II did not directly affect governance of French Polynesia. Unlike the French territory of New Caledonia, by the end of World War II relatively few people of European descent had settled in French Polynesia, and most were concentrated in the capital, Pape'ete, on Tahiti. Political control remained with the French governor and civil servants. There was no airport or landing strip in the islands. Outside the capital most people lived in traditional villages.

This picture changed dramatically with the commencement of the nuclear test programme. Within two years of the programme an estimated 20,000 French troops and profiteers had arrived in the islands (Danielsson and Danielsson 1977:45). Along with the massive influx of military and people in service industries principally in and around Pape'ete and the test sites, increasing numbers of Polynesians left their islands and agricultural subsistence base to become the labour force servicing the military, creating overcrowded and substandard living conditions in Pape'ete, in a pattern of increasing economic dependence on continuation of the test programme similar to that on Ebeye Island in Micronesia.

The French authority responsible for carrying out the test programme, France's Centre for Experimentation in the Pacific (CEP), began nuclear testing in 1966, exploding 41 nuclear devices above ground, 37 of which were at Mururoa, until in 1975, under intense international pressure including the 1973 International Court of Justice condemnation of tests, France agreed to cease atmospheric testing. France signed the 'Partial Test Ban Treaty' in 1975, 12 years after the other nuclear powers. In 1976 France resumed testing, exploding 137 devices underground between 1976 and 1992, of which 127 tests were at Mururoa, the remaining ten at Fangataufa Atoll. The majority of tests were conducted with devices lowered into holes drilled into the rock beneath the rim or in the lagoon of the atolls (De Planque 1998:21). In 1992 France halted the Pacific test programme, the same year the United States halted Nevada Desert tests and a year after the USSR ended their programme.

To the dismay of the Pacific nations and in the midst of international condemnation in mid-1995, the conservative French President Jacques Chirac announced that France would resume nuclear testing, conducting a series of eight underground tests at Mururoa Atoll. In their commentary on French nuclear testing in the Pacific, Alomes and Provis (1998:11) identify the 1995 resumption of testing as the last straw in 30 years of perceived indifference to the environment, health and future of the Pacific peoples. Following detonation of the first test which violated a moratorium observed by the nuclear powers (except China) since 1992, the largest and most violent protests ever seen in French Polynesia took place in Pape'ete. France was suspended as a dialogue partner from the South Pacific Forum and Australian, New Zealand, Japanese and some European parliamentarians marched in protest. After six nuclear tests between September 1995 and January 1996, France, stunned by the outrage expressed regionally and by international agencies and governments, bowed to pressure and on 30 January 1996 President Chirac announced the end to the French nuclear testing in the Pacific. In March 1996, France, Britain and the United States signed the Nuclear Free Pacific Zone Treaty (see below). The Fangataufa site is abandoned but Mururoa remains guarded by French Legionnaires.

DECOLONISATION, REGIONALISM AND A NUCLEAR-FREE PACIFIC: 1970–PRESENT

Throughout the 50 years of nuclear tests in the Pacific, Pacific Islanders have protested the right of foreign powers to test nuclear weapons and to be able to use their land to do so, not distinguishing between claims for self-government and for a nuclear-free Pacific. The modern era of the Pacific indigenous rights movement began immediately after World War II with the recognition of the right to self-determination for colonised peoples in the newly drafted Charter of the United Nations 1945 (Chapter XI, Article 73) and the onset of 50 years of Pacific nuclear testing (Blaisdell 1998).

In 1947 the colonial powers in the Pacific established the South Pacific Commission (SPC, which became the Secretariat of the Pacific Commission in 1997), to promote regional economic and social development towards self-government for the Pacific Island nations. Independent Pacific states were eligible to become members of the SPC but by the late 1960s, the organisation was still dominated by the colonial powers, including France. In 1971, the independent and self-governing Pacific Island countries plus Australia and Aotearoa/New Zealand established the Pacific Islands Forum to provide member nations with a forum to express their joint political views. A key factor leading to creation of the Forum was regional opposition to French testing. At the fourth annual Forum meeting in 1975, members adopted in principle a New Zealand proposal for a South Pacific Nuclear-Free Zone.

The Nuclear-Free and Independent Pacific Movement formally commenced that year with the first Nuclear-Free Pacific Conference held in Suva, Fiji. The movement was sponsored by a Pacific-wide network of antinuclear groups describing itself as a regional movement uniting indigenous and nonindigenous peoples campaigning for independence, sovereignty, human rights, demilitarisation, denuclearisation, true economic and social development, and environmental concerns (www.planet.org.nz/pacific_action.nfip.html). The nuclear-free Pacific movement 'became a modern crusade, uniting Pacific peoples in unprecedented numbers … and contributing to the creation of a shared Pacific identity' (Fischer 2002:238), compelling governments to take stronger antinuclear and anticolonial stands. Subsequent nuclear-free conferences were held in Pohnpei, Micronesia, in 1978, Hawai'i in 1980 and Port Villa, Vanuatu in 1983 from which was produced the People's Charter for a Nuclear-Free and Independent Pacific (NFIP) (the charter can be found at www.planet.org.nz/pacific_action.nfip.html). This called for a nuclear-free Pacific zone to be declared throughout the South Pacific and concluded that a nuclear-free Pacific could be attained only by independence from colonial imperialism. Development of a treaty establishing a nuclear-free zone in the Pacific was supported by the South Pacific Forum meeting in Tuvalu in 1984, and in 1985 nine Forum leaders meeting in Rarotonga signed the Pacific Nuclear-Free Zone Treaty ('Rarotonga Treaty') (www.forumsec.org.fj/). By the end of 1987, 13 Pacific nations had become signatories. The Treaty prohibits the acquisition of nuclear weapons by member states, testing of nuclear weapons, permanent stationing of nuclear weapons, waste dumping at sea and the threatened use of force against the Zone by the nuclear-armed powers (Smith 1991:98)

Regional and international support for a nuclear-free Pacific was further strengthened in July 1985 with the sinking of the Greenpeace flagship, the *Rainbow Warrior*, in Auckland Harbour by French Secret Service agents, killing a Greenpeace photographer. The *Rainbow Warrior* was en route to Mururoa where Greenpeace was to protest scheduled nuclear tests, having just returned from the Marshall Islands after evacuating all the population on Rongelap who were increasingly fearful of radioactive contamination following the discrediting of the earlier United States surveys on Bikini Atoll that had deemed the atoll safe for habitation (Weingartner 1991:19).

Within French Polynesia the 1980s saw an increasing alignment of the antinuclear and pro-independence agendas in political parties (von Strokirch 1991); however, protest about the test programme from within French Polynesia was complicated by economic dependence on the military presence. The same was true for the Marshall Islands in Micronesia. For both, sustainable economic development had not been the concern or interest of France or the United States respectively. The creation of a labour force dependent on military testing had been the aim, leading to an ambivalence in the populations in regard to demilitarisation alongside a fear that speaking out against the testing programmes would result in individual loss of income (Oldham 1999:11).

However, by 1995 opposition to the programme had strengthened, resulting in the violent protests in Pape'ete at the resumption of the French testing at Mururoa. The leading figure in the antinuclear and pro-independence movement in French Polynesia at this time was Oscar Temaru, himself a former worker on the Mururoa site. In 2004 and again in March 2005, Temaru was elected president of the Territorial Government of French Polynesia. He who considers French Polynesia to be 'French-occupied Polynesia' (Australian Broadcasting Corporation 2004) is now requesting access to files relating to the nuclear tests and in particular the health records of Polynesian workers at the site.

Fears that an end to the testing would bring an economic crisis to French Polynesia and in particular Tahiti were only partially realised. With the conclusion of the testing, a thousand Polynesian workers lost their jobs and the military contribution to the economy fell sharply. However, France continues to heavily subsidise the economy. In the Marshall Islands, continued United States military presence remains an economic mainstay for many Marshallese.

Although discussion in this chapter has been limited to places immediately and directly impacted by nuclear testing, the entire Pacific region has been affected by the potential leakage and spread of radioactive material from the test sites and transport of radioactive materials across the region by sea and in the air. In response, the South Pacific Forum initiated development of a further convention in 1994 known as the 'Waigani Convention' or Convention to Ban the Importation into Forum Island Countries of Hazardous and Radioactive Wastes and to Control the Transboundary Movement and Management of Hazardous Wastes within the South Pacific Region (www.forumsec.org.fj/). Sixteen Pacific nations including the Republic of the Marshall Islands, Republic of Palau, and the Federated States of Micronesia signed the Convention in 1995.

LEGACIES OF NUCLEAR TESTING IN THE PACIFIC

The environmental and health-related legacies of the French, British and United States test programmes in the Pacific are not easily determined due to the classified nature of much of the documentation relating to the tests, along with inadequate monitoring of the health of the people and the environments affected during and following the test programmes. This has made current and potential future health risks difficult to determine along with any links between the tests and current illnesses in both indigenous people and the veterans of the tests. Freedom of Information legislation in the United States and the United Kingdom has provided some access to previously classified documents relating to the tests. Most notably, this included evidence that the United States was aware some hours before the 1954 Bravo detonation over Bikini Atoll that changed directions in the prevailing winds would result in radioactive fallout over inhabited islands (Weingartner 1991:20). Much of the documentation on the French tests remains classified by the military.

Although there is lack of data on the effects of the tests on Pacific Islanders, and in particular those exposed to radiation during atmospheric testing in both the Marshall Islands and French Polynesia, there has been some success in claims for compensation over loss of land from people in the Marshall Islands and from veterans of the French tests for illness-related exposure to radioactive material during the tests.

Under the Compact of Free Association between the United States and the Republic of the Marshall Islands (1986), the United States agreed to reparations for damages to the Bikini Islanders as well as to other northern atolls in the Marshall Islands (see Smith 1991:73–77 for more details). Through the Bikini Claims Trust Fund, the Bikini Islanders were awarded $US75 million. In 2001, the Nuclear Claims Tribunal (also established under the Compact) handed down a decision in favour of the Bikini Islanders on a seven-year lawsuit the Bikinians had brought against the United States for damages done to their islands and their people during nuclear testing. However, the Nuclear Claims Tribunal, created by the Compact of Free Association, does not have the money to pay for this claim and the people of Bikini have petitioned the US Congress for the money (Niedenthal 2001).

Although part of the trust fund monies set up for the Bikini Islands was to assist their resettlement, clean-ups of the atoll have had only limited success in reducing the radioactivity to safe levels. In the mid-1990s, the government of the Marshall Islands requested the International Atomic Energy Association (IAEA) to undertake an independent review of radiological conditions on Bikini. The report recommended that Bikini Islanders should not resettle the atoll under the present conditions on the assumption that persons resettling the island would consume a diet of locally produced food leading to unacceptably high doses of radiation. The review recommended 'clean up' procedures that would limit the radioactivity uptake in plants (Stegnar 1998). Bikini Islanders regularly return to Bikini Atoll (Figure 4.2) to run the dive tours they operate on the wrecks of the numerous ships that were purposely sunk around the atoll during the nuclear tests (www.bikiniatoll.com/divetour.html). Many of these are well-known World War II battleships. The archaeology of nuclear testing provides a vehicle through which Bikini Islanders can raise awareness of their history and culture and generate employment and income. The Republic of the Marshall Islands in association with the Bikini government are developing a nomination of Bikini Atoll for inclusion on the UNESCO World Heritage List.

The United States Department of Energy is also assisting in resettlement programmes on Enewetak and Rongelap, providing monitoring of radiation levels for resettled populations and open access to results of the surveys. Through the Rongelap Resettlement Act of 1999, the US Congress approved and continued a 1996 resettlement agreement that saw Phase I of the resettlement programme initiated in 1998. Rongelap leaders engaged the US Department of Energy in developing a resettlement support plan to provide environmental monitoring to verify the effectiveness of cleanup methods on the island, and to develop local resources and expertise in radiation monitoring (eed.llnl.gov/mi/introduction.php; www.visitrongelap.com/index.html).

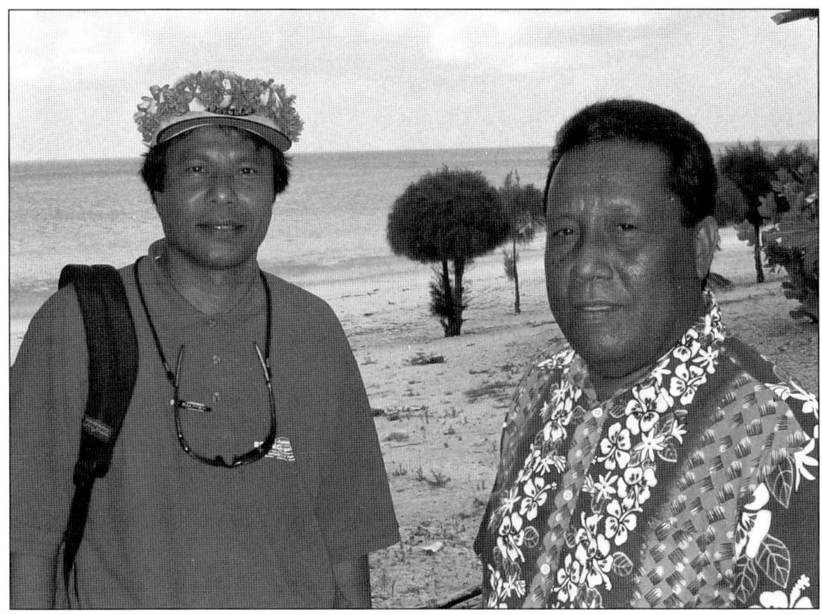

Figure 4.2. Bikinian Mayor Eldon Note and Bikinian Senator Tomaki Juda on Bikini Atoll on the 50th anniversary of the Castle Bravo detonation in March 2004. © Jack Niedenthal 2004

Serious health problems began to appear in the Rongelapese community immediately following the Bravo test. According to Weingartner (1991:20), by 1958 the rate of birth defects and miscarriages in Rongelap women was double that elsewhere in Micronesia; in 1963 the first thyroid tumour appeared and the number of these increased each year; and by 1985 nearly 80 percent of all Rongelapese under 10 years old in 1954 had developed tumours requiring surgery. Growth retardation and other physical and mental deformities have been increasing. Medical researchers for the United States Department of Energy have found that more than half of the Rongelapese suffer from a rare form of chromosome damage. A major concern continues to be whether children with stunted growth and other abnormalities are receiving their radiation dosage through their genes or from their environment (Pollock 2004).

The IAEA also undertook a study of the radiological levels at Mururoa and Fangataufa Atolls following closure of the test programme in 1996. The aim was to assess residual radiological conditions on the atoll and the potential for use of natural resources on the atolls in the future. The study concluded that residual radioactive material on the atolls was insufficient to harm health through radiation, no remedial action was necessary in regard to radiological level on the atolls, and no further environmental monitoring of the atolls is needed for purposes of radiological protection (De Planque 1998:23). Although a 'relatively large' amount of plutonium is present in the lagoons of both atolls, this delivers only very small doses of radiation due to its low rate of transfer to humans and the fact that the plutonium is being gradually washed out of the lagoon (Lindsay and McEwan 1998).

The findings of the IAEA study were similar to those of previous studies in the 1980s (Weingartner 1991:21) and at the recommencement of testing in 1995 (Office of the Chief Scientist 1995). Although recorded levels of radiation at the site are considered to pose no threat, concern remains about the long-term environmental effects of the tests because of the potential for leakage of radioactive material from underground tests. In 1995 it was unclear to what extent the structural integrity of the volcanic stone beneath the coral limestone atoll had been impaired by the tests (Office of the Chief Scientist 1995: 9). A substantial amount of radioactive material from the tests is trapped within this rock.

During the period of atmospheric testing, the French military set in place evacuation plans for people on nearby islands. On Mangareva Island, 400 km east of Mururoa, concrete shelters were constructed in which the island population would shelter for a number of days during tests at the order of the French military (Daeron 1996). It is the period of atmospheric testing that is of most concern for the health of Polynesian people who worked at the sites and for French veterans. Although the French authorities have always presented the test sites as a scientific laboratory, research on the long-term effects of the nuclear testing programme on the health of the test site workers was not contemplated during the programme or since (INESAP 1998). At times during the tests fishing was banned on Mururoa, but many Polynesian workers continued to catch and eat the fish. There is anecdotal evidence of an increase in birth defects in children of Polynesian men who worked at the sites. French Polynesia has the highest rate of thyroid cancer in the world. Until 1998 all hospitals in Pape'ete were controlled by the military, and the personal health records and even the names of French military and civil servants and Polynesians who worked on the test sites are classified by the French government.

Pressure from French veterans groups and the Mururoa Association of test site workers to release these records is mounting (Australian Broadcasting Commission 2004). The Association, led by Roland Oldham, has established a register for the estimated 10,000 Polynesians who worked at the sites over the 30 years of testing. In a landmark decision in 2003, the French military pensions tribunal ruled for the first time that an illness (a form of leukaemia) suffered by a French naval serviceman who spent 18 months on the Mururoa test site in 1961 was attributable to exposure to radiation during this time (Field 2003), opening the way for further cases to be heard. French veterans living in France claim to suffer twice the expected rate of cancer and a high rate of birth defects in their children (Australian Broadcasting Commission 2004).

During a recent visit to Paris as the newly elected president of French Polynesia, Oscar Temaru sought audience with President Chirac to request compensation for the Polynesian workers. The audience was not granted (Australian Broadcasting Commission 2004).

Johnston Atoll, site of United States atmospheric tests in the Central Pacific, is still polluted by plutonium from the tests. Johnston was also used for storage of Agent Orange after the Vietnam War and as a disposal site for United States chemical weapons, including those removed from Germany at the end of the Cold War. The facility has now been closed and cleanup of the atoll was completed in 2004 (www.cia.gov/cia/publications/factbook/geos/jq.html).

CONCLUSION

The Cold War provided the overriding rationale for weapons testing in the Pacific, but seen within the context of nineteenth- and twentieth-century colonialism, the test programmes are but one manifestation of the imposition of foreign economic, political and military regimes that can be read in the archaeological landscapes of the Pacific Islands. For those people of the Pacific directly affected by nuclear weapons testing, whether in ongoing individual and intergenerational health problems, loss of traditional lands and resources, or in a colonisation of the mind through fear of the effects of exposure to radioactive material (INESAP 1998), the second half of the twentieth century is an especially destructive period. However, any conceptualisation of the Cold War as an historic era in the Pacific would mask the reality of weapons testing and militarisation that has continued long after the formal end of Cold War hostilities. The long-term environmental and health effects of nuclear weapons testing are largely unknown and compensation, most notably moral compensation, has not been paid. French Polynesia is still an 'Overseas Land of France' and the independent Micronesian nations remain economically dependent on the United States.

ACKNOWLEDGEMENT

My thanks to Jack Niedenthal who generously provided images for this chapter.

REFERENCES

Alomes, S and Provis, M (1998) *French Worlds, Pacific Worlds: French Nuclear Testing in Australia's Backyard*, Port Melbourne, Vic.: Institute of French Australian Relations in association with Two Rivers Press

Australian Broadcasting Commission (2004) 'Tahiti: the bomb, the President and the French connection', *Foreign Correspondent*, Reporter: Trevor Borman

Blaisdell, K (1998) 'The Human Rights Movement in the Pacific', *In Motion Magazine, May 25,* http://www.inmotionmagazine.com/pacific.html (last accessed December 2006)

Daeron, M (1996) *Moruroa le grand secret*, a documentary film directed by Daeron and produced by Point du Jour International, released in 1996

Danielsson, B and Danielsson, M (1977) *Moruroa, Mon Amour: The French Nuclear Tests in the Pacific,* New York: Penguin Books

De Planque, E G (1998) 'International study of the radiological situation at the Atolls of Muroroa and Fangataufa. The Muroroa study', *International Atomic Energy Agency Bulletin* 40 (April 1998), 21–23

Field, C (2003) 'Mururoa nuclear blasts lethal, French tribunal rules', *New Zealand Herald,* 8 February

Fischer, SR (2002) *A History of the Pacific Islands,* New York: Palgrave Press

Hanlon, D (1998) *Remaking Micronesia: Discources over Development in a Pacific Trust Territory 1944–1982,* Honolulu: University of Hawai'i Press

Hayes, P, Zarsky, L and Bello, W (1986) *American Lake: Nuclear Peril in the Pacific,* Melbourne: Penguin Books

International Network of Engineers and Scientists Against Proliferation (INESAP) (1998) 'Muroroa and United States', *INESAP Bulletin*, 15 April 1998, http://www.inesap.org/bulletin15/bulletin15.htm (last accessed December 2006)

Lindsay, G and McEwan, A (1998) 'Potential doses at the Atolls. Assessing radiation doses attributed to residual radioactive material', *IAEA Bulletin* 40 (April 1998), 38–42

McDonald, B (1982) *Cinderellas of the Empire: Towards a History of Kiribati and Tuvalu*, Canberra: Australian National University Press

Niedenthal, J (2001) *For the Good of Mankind: a History of the People of Bikini and Their Islands*, Honolulu: University of Hawai'i Press

Office of the Chief Scientist (1995) The Impact of Nuclear Testing at Muroroa and Fangataufa. Paper prepared for the South Pacific Environment Minister's Meeting by a scientific advisory group, Brisbane, 16–17 August, Canberra: Department of the Prime Minister and Cabinet

Oldham, R (1999) 'Economic consequences of the end of the tests in Polynesia', in Proceedings of the Symposium *The French Nuclear Tests in Polynesia: Demanding the Truth and Proposal for the Future*, 20 February, Lyon: Centre of Documentation and Research on Peace and Conflicts

Pollock, N (2004) Marshall Islands Women's Health Issues Nuclear Fallout Paper, presented at Asia-Pacific Regional Meeting, Women's International League for Peace and Freedom, Christchurch, 28 February

Smith, G (1991) *Micronesia. Decolonisation and United States Military Interests in the Trust Territories of the Pacific Islands,* Canberra: Peach Research Centre, Australian National University

Stegnar, P (1998) 'Review at Bikini: Assessing radiological conditions at Bikini Atoll and the prospects for resettlement', *IAEA Bulletin*, April, 15–17

UNESCO (2003) Report of the Central Pacific World Heritage Project International Workshop, Honolulu, 2–6 June

US Army Space and Missile Defense Command Web site, www.smdc.army.mil/RTS.html (last accessed December 2006)

Von Strokirch, K (1991) 'The impacts of nuclear testing on politics in French Polynesia', *Journal of Pacific History* 26(2): 330–346

Weingartner, E (1991) *The Pacific Nuclear Testing and Minorities,* London: Minorities Rights Group

An ideological vacuum: The Cold War in outer space

ALICE GORMAN and BETH O'LEARY

INTRODUCTION

In 1945, as the Allies advanced into Germany, one of the early battles of the Cold War was fought. The USA and the USSR engaged in a race to acquire German rockets and rocket scientists (Lasby 1971; Neufeld 1996). The V2 rocket, developed by Wernher von Braun and his team, was to become the basis of Cold War missile technology. Over a decade later the descendants of the V2 rocket launched the first Earth satellites, and twenty-five years later, they propelled the first humans towards the Moon. In this chapter we look at the oldest surviving satellite, *Vanguard 1*, and the lunar landing site Tranquility Base, as part of the cultural heritage of the Cold War.

The Cold War was played out not only on the surface of the Earth, through military, political and social manoeuvres, but in space as well. One of the objectives of the International Geophysical Year (IGY) in 1957–1958 was to place a satellite into Earth orbit, an objective which provided a new arena for ideological antagonism between the USA and the USSR. When Russia successfully launched *Sputnik I* into orbit in 1957, the excitement of the first verifiable human entry into space was overshadowed by the fear of potential military threats. As a result, the US government redirected its support from the IGY scientific satellite *Vanguard* to the military *Explorer* satellite. When it was finally launched in 1958, *Vanguard 1*'s instrumentation reflected the conflicting views of space that surrounded its creation.

The 'Space Race' culminated with NASA's Apollo program and its crewed moon landings (1969–1972). Although much of the rhetoric surrounding this achievement emphasised (and continues to emphasise) the peaceful uses of space for 'all mankind' (Gorman 2003), the astronauts themselves were very aware that they were warriors in yet another battle of the Cold War (O'Leary et al 2003). In addition to the descent stage of the Lunar Module, the American flag, and the boot prints representing the first human steps on the surface of another world, Tranquility Base is littered with equipment and refuse from the mission. While it can be argued that this site is one of the most important cultural heritage places of the 20th century, it also represents the financial and political commitment made by the US government to demonstrate the ideological superiority of western technology and capitalism. As with frontiers on Earth, the empty expanse beyond the atmosphere was perceived as morally or ideologically empty as well: a space to be filled with the political and material culture of the victor in the Cold War.

THE IDEOLOGICAL VACUUM

Space is usually perceived as an empty vacuum; and indeed, prior to the International Geophysical Year, what actually lay beyond the Earth's atmosphere was a matter of conjecture. But if space was empty of life, of atmosphere, and of history, it was also empty of human values. Imprinting the cosmos with meaning was a driving force of 'the conquest of space' (Bryld and Lykke 2000:53).

In the USA, space was seen as the High Frontier, a new wilderness, not only a physical vacuum but also a 'moral vacuum' waiting to be filled. This was a tradition dating from the European colonisation of the North American continent. For the early colonists in the New World,

> Wilderness ... acquired significance as a dark and sinister symbol. [The pioneers] shared the long Western tradition of imagining the country as a moral vacuum, a cursed and chaotic wasteland. As a consequence, frontiersmen acutely sensed that they battled wild country not only for personal survival but in the name of nation, race, and God. Civilizing the New World meant enlightening darkness, ordering chaos and changing evil into good. (Nash 1967:24)

There was one significant difference between the New World wilderness and the wilderness of outer space: the absence of Indigenous subjects of conquest. Despite this, the goal of acquiring a new physical or ideological territory was identical. The metaphor of the Western frontier applied equally to the Cold War conquest of space (McCurdy 1997:159) and accorded well with two defining ideas at the foundation of US nationhood: manifest destiny and mission. Manifest destiny became current in the 1840s and was invoked to justify a colonial expansion 'prearranged by Heaven' (Merk and Merk 1963:24). The American pioneers combined this notion of their destiny with a mission to redeem the sins of the Old World by example, in the creation of a new order (Merk and Merk 1963:3). In the Cold War, this mission was expressed in the desire to gain the allegiance of Third World nations through the demonstration of high science.

The values that influenced early space technology – whether military or civilian, scientific or symbolic, capitalist or communist – mattered enormously, and would colour the future course of human interactions with space. Throughout the 'Space Race' of the 1950s and 1960s, the symbolic impact of space achievements shaped space policy far more than scientific considerations. This was true from the launch of the first Earth satellites in 1957 to the Apollo moon landings over a decade later. The earliest Soviet satellites have long since re-entered the atmosphere and thus been destroyed; but one satellite, the American *Vanguard 1*, remains in orbit as the oldest human object in space. The values this satellite carried into orbit reflect the conflicts, hopes and political realities of the late 1950s.

THE INTERNATIONAL GEOPHYSICAL YEAR

In 1950, as missile ranges and nuclear weapons were being developed around the world, a group of scientists decided that there should be a follow-up to the International Polar Years of 1882–1883 and 1932–1933. A solar maximum would occur in 1957–1958, and understanding the Arctic region had assumed an even greater importance for weather forecasting and radio communications since 1933. A proposal was prepared and in 1952 the International Council of Scientific Unions appointed the IGY committee, or CSAGI (Comité Spéciale de l'Année Géophysique Internationale). The original idea was expanded to include the study of the whole Earth, particularly the sun's influence on the Earth during the solar maximum (Chapman 1959:11, 101; Roberts 1958:1; Evans 1958).

The IGY was a massive effort of international scientific cooperation on a scale never before undertaken (Evans 1958:30). Major components of IGY studies were oceanography, glaciology, seismology, meteorology, the upper atmosphere and cosmic rays (Chapman 1959). By the time the IGY was announced, several countries were using rockets for both military purposes and upper atmosphere research. These included the USA, USSR, Britain, Australia, Japan and France (Wyckoff 1958:107). By inference, any of these nascent space-faring nations might develop a satellite launch capability. By 1954 the feasibility of a satellite launch appeared strong enough to include it in the IGY programme (Van Allen 1988:12-13; Chapman 1959:105; Green and Lomask 1970:23), and the image of a 'world-circling spaceship' was incorporated into the IGY's logo (Figure 5.1).

Figure 5.1. The IGY logo, featuring an earth satellite. Photograph courtesy of NASA

SOVIET AND UNITED STATES SATELLITE PROGRAMMES

On 29 July 1955, US President Eisenhower announced approval of plans for an IGY satellite programme. The Army, Air Force and Navy all had satellite projects in development. However, Eisenhower was concerned about initiating space exploration as a military enterprise. The Naval Research Laboratory's Vanguard project was based on sounding rocket technology and received preference over launch vehicles based on military missiles such as the Army Ballistic Missile Agency's proposal (von Braun and Ordway 1985:154). Scientific instrumentation was an important part of presenting the satellite as a peaceful object (Osgood 2000:209). Moreover, the Vanguard project would not use materials or technology needed for missile development (von Braun and Ordway 1985:155). Although there is some debate over its importance in the rationale for choosing Vanguard, it seems that the principle of 'overflight' was also a factor in preferring a 'civilian flavour' for the US satellite programme:

> Establishing the precedent of 'freedom of space' with a peaceful scientific satellite would smooth the way to overflying the Soviet Union with military reconnaissance satellites. (Neufeld 2000:232)

In the Soviet Union, official approval for a satellite programme had been given prior to the inclusion of an Earth satellite in the IGY programme (Gorin 2000). On 30 January 1956, a secret decree authorised the development of *Object D*, a heavy satellite loaded with scientific instruments designed for IGY research. *Object D* would become *Sputnik 3* in 1958. But *Object D* ran behind schedule, and the mastermind of the Soviet space programme, Sergei Korolev, began work on the 'Simple Satellite', specifically designed to become the first human object in space (Gorin 2000:38).

As the IGY approached in 1957, the USSR was prioritising a satellite launch while the USA concentrated on missile capabilities. At several points in the lead-up to IGY, Eisenhower and other military leaders were advised of the psychological impact of being second in space (Killian 1977:10; Osgood 2000). However, it was simply assumed that *Vanguard* would be the first; at this stage it was inconceivable to the USA that the USSR could take the lead in space development (Osgood 2000:212).

PROJECT VANGUARD

Vanguard 1 was a 15.2 cm aluminium sphere with four spring-released antennae mounted at 90 degrees to the 'equator', and weighing just 1.47 kg (Figure 5.2). It carried solar batteries that transmitted for over

Figure 5.2. The Vanguard satellite. Photograph courtesy of NASA

seven years (Green and Lomask 1970:49) and a battery-powered Minitrack transmitter that ended up only lasting three weeks (Hagen 1958:132). The satellite, its launch and orbit were designed to maximise scientific outcomes (eg Hagen 1958, Green and Lomask 1970:33–34). As the exact shape of the Earth and the distribution of its mass were unknown, a major contribution to geodesy could be made simply by observing *Vanguard's* orbital perturbations (Chapman 1959:14–18; Pickering 1958:133). In addition, four experiments were selected to fly on the satellite, one of which was designed by James Van Allen to measure cosmic ray intensity.

In addition to the actual satellite itself, the project involved a launch site (Cape Canaveral, Florida), the Viking/Aerobee-based launch vehicle, and an international tracking network. As the IGY was an international cooperative effort, the American IGY committee wanted to involve other countries and volunteers. This also contributed to the 'civilian flavour' of the project. Project Moonwatch, directed by the Smithsonian Astrophysical Observatory, comprised volunteers from 23 countries trained to provide highly accurate visual observations of *Vanguard's* orbit (Pickering 1958:133). Visual tracking would become especially important when the Minitrack batteries failed and radio tracking was impossible. Amateur radio groups and stations within the USA were invited to volunteer for radio tracking in Project Moonbeam (Green and Lomask 1970:101).

Eight countries established Minitrack stations to receive *Vanguard's* radio signals. Professional visual tracking was carried out with specially designed Baker-Nunn cameras located in nine countries. Because of its ideal location, the Woomera rocket range in South Australia was the only place with both a Minitrack station and a Baker-Nunn camera. Although the USA provided and transported the equipment, local scientists were vital to the establishment and operation of these tracking stations.

But *Vanguard* was not the first Earth satellite. It was not even the first American satellite. In the end, the launch and mission of the satellite were to be determined more by political considerations than those of scientific enquiry.

SPUTNIK 1 AND ITS IMPACT

Both the USA and the USSR outlined their satellite plans at an IGY conference in Barcelona in 1956 (Van Allen 1988:13; Chapman 1959:105; Gorin 2000:39). Despite this, when the Simple Satellite was launched as *Sputnik 1* on 4 October 1957, the USA was caught off-guard. Not only had the USSR successfully launched a satellite, but, at 83.6 kg, it was far larger than thought possible (Figure 5.3). None of the Baker-Nunn

Figure 5.3. *Sputnik 1*. Photograph courtesy of NASA

cameras organised for *Vanguard* were yet operational; instead, US scientists relied on the volunteer Moonwatch teams for visual acquisition of *Sputnik's* orbit (Green and Lomask 1970:194). A month later, on 3 November, the even larger *Sputnik II* (with the unfortunate dog Laika aboard) was launched. The rockets that had placed such massive payloads into orbit were, to the US government, frightening evidence of the 'missile gap'.

The shock with which the American public greeted the news of *Sputnik 1* has become the stuff of legend (eg Killian 1977). Many Americans felt that *Sputnik 1* was an affront to national pride and a violation of manifest destiny (Killian 1977:9). Nuclear weapons advocate Edward Teller's reactions were perhaps extreme, but reflected actual fears. He said that the United States had lost 'a battle more important and greater than Pearl Harbour', and when asked what might be found on the Moon, replied 'Russians' (Killian 1977:7–8). The USA was forced to recognise the existence of a competition, not just for missile superiority but, as Lyndon Johnson said in early 1958, for 'the position of total control over Earth' (quoted in Killian 1977:9).

LAUNCHING A US SATELLITE

While the Sputniks circled the Earth, *Vanguard* had its third test launch on 6 December 1957. It was a disaster: the launch vehicle blew up four feet from the ground in the full glare of publicity. The press labelled it *Flopnik* and *Kaputnik* (Killian 1977:119); in New York, the Soviet delegation to the United Nations asked if the USA would be interested in receiving aid as a technically backward nation (Green and Lomask 1970:210).

The commitment to the IGY and the carefully selected experiments planned for *Vanguard* followed a similar path to *Object D* in the USSR. Three weeks after *Sputnik 1* had been launched, Wernher von Braun's *Explorer* satellite project, at the Army Ballistic Missile Agency in Alabama, was authorised. This satellite would be launched on a military rocket: the Redstone-based *Jupiter C*. Keeping satellites free from military taint was no longer an important factor in the light of loss of national prestige (Killian 1977:121). *Sputnik 1* had created a military challenge for the USA.

On 31 January 1958, *Explorer 1* became the first US satellite in orbit. James Van Allen's cosmic ray instrumentation had been made compatible with either *Vanguard* or *Explorer*, and flew on the rival satellite (Van Allen 1988:13). And so it was the *Explorers I* and *II* that discovered the Van Allen radiation belts, considered to be one of the major achievements of the IGY (Chapman 1959:85, 106). The Explorer series of satellites also made full use of the tracking facilities and protocols established for *Vanguard*.

In the end, when *Vanguard 1* was successfully launched on 17 March of that year, it carried no internal scientific instrumentation (Van Allen 1988:13). But its scientific mission was not in vain. Analysis of *Vanguard's* orbit revealed that, as well as bulging around the equator, the Earth was pear-shaped. Part of the success of this component of the mission must be attributed to the dedication of the volunteer Moonwatch groups around the world. Analysis of atmospheric drag on *Vanguard* also proved the atmosphere to be far more extensive than previously thought.

THE SIGNIFICANCE OF *VANGUARD*

Vanguard was not the 'vanguard' after all; it is the satellite remembered for coming third, forever in the shadow of *Sputnik* and *Explorer*. But all the other early satellites have long since vanished in a fiery death. Only *Vanguard 1*, stable for perhaps another 600 years, continues to orbit the Earth as a physical testimony to the year when humans first ventured beyond the atmosphere. It has left a technological and scientific legacy that continues into the present.

In terms of the development of space systems, the *Vanguard* team worked out the principles and methods of thermal control, and devised electronic equipment of exceptional reliability (Green and Lomask 1970:252). For all stages of the satellite including the launch vehicle, a major innovation was miniaturised circuits. The solar cells placed on the satellite shell 'set a new standard of efficiency and accounted for the long operating life of *Vanguard 1*' (Green and Lomask 1970:254). Solar-powered batteries have since become a standard feature of satellites. The Minitrack network, set up for *Vanguard*, became the backbone of the NASA Satellite Tracking and Data Acquisition Network (Green and Lomask 1970:255). Despite its failure to be first in the 'Space Race', Project Vanguard is acknowledged as 'the progenitor of all American space exploration today' (Green and Lomask 1970:256).

As the sole survivor of those early days of space exploration, *Vanguard 1* represents a model of what space enterprise could be: cooperative, peaceful and inclusive. The influential Purcell committee, which advised Eisenhower after *Sputnik 1*, suggested this in 1958: 'Perhaps the International Geophysical Year will suggest a model for the international exploration of space in the years and decades to come' (PSAC 1958).

But *Vanguard* was also an ideological weapon, combining the paradoxical aims of presenting US space ambitions as peaceful and scientific, while demonstrating a technological superiority vital to maintaining the confidence of the free world and containing Communist expansion (Osgood 2000:213–14; see also Green and Lomask 1970:32). As 'a visible display of technological prowess', *Vanguard* was intended to be a deterrent (Osgood 2000:216). Charles Lindbergh sums up the significance of *Vanguard* in his foreword to Green and Lomask's history: '[I]t is a record of conflicting values, policies and ideas … an environment including atomic weapons, *Sputnik* and Cold War with the Soviet Union' (Lindbergh 1970:v).

APOLLO TO THE MOON

In May 1961 President Kennedy addressed the US Congress with a bold new proposal: 'I believe this nation should commit itself to achieving the goal, before this decade is out, of landing a man on the moon and returning him safely to the earth' (Chaikin 1994:15). Humans had first left marks on the lunar surface in 1959 with the Russian *Luna 2*, but three attempts by the USA to land survivable instrument packages on the Moon in 1962 failed (Johnson 1999). In 1961 Astronaut Alan Shepard had taken a 15-minute suborbital flight. Yet, in less than nine years, the USA was supposed to place a human on the Moon.

The Apollo program (1967–1972) was born in the context of the space race where, at its inception, the Soviets appeared to be winning. Although the Apollo program was considered to be a great catalyst for future scientific exploration of the cosmos, that was not its primary goal: it was part of a technological propaganda battle between the United States and the Soviet Union. A successful flight to the Moon would be considered a decisive win in a major battle of the Cold War.

As one of the most complicated endeavours in space, the race to the Moon had many stages. Both the earlier Soviet *Luna* and American *Ranger* uncrewed missions were necessary to achieving lunar orbit. The lead in reaching the Moon see-sawed back and forth, with the Russians usually ahead. The Soviet Union's *Luna 10* spacecraft was the first human object put into lunar orbit on 3 April 1966; it was duplicated four months later by the USA's *Lunar Orbiter 1* spacecraft, designed to find suitable Apollo landing sites (Johnson 1999). The temporary stay of the *Apollo 8* mission in lunar orbit in December 1968 opened a new period of intense lunar orbit operation. Lunar landings 'would come only after brief stays in lunar orbits to complete final preparations' (Johnson 1999).

A NEW BREED OF COLD WARRIOR

The astronauts who made up the Apollo program were all military men. Several were veterans of earlier space programmes such as Gemini. Their selection as participants in the voyages to the Moon was in many ways the product of a series of related events, and the luck of the draw. But not all were lucky. In 1967, the Apollo I crew of astronauts Grissom, White and Chaffee was killed in a launchpad fire; a faulty hatch design prevented their escape. Their deaths were treated as a national tragedy. The men who died were heroes, buried with full military honours. The incident was a terrible setback, but in less than a year *Apollo 8* astronauts Borman, Lovell and Anders became the first humans to leave Earth's orbit and orbit the Moon. The flight took place after such a short time because, according to Borman,

> There was an enormous drive to accomplish this before the Russians. That's why *Apollo 8's* mission was changed from an Earth Orbital to a Lunar Orbital Mission because NASA had word that – from the CIA – that the Russians were going to go around the moon before the end of '68. So they changed our mission. (videotaped interview with Frank Borman, 23 January 2001)

Borman, commander of the mission, saw the risk in the more ambitious flight plan but accepted it as absolutely necessary to getting a man on the Moon first, before the Soviets. In an interview in 2001, Borman said, 'The Apollo program wasn't a voyage of exploration or … expertise in advancing technology. It was a battle in the Cold War' (videotaped Interview with Frank Borman, 23 January 2001). With untested technology and skills, the *Apollo 8* crew successfully orbited the Moon, flying 70 miles above its surface, to locate a place for future missions to land. On Christmas Eve 1968 they sent back pictures and a quote from Genesis as they gazed at the Earth – as if it had just been created. When picked up after splashdown in the ocean and asked if the Moon was made of Limburger cheese, Astronaut Anders answered, 'No, it's made of American cheese' (Chaikin 1994:197).

Even after *Apollo 8's* success, the Soviets continued to plan a crewed Moon mission. But four Soviet uncrewed launches ended in disaster. The third Soviet launch occurred only thirteen days before the scheduled launch of *Apollo 11* (Chaikin 1994:358).

THE OUTER SPACE TREATY AND CLAIMS TO THE MOON

The final stage in claiming the Moon was standing on it. That event happened on 20 July 1969 (Figure 5.4).

The landing by the *Apollo 11* crew of Collins, Armstrong and Aldrin was an achievement watched by 600 million people worldwide (Burrows 1998). Although hailed by astronaut Armstrong as 'one small step for man, one giant leap for mankind', it was an American who stepped

Figure 5.4. *Apollo 11* astronaut footprint. Photograph courtesy of NASA

on the Moon and much of the material culture put there symbolised its national presence.

According to Article II of the United Nations *Treaty on Principles Governing the Activities of States in the Exploration and Uses of Outer Space, Including the Moon and Other Celestial Bodies* (the Outer Space Treaty) of 1967, the Moon is 'not subject to national appropriation by claim of sovereignty by means of use or occupation, or by any other means'. Essentially, no one can claim or own the Moon. But Article VIII of the Outer Space Treaty allows objects or parts of objects and personnel in space to remain the property of the nation that put them there. The objects brought to the lunar surface by Armstrong and Aldrin remain under the jurisdiction of the United States (Gibson 2001:21). Although the legal tenets of the Outer Space Treaty and rhetoric of Armstrong's statement point to an ownership and achievement of all humankind on the Moon, NASA decided that the American flag would be raised during the first walk on the Moon (Chaikin 1994:316). It was one of the first activities the astronauts engaged in after landing (Figure 5.5).

This act was symbolic of claiming territory and victory set by historic precedent. The names of the spacecraft involved in the first lunar landing – *Columbia* and *Eagle* – were also metaphors for America. The flag was even engineered to appear to wave in the breeze on the windless surface of the Moon. When President Nixon called to congratulate them, the two astronauts in front of the flag saluted their commander-in-chief. To nations other than the USA, and even to some of those involved in the American effort, the flag on the Moon was an unwarranted gesture. To the Soviets it must have signalled a defeat in space.

TRANQUILITY BASE AS AN ARCHAEOLOGICAL SITE

As well as producing thousands of images, a small sketch map was later made of the Tranquility Base landing site by the United States Geological Survey. Over 106 objects were left on the Moon's surface during the *Apollo 11* mission (Lunar Legacy web site). It had been necessary to jettison a large amount of material to ensure that the weight of lunar rock and soil samples collected did not prevent the *Eagle* from leaving the surface of the Moon. The inventory left on the Moon by the *Apollo 11* mission varies from tongs and overshoes to emesis (human vomit) bags and a Laser Ranging Retroreflector that measured precisely the distance between Earth and the Moon (Gibson 2001:133–135). A mission patch with the names of the deceased *Apollo 1* astronauts was also

---

Figure 5.5. Astronaut with flag. Photograph courtesy of NASA

Figure 5.6. *Apollo 1* Mission Patch. Photograph courtesy of NASA

left (Figure 5.6). Even the craft which had carried the two astronauts to the Moon was jettisoned, and later de-orbited and crashed on the surface.

An archaeologist visiting the Tranquility Base lunar landing site a thousand years in the future would view the assemblage as American material culture representing the international community. The plaque on the *Eagle's* descent stage reads 'Here men from the planet Earth first set foot upon the moon. July 1969 AD. We came in peace for all mankind'. Below the signatures of the astronauts are the printed name, title and signature of US President Nixon. Goodwill messages from 73 world nations etched on the silicon disk deposited at the site turn the focus of *Apollo 11* to a mission of peace and human endeavour. But there was no message from the Soviet Union (Gibson 2001:66).

When *Apollo 17* astronauts returned home in mid-December of 1972, they left behind the last deposit of cultural resources associated with the Apollo program on the Moon. The Apollo program ended because of budget cuts, the diversion of political and public support by events in Vietnam, and domestic concerns in the USA. It has been argued that the Apollo program was never more than another battlefront in the Cold War (Gibson 2001:56). Once the USA had won that battle by first placing men on the Moon and returning them safely to Earth, the Cold War in space had been won.

CULTURAL HERITAGE MANAGEMENT IN SPACE

The record of human material culture in space began with the launch of the first artificial satellite from Earth on 4 October 1957 (Johnson 1999:1). Although space now contains many more objects and debris, including the recent tracks of the Rover on the planet Mars, the majority of space sites whether in orbit or on other celestial bodies were created within the historical context of the Cold War. The Cold War resulted from political and economic destabilization worldwide after World War II, and global conflicts between democratic nations in the West and communist nations in the East (Walker 1993). As a result of the development of nuclear weapons, long-range missiles and new forms of espionage, outer space became an area where the conflict between the USA and USSR was played out.

In the USA there has been recognition of the importance of space heritage in the Cold War period (1946–1989) by many federal agencies, and some sites have been identified as National Historic Landmarks including the Saturn V Dynamic Test Stand in Huntsville, Alabama, and the Apollo Mission Control Center in Houston, Texas. All significant Cold War sites, however, have been in the United States and on Earth. US Federal Cultural Resource Management Law affords consideration and protection to significant sites under several acts and implementing regulations (ie NHPA, 36 CFR 800, 36 CFR 60) but has never been applied to objects in space or on the Moon.

As yet, no state has attempted to extend national heritage protection to orbital objects like *Vanguard 1*. But this principle has been tested on the Moon. Funded by a small research grant from the New Mexico Space Grant Consortium under NASA in 2000, O'Leary, Gibson and Versluis prepared an archaeological inventory and base sketch map of the Apollo 11 Tranquility Base Lunar Landing Site and proposed to nominate the objects, structures and features at the site as a National Historic Landmark (NHL) (Figure 5.7; O'Leary et al 2003). This was proposed as a first step in nominating the Apollo 11 site for UNESCO's World Heritage List. Other Apollo sites and Russian sites on the Moon also clearly qualify. This first lunar landing site met all US federal preservation law criteria, but both NASA, as the federal agency responsible for the nomination, and the National Park Service, as the Keeper of the National Register of Historic Places, were not supportive of the nomination. In brief, the Deputy General Counsel for NASA, Robert Stephens, declined to pursue the nomination, stating that 'listing of lunar areas as NHL's is likely to be perceived by the international community as a claim over the moon' (personal correspondence, R. Stephens, 18 Aug 2000). The Keeper of the National Register of Historic Places, Carol Shull, wrote

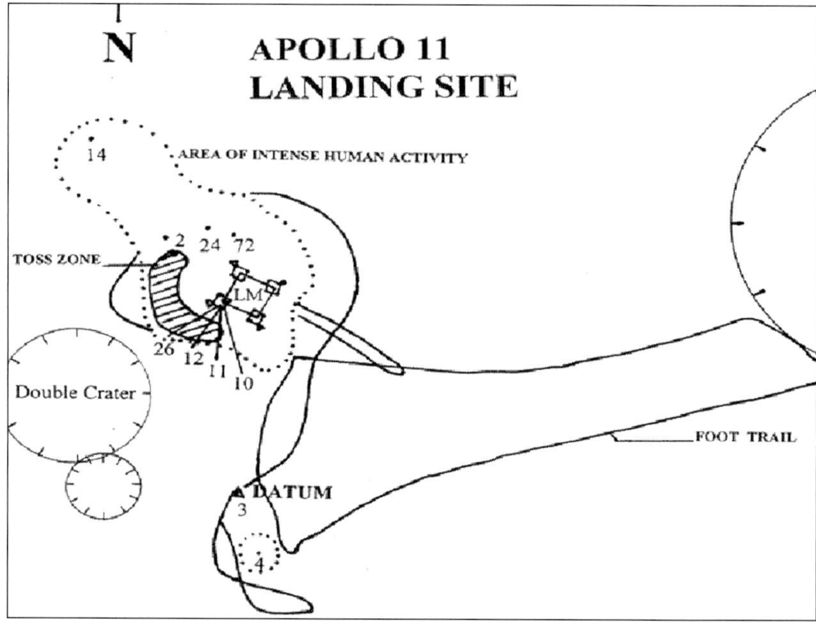

Figure 5.7. The diagram is based on revisions to the Apollo 11 Lunar Traverse map prepared by the U.S. Geological Survey and published by the Defense Mapping Agency for NASA. Courtesy of NASA and the Lunar and Planetary Institute

that 'it has been determined as a matter of policy that it would not be appropriate to designate NHL's on the moon.... we do not consider we have sufficient jurisdiction and authority over the land mass of the moon' (personal correspondence, C. Shull, 8 June 2000). Clearly the US federal preservation authorities do not want the responsibility for having a space heritage site as part of the US National Register even though the Outer Space Treaty gives them jurisdiction over the artefacts.

CONCLUSIONS

The two space sites discussed here, the *Vanguard 1* satellite and Tranquility Base, represent different aspects of the Cold War political landscape. *Vanguard 1* was conceived as a civilian, scientific and co-operative enterprise that could provide a model of the human future in space. *Sputnik 1* burned another trajectory – competitive, adversarial and ideological – which throve on the divisions between the Eastern and Western blocs. It was in this spirit that the *Apollo 11* mission placed the US flag on the surface of the Moon, and left the *Apollo 1* mission patch (Figure

5.6) to commemorate the Cold War warriors who met their deaths in the conquest of space.

By placing human material culture in orbit and on the surface of the Moon, lasting monuments of human meaning became part of the fabric of outer space. Space was no longer 'empty'; the frontier had been traversed and conquered. The Apollo missions proved that manifest destiny had not been violated by the Russian Sputniks. American values had been planted in the soil of a new world through the flag, the furrows and the footprints left by the lunar missions. Between *Vanguard 1* and *Apollo 11*, the escalation of the Cold War on Earth transformed space from the province of all humanity, as envisioned in the Outer Space Treaty, to a territory to be won for the most technologically advanced state. *Vanguard 1* and Tranquility Base illustrate the symbolic meanings that the material culture of space exploration was expected to convey, both then and now. Ironically, it is the very symbolism of the *Apollo 11* flag as a territorial claim that prevents the USA from extending heritage protection to Tranquility Base today.

The material culture of recent history is perhaps the most difficult to preserve. For some who lived in the era of the Cold War, the site's objects and structures appear to be outdated, obsolete trash. With multiple multimedia images and records of space endeavours, such as the Apollo program, the preservation of objects and structures on the Moon may seem redundant. After all, they have lain undisturbed for 37 years. One of the most acceptable and prevalent methods of cultural heritage management is avoidance of impacts to sites. So far, there have been no human impacts on the Apollo lunar sites or on nonfunctioning satellites since they were first created, but as space industries and eventual space colonisation develop in the 21st century, it is necessary to consider what and how elements of this cultural heritage should be preserved for the benefit of future generations (World Archaeological Congress Space Heritage Task Force website). Artefacts *in situ* on the Moon and in orbit around celestial bodies, like *Vanguard 1*, possess integrity of location, setting, association and feeling that make them significant to an important and as yet underinvestigated part of Cold War material culture – outer space. At this time, space heritage properties, with the exception of some of their components on Earth, remain without preservation protection.

The symbolic dimensions of Cold War material culture in space continue to resonate in the 21st century. *Vanguard 1* was designed to be a peaceful, scientific mission representing international cooperation, and also an ideological weapon to contain communist expansion in the Third World. The *Apollo 11* mission 'came in peace for all mankind' and yet left the Moon marked with national symbols. These conflicting values affect more practical considerations of how, and why, space sites should be protected. The way in which space-faring states treat the heritage of space exploration, as the Lunar Legacy Project so clearly demonstrates, is strongly linked to how they perceive their future in space. Assertions of national heritage significance risk being interpreted as territorial claims by extending a national jurisdiction into space. On the other hand, to claim that these sites have a global significance is to reinforce the inclusive definition of space as the province of all humanity irrespective of economic or scientific development, promoted by the Outer Space Treaty. The dominant ideology in the vacuum of outer space is still contested as a new era of space exploration begins.

REFERENCES

Borman, F (2001) Videotaped interview on 23 January 2001 with Beth O'Leary and Ralph Gibson. On file at the Rio Grande Archives, New Mexico State University, Las Cruces.

Burrows, W (1998) *This New Ocean*, New York: Random House

Bryld, M and Lykke, N (2000) *Cosmodolphins: Feminist Cultural Studies of Technology, Animals, and the Sacred*, New York: Zed Books

Chaikin, A (1994) *A Man on the Moon*, Alexandria, Va.: Time-Life Books

Chapman, S (1959) *IGY: Year of Discovery: The Story of the International Geophysical Year*, Ann Arbor: University of Michigan Press

Evans, JW (1958) 'Instrumentation for global observation of the sun during the IGY', in Odishaw, H and Ruttenberg, S (eds) *Geophysics and the IGY: Proceedings of the symposium at the opening of the International Geophysical Year, 28–29 June 1957*, Washington DC, American Geophysical Union of the National Academy of Sciences – National Research Council. Publication No. 590, 21–30

Gibson, RD (2001) *Lunar Archaeology: The Application of Federal Historic Preservation Law to the Site Where Humans First Set Foot upon the Moon*, Las Cruces: M.A. Thesis. Department of Sociology and Anthropology, New Mexico State University

Gorin, PA (2000) 'Rising from the cradle: Soviet perceptions of spaceflight before Sputnik'. In Launius, RD, Logsdon, JM and Smith RW (eds) *Reconsidering Sputnik: Forty Years Since the Soviet Satellite*, London: Harwood Academic Publishers, 11–42

Gorman, AC (2003) 'The cultural landscape of space', Paper presented at the Fifth World Archaeological Congress, Washington DC

Green, C and Lomask, M (1970) *Vanguard: A History*, Washington DC: NASA SP-4204. The NASA Historical Series

Hagen, JP (1958) 'The Vanguard Satellite Launching Vehicle – placing the satellite in orbit', in Odishaw, H and Ruttenberg, S (eds) *Geophysics and the IGY: Proceedings of the symposium at the opening of the International Geophysical Year, 28–29 June 1957*, Washington DC, American Geophysical Union of the National Academy of Sciences – National Research Council. Publication No. 590, 119–132

Johnson, N (1999) *Man-made Debris in and from Lunar Orbit*, American Institute of Aeronautics and Astronautics. IAA-99-IAA.7.1.03

Killian, JR, Jr (1977) *Sputnik, Scientists and Eisenhower: A Memoir of the First Special Assistant to the President for Science and Technology*, Cambridge, MA: MIT Press

Lasby, CG (1971) *Project Paperclip: German Scientists and the Cold War*, New York: Atheneum

Lindbergh, C (1970) 'Foreword', in Green, C and Lomask, M (1970) *Vanguard: A History*, NASA SP-4204. Washington, DC: The NASA Historical Series, v–viii

Lunar Legacy Web site (2001) http://spacegrant.nmsu.edu/lunarlegacies/ (last accessed December 2006)

McCurdy, HE (1997) *Space and the American Imagination*, Washington: Smithsonian Institution Press

Merk, F and Merk, LB (1963) *Manifest Destiny and Mission in American History: A Reinterpretation*, New York: Alfred A. Knopf

Nash, R (1967) *The Wilderness and the American Mind*, London: Yale University Press

Neufeld, MJ (1996) *The Rocket and the Reich: Peenemünde and the Coming of the Ballistic Missile Era*, Cambridge: Harvard University Press

Neufeld, MJ (2000) 'Orbiter, overflight and the first satellite: New light on the Vanguard decision', in Launius, RD, Logsdon, JM and Smith, RW (eds) *Reconsidering Sputnik: Forty Years Since the Soviet Satellite*, London: Harwood Academic Publishers, 231–257

O'Leary, B, Gibson, R, Versluis, J and Brown, L (2003) 'Lunar archaeology: A view of Federal US Historic Preservation law on the moon', Paper presented at the Fifth World Archaeological Congress, Washington DC

Osgood, KA (2000) 'Before Sputnik: National security and the formation of US outer space policy', in Launius, RD, Logsdon, JM and Smith, RW (eds) *Reconsidering Sputnik: Forty Years Since the Soviet Satellite*, London: Harwood Academic Publishers, 197–229

Pickering, WH (1958) 'The United States satellite tracking program', in Odishaw, H and Ruttenberg, S (eds) *Geophysics and the IGY: Proceedings of the symposium at the opening of the International Geophysical Year, 28–29 June 1957*, Washington DC, American Geophysical Union of the National Academy of Sciences – National Research Council. Publication No. 590, 133–141

President's Science Advisory Committee (1958) *Introduction to Outer Space*, Reprinted in Killian 1977

Roberts, WO (1958) 'Solar-terrestrial relationships', in Odishaw, H and Ruttenberg, S (eds) *Geophysics and the IGY: Proceedings of the symposium at the opening of the International Geophysical Year, 28–29 June 1957*, Washington DC, American Geophysical Union of the National Academy of Sciences – National Research Council. Publication No. 590, 1–5

Shull, C (2001) Personal correspondence dated 8 June 2000. On file at the Rio Grande Archives, New Mexico State University, Las Cruces.

Space Heritage Task Force Web site (2003) http://www.worldarchaeologicalcongress.org/site/active_spac.php (last accessed December 2006)

Stephens, RM (2001) Personal correspondence dated 18 August 2000. On file at the Rio Grande Archives, New Mexico State University, Las Cruces.

United Nations (1967) *Treaty on the Principles Governing the Activities of States in the Exploration and Use of Outer Space, Including the Moon and Other Celestial Bodies*, New York: United Nations

Van Allen, JA (1988) 'Early days of space science', *Journal of the British Interplanetary Society* 41: 11–15

von Braun, W and Ordway, F (1985) *Space Travel: A History*, New York: Harper and Row

Walker, M (1993) *The Cold War*, New York: Henry Holt and Company

Wyckoff, PH (1958) 'The rocket as research vehicle', in Odishaw, H and Ruttenberg, S (eds) *Geophysics and the IGY: Proceedings of the symposium at the opening of the International Geophysical Year, 28–29 June 1957,* Washington DC, American Geophysical Union of the National Academy of Sciences – National Research Council. Publication No. 590, 102–107

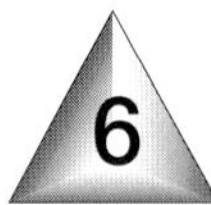

Shaping military women since World War II

MARGARET VINING

INTRODUCTION

Uniforms that defined military women in the Cold War belong to the larger story of military service and citizenship, mass mobilisation, and the concept of total war. Since the seventeenth century, soldiers' uniforms have shaped the actions and habits of men, imposing a discipline that transforms individual strength into collective power. Central to the foundation of the military, uniforms are proof of an imposed discipline; they are also indisputably masculine (Roche 1994: 228–239). This study uses a form of material culture, the clothing of everyday life, which is usually unavailable to traditional archaeologists and which they are forced to reconstruct from perhaps a few bone buttons, brooches and lace ends.

During the nineteenth century, martial clothing and uniforms in general proliferated among civilians. Public servants such as police, postmen, firemen, and railroad employees, became uniformed. Occupational uniforms and other types of standardised clothing also differentiated workers, professionals, youth groups, and members of fraternal and social organisations.

Uniforms, then as now, distinguished members of groups and organisations from nonmembers, implying commitment and influencing or constraining behavior. What constitutes a uniform has no easy answer. Basic questions about uniforms have gone unresolved despite their social and cultural importance. Civilian uniforms often adopt a military-style hierarchy of rank, frequently gendered. Men are more likely to be seen wearing 'the uniforms of hierarchical authority' – doctors in lab coats, for instance – women 'the uniforms of service' – nurses in caps and aprons (Steele 1989:68; Crane 2000:87–94).

The resources for this chapter are drawn from the outstanding collection of uniforms and accessories in the Division of Military and

Diplomatic History (formerly Armed Forces History) Collections at the National Museum of American History. Among them, one unique group of approximately fifty uniforms worn by women volunteers during World War I, civilian and military, provides a useful backdrop for this discussion about women's military apparel in the Cold War.

WORLD WAR I

In World War I, at least in the United States, women volunteers by the tens of thousands—civilian as well as quasi-military and a few military—wore uniforms that exhibited overt military features and suppressed gender distinctions. Most women wore skirts—those in motor corps were exceptions—but otherwise their uniforms were visibly modeled on men's: service-coloured (khaki, olive green, navy, black, grey whipcord) overseas caps or service hats, belted coats with four front pockets, lapels with insignia, shoulder straps with 'US' and organisational insignia, braid

Figure 6.1. One of eighteen cases displaying the uniforms worn by women in World War I in an exhibition in the Smithsonian's National Museum, ca 1925. National Museum of American History, Division of Military and Diplomatic History

trim, overseas stripes on the lower sleeve, and official shoulder sleeve insignia.

The army and the navy in World War I authorised an outdoor uniform for their nurse corps. The Army Nurse Corps became an official component of the military in 1901, the Navy Nurse Corps in 1908. The new uniform supplemented traditional regulation nurses' work uniforms of starched dresses, aprons and caps, which had changed little since Florence Nightingale decreed uniforms for nurses in the Crimean War more than half a century before. It was markedly similar to the outdoor uniforms of the thousands of Red Cross nurses who were contracted for the war effort.

In the mass mobilisation for World War I, neither the presence of uniformed women nor the suitability of their uniforms stirred controversy. Nor did the wearers gain a lasting place in the armed forces despite their impressive and enthusiastic service. They were generally educated middle- and upper-class women who, at the end of the war (with the exception of nurses) put aside uniforms and disappeared from the military. Yet, the uniforms women had donned for war work confirmed a major social change. Uniforms in the war were as important to women as they were to men, central to their military experience, identifying them and defining their roles. Clearly, women regarded their war work morally equivalent to military service (Lurie 1981:17–20; Ewing 1975:11–12).

That their wartime service accounted, at least in part, for the passage of the woman's suffrage constitutional amendment underscored the uniforms' significance, as did the extension of the franchise to women in Britain, Germany, and several other countries (Frevert 1989:151–167; Law 1997; Holton 1996:205–226). Given the ancient link between military service and citizenship, the wearing of uniforms can be regarded as a statement of loyalty and patriotism and a symbolic claim to citizenship.

WORLD WAR II

With the onset of World War II, women in civilian agencies again organised for war work, many in the same organisations whose members had worn smart paramilitary uniforms in the earlier war. This time, however, volunteer efforts were largely overshadowed by the unprecedented and highly contested recruitment of women into the armed forces. But the women who flocked to join the military were considered a wartime exigency, their wardrobe a concern only 'for the duration'. It was unthinkable that the uniforms developed for women in World War II might become the standard dress for US military women for decades following the war.

Figure 6.2. The first uniform design for the WAAC, officer and enlisted, showing plastic buttons and insignia, and belted jacket. National Archives and Records Administration

Military supply systems in the United States that had for almost two centuries procured uniforms for soldiers, approached the challenge of women's uniforms arbitrarily, drawing little from previous experience with nurses' uniforms. From the start, a preoccupation with femininity among decision-makers – army officials and motherly directors of the women's contingents – characterised selections of uniforms for all services. The notion of imposing femininity on women in the military pointed up the acute disjuncture between expectations of society and demands of military service. Women recruited to 'free a soldier to fight' took over support jobs in a wide variety of fields wearing uniforms deemed appropriate for ladies, rather than functional apparel designed for the work they would do (Risch 1945:37–89; Holm 1982:39–43; Morden 1990:437–440). Women's World War II uniforms imposed a ladylike comportment that would continue to set them apart through most of the Cold War, belying their integration into the military institution.

The army, where most women were recruited, moved first among the services early in World War II, establishing the Women's Army Auxiliary Corps (WAAC) in May 1942. The WAAC was run by the army but it was not quite part of the army. Pressured on issues of fairness, the WAAC was converted to the Women's Army Corps (WAC) in September 1943, a change that gave its members pay comparable to their male counterparts and more military privileges.

To keep costs low and help women blend into soldierly environments, the army designated a no-nonsense quartermaster-designed wardrobe for its women. By long-accepted practice, the army's quartermaster was obligated to provide whatever it required soldiers to wear. For women this included not only the standard uniform – jacket, skirt, and shirt, of the same colour and fabric as men's uniforms – but also regulation accessories: the unpopular 'Hobby hat' (named for the first director of the

Figure 6.3. The WAAC uniform in service, worn by an actual servicewoman rather than a model. The belt was soon discarded. National Museum of American History, Division of Military and Diplomatic History

Figure 6.4. Snapshot from the WAC scrapbook of Corporal Margaret Godbold. The inscription on this snapshot reads: 'Issue underwear. Real glamour girls'. National Museum of American History, Division of Military and Diplomatic History

Figure 6.5. Snapshot from the WAC scrapbook of Corporal Margaret Godbold. Contemporary comment noted on reverse is: 'Hobby hat on end girl was not popular. We like caps'. National Museum of American History, gift of Margaret Godbold

WAAC and WAC), rayon and cotton stockings in a suntan shade, gloves, purses, even khaki foundation garments (brassieres and girdles) for a 'neat and military appearance', as well as khaki nylon tricot undergarments (Treadwell 1954:38–39).

Attractive on the drawing board and ambitious in the array of regulation accessories presented, the Women's Army Auxiliary Corps' first uniform nonetheless required endless revisions to make it conform to the shapes and sizes of its wearers (Risch 1945:37–89). The belted jacket was quickly deemed unflattering and too bulky; plastic buttons embossed with a lopsided eagle known as the WAAC 'buzzard' were soon replaced with gold-coloured buttons bearing the US coat of arms. A garrison or overseas cap was added to the wardrobe to supplement the uniform's Hobby hat, which required special blocking and too much maintenance. Modifications and supplements continued throughout the war, compounding already chronic problems of short supply.

At the same time, the army's Quartermaster Research and Development office developed innovative fabrics and types of clothing for soldiers that could be worn in layers, enabling men to use combinations of the same uniform in a variety of climates. Near the end of the war, the Quartermaster began to issue female versions of standardised field clothing to a select few nurses and women motor transport personnel in tropical climates. However, theatre regulations required women to carry a special daily pass attesting the necessity for such uniforms (Risch 1945:135).

THE COLD WAR

By the beginning of the Cold War, army women could have a closet full of regulation clothing – a female version of the 'Ike' jacket; a white dress uniform; utility parka, slacks, shirts, and caps for outdoor work and for cold weather climates; helmets; athletic wear and more, depending upon availability. They could also purchase their own undergarments. Still, the most frequent complaints reportedly made by women in the field during World War II, Korea, and Vietnam centred on inappropriate clothing and the necessity of wearing men's sturdier utility shirts, trousers, and boots in harsh work environments (Holm 1992:238–240).

The navy and coast guard brought women recruits into their reserves from the summer of 1942, and the marines in 1943, according them the same military privileges as men. Unlike the army, the navy turned to women and professionals to make critical uniform decisions for women members of the navy and Marine Corps. By 1952 they wore 'haute couture' uniforms by New York designer Mainbocher, high fashion that endured well into the Cold War as the mainstay of the wardrobe for navy women. A clothing allowance permitted them to purchase specified uniforms, underwear, and accessories; women marines were also required to purchase and wear a special brand and hue of lipstick and nail polish, 'Montezuma Red', to conform to the colour of the red cord on the uniform hat (Stremlow 1994:17–19).

Concurrent with the developing Cold War, the Women's Armed Services Integration Act of June 1948 made women permanent members of the armed forces of the United States. The new United States Air Force, recently independent from the army and determinedly elitist, accepted women in 1947. Designated the Women's Air Force (WAF), women in the air force did not form a separate corps as did the postwar Women's Army Corps (WAC). The air force professed to be more inclusive of its women members than the other services but soon fell back, rationalising the peacetime closing to women of many of its specialties.

Major Muriel Ardery, USAF retired, a member of the ad hoc USAF uniform board, relates that General Hoyt Vandenberg, Chief of Staff of the Air Force, took a personal interest in the development of uniforms for the new service. He advanced his perception of appropriate women's uniforms for a new military elite – the glamorous jet-age air force – calling for chic, stylish outfits similar to those of contemporary airline stewardesses. Colours for the first air force uniforms for men and women set in place the US Air Force tradition of silvery grey and blue (Ardery 1988:4).

The postwar army, linking enlistment of women and force retention to an appealing uniform, followed the other services to provide a 'power suit' uniform for the Women's Army Corps. Designed by a noted fashion creator, Hattie Carnegie, the fashionable taupe uniform proved to be extremely unpopular, drawing strongest objections from women because it was not military enough. The army made several unfortunate attempts in the 1950s, 1960s, and 1970s to settle on suitable clothing for women before finally issuing service uniforms similar to those of male soldiers and adopting universally sized work clothing (Morden 1990:457).

Artificial distinctions in the treatment of female and male soldiers were called into question increasingly in the early 1970s after

---

Figure 6.6. Noted clothing designer Hattie Carnegie included four women's uniforms in her 1951 collection. National Museum of American History, Division of Costumes

Figures 6.7–6.10. In 1969, the Defense Advisory Committee on Women in the Service (DACOWITS) sponsored a fashion show highlighting women's uniforms past and present. These four represent current uniforms for the navy, air force, army nurse corps, and the army summer uniform. National Museum of American History, Division of Military and Diplomatic History

Figure 6.11. Women cadets at the United States Air Force Academy, ca 1989. National Museum of American History, Division of Military and Diplomatic History

Figure 6.12. Major General Tiiu Kera, second from left, with members of a general officer's tour at Langley Air Force Base, Virginia. Courtesy of MG Tiiu Kera, USAF Ret.

congressional approval of the Equal Rights Amendment. Court challenges to the constitutionality of discriminatory practices by the military also eliminated some inequities during the 1970s; women were admitted to the national service academies.

By the end of the decade, all branches of the services abolished separate women's units, integrating women into the regular forces. Military uniforms document many of these major developments: Insignia representing expanding job opportunities; eagles and stars on shoulder straps illustrating the lifting of the grade ceiling (1967); maternity uniforms reflecting options for career and family (1975); and women's military academy uniforms (1976); pantsuit option for Class A or service dress (1978), and more (Holm 1982:192–200).

A recent gift to the collections in the Division of Military and Diplomatic History is the standard USAF flight suit worn by Major General Tiiu Kera. A potent example of women's apparel reflecting expanded military duty, it was worn by General Kera when she served as commander of the EC-135 Looking Glass during the Cold War. In that capacity, she was authorised to act on behalf of the commander in chief or the chairman of the Joint Chiefs of Staff to employ US strategic deterrent forces in the event of a nuclear attack.

Until women became part of the habit and tradition of the military, their uniforms in all service branches mirrored uncertainty about the appropriate martial appearance for women in the armed forces. Cold War uniforms document the fundamental shift in society and military policy from reluctance to the presence of any women in the armed forces outside the medical occupations to women serving in most occupations.

REFERENCES

Ardery, M (1988) 'Account of the development of the uniform for women in the Air Force 1948–1951', Washington, DC: National Museum of American History, Smithsonian Institution, internal research document

Crane, D (2000) *Fashion and Its Social Agendas: Class, Gender, and Identity in Clothing*, Chicago: University of Chicago Press

Ewing, E (1975) *Women in Uniform*, Totowa, NJ: Rowman and Littlefield

Frevert, U (1989) *Women in German History: From Bourgeois Emancipation to Sexual Liberation*, trans. McKinnon-Evans, S et al, Oxford: Berg

Holm, J (1982) *Women in the Military: An Unfinished Revolution*, Novato, CA: Presidio Press

Holton, SS (1996) *Suffrage Days: Stores from the Women's Suffrage Movement*, London: Routledge

Law, C (1997) *Suffrage and Power: The Women's Movement, 1918–1928*, London: IB Taurus

Lurie, A (1981) *The Language of Clothes*, New York: Henry Holt

Morden, BJ (1990) *The Women's Army Corps 1945–1978*, Washington DC: Center of Military History, United States Army

Risch, E (1945) *A Wardrobe for the Women of the Army*, Washington DC: Office of the Quartermaster General, QMC Historical Studies 12

Roche, D (1994) *The Culture of Clothing: Dress and Fashion in the Ancien Regime*, London: Cambridge University Press

Steele, V (1989) 'Dressing for work', in Kidwell, CB and Steele, V (eds) *Men and Women: Dressing the Part*, Washington DC: Smithsonian Institution Press

Stremlow, M (1994) 'Free a marine to fight: Women marines in World War II', *World War II Commemorative Series*, Washington DC: Marine Corps Historical Center

Treadwell, ME (1954) *United States Army in World War II: Special Studies, the Women's Army Corps*, Washington DC: Office of the Chief of Military History, Department of the Army

Defining the national archaeological character of Cold War remains

WAYNE COCROFT

INTRODUCTION

The end of the Cold War has left an extensive global legacy of abandoned military installations, ranging from small monitoring posts to vast militarised landscapes. For most of their history, these were top-secret facilities and in many instances their passing has been unacknowledged. The Cold War was a universal global phenomenon; its physical remains in each country may be seen as a reflection of a unique national experience of the political and military stand-off between the Superpowers.

This chapter describes the recent recording of Cold War sites in England and their subsequent assessment to determine the most significant sites for conservation and preservation. This appraisal maintained that the remains represented a distinctive national assemblage, determined by a range of interconnected factors, including geography – both the United Kingdom's position as an offshore island ('the unsinkable aircraft carrier') and the legacy of existing military infrastructure. Britain's postwar political aspirations are embedded in the concrete of its Cold War installations; they reflect the country's desire to retain a leading international role and its 'special' relationship with the United States. These ambitions were supported by a vigorous indigenous scientific and technological sector, but tempered by the declining ability of the national economy to pay for ever more expensive defence projects, evident in the forlorn remains of technologically successful, yet abandoned, projects. It is argued that this assessment methodology might be applied to other countries' experiences of the Cold War, as a basis for both comparative studies and defining the most internationally significant Cold War remains.

BACKGROUND

Globally, it has been estimated that in the decade following the fall of the Berlin Wall, in November 1989, around 8,000 military installations have been closed, releasing over one million hectares (the true figure may be even greater) of land for civilian use (IABG 1997:2). One of the positive consequences of this change has been that for the first time in perhaps over fifty years, many formerly prohibited areas in eastern and western Europe are now accessible to archaeologists and others, while the application of aerial reconnaissance in particular has resulted in the discovery of many hundreds of new archaeological sites (Braasch 2002:19–22). The latest layer of activity left by the military has, however, often been neglected in favour of the remains of earlier periods.

The most obvious physical legacy of the Cold War is its abandoned military installations. Many of the establishments, which were closed as a consequence of the end of the Cold War, are of undisputed historical value. These include the former Royal Hospital at Greenwich, sections of the naval dockyards at Plymouth and Portsmouth, and internationally significant armament-manufacturing centres at the Royal Arsenal, Woolwich, and the Royal Gunpowder Factory, Waltham Abbey (Cocroft 2000; Bold et al 2001). These often architecturally distinguished sites with attractive waterside locations have found new leases of life as commercial office spaces, academic institutions, sites for distinctive housing developments, and heritage centres, whilst maintaining their historic character (Clark 2000). A similar picture is found in Europe, where in Germany, for example, at Zossen Wünsdorf, Brandenburg, imperial and 1930s army houses and barracks have provided good-quality dwellings in an attractive woodland setting. At Tallinn, Estonia, well-built Tsarist-era barracks offer similar potential for conversion into civilian apartments (Cunningham 1997:57).

In contrast, many Cold War structures are seen as stark, ugly, and inhuman reminders of a confrontation that might have wiped out life on earth. Other structures, such as the white radomes (the 'golf balls') of the Ballistic Missile Early Warning Station at Fylindales, North Yorkshire, became cherished landmarks, whose demolition was met with regret.

In dereliction, other sites have acquired their own aesthetic and are increasingly attracting the attentions of contemporary artists (see Boulton and Wilson, this volume; also Kippin 2001; Schjeldahl 1999; Watson 2004). In the early 1990s, the initial desire was often to sweep these

---

Figure 7.1. RAF Fylindales, North Yorkshire, 1963, Ballistic Missile Early Warning System; part of a global monitoring network, the distinctive golf ball-shaped radomes cover sensitive radar equipment. © Crown copyright NMR BB97/09913

structures and places away, without any thought to their historic significance. This was most publicly played out in Germany, with the hasty removal of the Berlin Wall, the most enduring symbol of the Cold Wall divide between east and west (Feversham and Schmidt 1999; this volume). Most Cold War installations were, however, secret places, remote from large conurbations and their functions unknown even to the communities who lived around them.

THE ASSESSMENT OF COLD WAR SITES IN ENGLAND

The assessment of Cold War sites by English Heritage's Monuments Protection Programme (MPP) was part of a wider project to reassess all the known archaeological resources in England (English Heritage 2000); it followed on from, and complements, a series of projects to assess England's earlier twentieth-century defence heritage (see Dobinson et al 1997: 288–99; Schofield 2002: 269–82). This assessment presented a unique challenge and opportunity to recommend a class of interrelated sites for conservation very soon after the primary reason for their existence had ceased. Nevertheless, even in an archaeologically imperceptible period of time, between the fall of the Berlin Wall and the time of this study in the late 1990s, there were losses to the total number of sites and structures. On most sites prior to disposal, the majority of structures were stripped of their furniture, fittings and equipment, leaving vacant spaces often devoid of meaning.

Politically, the work had the potential to be one of the most contentious MPP assessment projects. It was carried out against the background of the largest government defence lands disposals programme since the end of the Second World War. Generally, the Ministry of Defence, through its land agents Defence Estates, and other government departments, are obliged to achieve the best possible price for surplus property, usually through sale by auction. The designation of sites and structures as Scheduled Monuments or Listed Buildings could potentially seriously affect market value. Another concern was how the public would perceive this work. Was the Cold War too recent to be considered as heritage? Cold War sites may be seen to lack conventional aesthetic, but does this alone make them unworthy of preservation, or do new aesthetic and other values need to be explored? Nevertheless, there has been a growing interest in this project, probably partly through curiosity that English Heritage was concerning itself with the very recent past or inquisitiveness about these very secret places that were being revealed for the first time. Few Cold War sites in England engendered the hatred felt for the Berlin Wall, where people were moved to take a hammer and chisel to remove it. In England, where sites were damaged, it was more for economic gain than a wish to be rid of the sites for what they represented.

THE ASSESSMENT PROCESS

The first challenge of any archaeological study is to identify the source material. Sites and structures included in the study were defined as those built between the end of the Second World War and the fall of the Berlin Wall specifically to meet the threat posed by the Soviet Union and her allies. Many of the sites occupied by armed forces during the Cold War were often centuries old and poorly suited to modern military needs. These older sites were specifically excluded from this assessment and were evaluated by other programmes.

As with previous studies of Second World War sites (Schofield 2002), documents at the National Archives were an important source of information for many of those of Cold War date. A number of these records were investigated for English Heritage as part of a wider study of twentieth-century military sites (Dobinson 1998). The Cold War also greatly benefited from the recording work on Ministry of Defence disposal sites initiated by the Royal Commission on the Historical Monuments of England and continued by English Heritage after the merger of the two organisations in 1999 (Cocroft and Thomas 2003). During this project, a wide search of the secondary literature was undertaken, including official histories, pamphlets and web sites produced by enthusiasts' groups. Using this wealth of sources, lists of the total numbers of different classes of sites and structures were developed and cross-checked. One of the great strengths of this project was that it was a field-based exercise, which provided a detailed picture of the nature of the remains and their current condition. For many of the more recent structures, particularly those built during the 1980s, site visits were the only practical method to gather information, as the supporting documentation was often subject to the '30-year' release rule governing official documents in the United Kingdom.

From this information it was possible to classify Cold War sites and structures into nine main categories, which, if necessary, were subdivided into groups and then into thirty-one monument classes.

In nearly all instances it was possible to identify the total numbers of sites built using documentary sources. For each monument class, a 'class assessment of importance' was written, providing a brief history and discussion of the role of each class and any typological variants. For most monument classes it was possible to list all the sites and provide a rough assessment of their current condition. An important concept established by the Monuments Protection Programme, especially when considering industrial sites, was to determine the standard range of

Table 7.1. Summary of Cold War structures and sites listed by Category, Group and Class

Air Defence

1 Radar
- Rotor 1950s
- Linesman 1960s–1980s
- Improved UK Air Defence Ground Environment, Late 1980s

2 Royal Observer Corps
- Visual Reporting Posts
- Underground Monitoring Posts
- Group Headquarters

3 Anti-Aircraft Guns
- Anti-Aircraft Operations Rooms
- Postwar Heavy Anti-Aircraft Batteries
- Postwar Light Anti-Aircraft Batteries

4 Surface to Air Missiles
- Bloodhound Missile Mark I Sites
- Tactical Control Centres
- Bloodhound Missile Mark II Sites

5 Fighter Interceptor Airfields
- Hardened Aircraft Shelters
- Hardened Airfield Structures

Nuclear Deterrent

6 V-Bomber Airfields
7 Nuclear Weapons Stores
8 Thor Missiles Sites

United States Air Force

9 Airfields
10 Cruise Missile Sites

Defence Research Establishments

11 Aviation
12 Naval
13 Rockets, Guided Weapons
14 Nuclear
15 Miscellaneous

Defence Manufacturing Sites

16 Defence Manufacturing Sites

Emergency Civil Government

17 Early 1950s War Rooms
18 Regional Seats of Government
19 Subregional Headquarters
20 Regional Government Headquarters
21 Local Authority Emergency Headquarters
22 Civil Defence Structures
23 The Utilities
24 Private Nuclear Shelters

Emergency Provisions Stores

25 Grain Silos
26 Cold Stores
27 General Purpose Stores
28 Fuel Depots

Communications

29 Underground Telephone Exchanges
30 Microwave Tower Network

Miscellaneous

31 The Peace Movement

component pieces that characterise each site type. Using this information, sites may quickly be assessed for completeness and anomalies identified, which may in turn merit more investigation. The next step in the process was for English Heritage staff to visit the owners of the sites to check the validity of the essentially desk-based evaluation, to discuss how the recommendations in the report might affect the sites, and how a sustainable future for the sites might be achieved.

Table 7.2. Summary of assessment criteria

Survival/condition

1 Structural integrity and survival of original internal configuration, plant and fittings.

2 Monuments have been generally assessed to reflect their original purpose and function, which dictated their form. Nevertheless, reuse for another purpose at a later time may add to the historical value of a structure.

3 Survival of contemporary setting, character, spatial relationships – group value.

Period

4 Representativeness of a particular phase of the Cold War.

5 Centrality to British and/or NATO defence policy.

6 Technological significance. As well as being military structures, many sites are important monuments to postwar British achievements in science and technology.

Rarity

7 In nearly all cases the individual monument types may be regarded as rare, with no more than a handful of surviving examples. Many of the structures or sites also carried out unique functions. While rarity and uniqueness are criteria for protection, they will be supported by other, usually technological, reasons.

Diversity

8 Diversity of form – where a given site or structural type might exhibit a number of different structural forms, although designed to fulfil an identical or similar function.

Cultural and Amenity Value

9 Cultural and amenity value – education, understanding, tourism, public access.

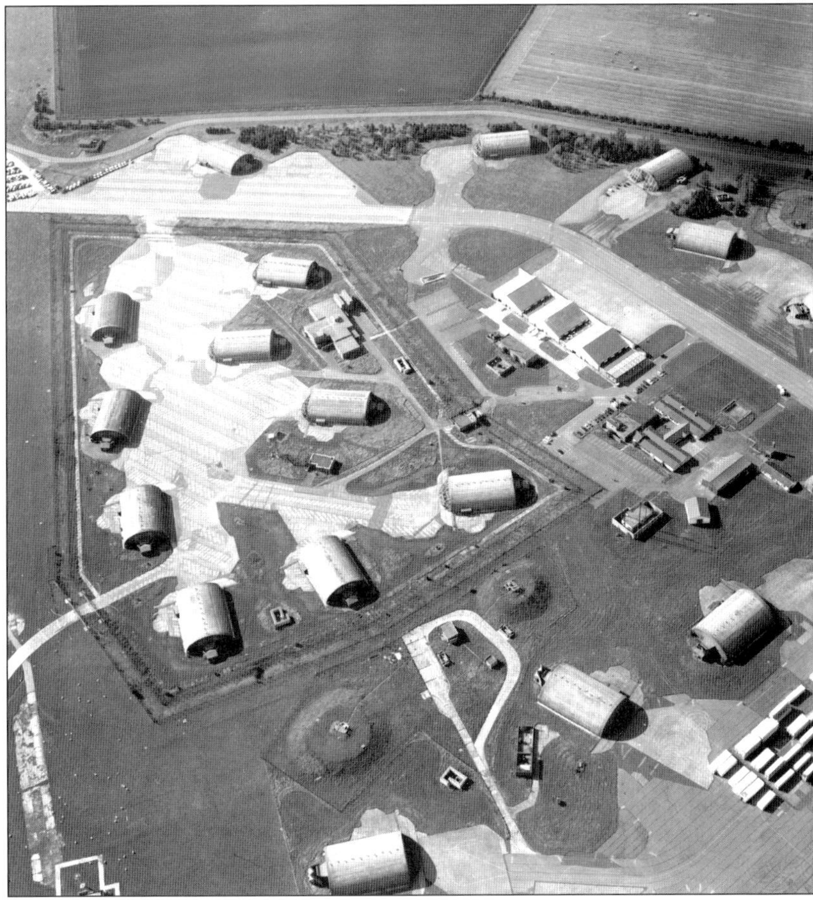

Figure 7.2. RAF Upper Heyford, Oxfordshire. In the 1970s, the squadron of nine nuclear-armed F-111 aircraft held at constant readiness in this area would have been amongst the first NATO units to respond to a Warsaw Pact attack on Western Europe. © Crown copyright NMR 18537/18

SELECTION CRITERIA

As outlined above, this study was potentially controversial and any designations might be subject to challenge. For this reason it was necessary to ensure that the assessment criteria were particularly robust. In addition to the standard nonstatutory assessment criteria (cited in PPG16, DoE 1990), additional tests were also applied.

An early study of Cold War resources by the United States Department of Defense (1994) established an important principle to define sites and structures, which was central to the Cold War mission. This principle may be applied at national level to identify key sites and structures, but is equally valid at site level, where for example it might be applied to determine the most significant structures which defined a particular type of mission at a given point during the Cold War.

Where sites comprise a number of key components, the preferred option has been to recommend the whole site for preservation, maintaining the functional and chronological relationships between the structures and their period setting, which could include for example deliberate ornamental planting. However, not all components of a site have equal value in interpreting its primary function, and some prefabricated elements may have no sustainable future. Their footprint may, nevertheless, continue to contribute to understanding the site's layout and function. In exceptional circumstances, some structures may be significant technological monuments in their own right and merit preservation despite damage to their local setting. The scale of some Cold War sites, such as airfields covering many hundreds of hectares, poses distinct problems. The preservation of an entire airfield in a manner that would both be sustainable and maintain its Cold War character may be an unrealistic objective. Recommendations for preservation have therefore focused on key elements to exemplify changing Cold War strategy, aviation technology, or the principal role of a particular base at a given point of the Cold War. At Upper Heyford, Oxfordshire, for example, it is proposed to retain the alert area for nuclear-armed F-111 aircraft (Figure 7.2).

This facility was central to NATO deterrent policy during the 1970s and was where some of the first nuclear-armed sorties of the Third World War might have been flown from. In preserving this group of nine hardened aircraft shelters, squadron headquarters, multiple fence lines and controlled entry points, not only are examples of standard hardened NATO structures of the 1970s retained; it also reflects the scale of defence investment at this date and the complexity of the operation being undertaken.

For most of the Cold War the principal role of aircraft stationed at RAF Alconbury, Cambridgeshire, was strategic reconnaissance. In the early 1980s this task was taken over by U2/TR1 'spy planes'. These required what are believed to be unique extra-wide hardened aircraft shelters, and a massive double-storey bunker to maintain their complex avionics, and to download and analyse the gathered data, potentially while operating in a heavily contaminated environment. Their preservation at Alconbury would reflect the functional relationships between the aircraft and the bunker, the principal Cold War role of Alconbury and the wider global theme of constant surveillance.

Table 7.3. Principal factors determining the character of Cold War remains

Geography
National aspirations
Legacy of existing defence infrastructure
Relationship with Superpower
Access to technology
Economy – ability, or not, to pay for desired defence assets
Military culture
Intelligence assessments (valid or not) of the adversary's capabilities and intentions
Technology of weapons system
Evolving military doctrine on how a nuclear war might be fought
Understanding of nuclear weapon effects and ways to counter them

DEFINING CHARACTER

In addition to ensuring that well-preserved representative examples of the different types of sites and structures were identified for designation as protected sites, sites were also selected that reflected the unique British experience of the Cold War.

The assemblage of Cold War structures which survives in any country may be seen as a reflection of its national experience of the Cold War. The dominant Superpower on either side controlled access to the most technologically advanced weapons systems, and often stationed its forces on the territory of its alliance members. These allegiances are reflected in the use of similar types of weapons, which in turn required comparable infrastructure. This is most marked in North Atlantic Treaty Organisation (NATO) areas during the 1970s and 1980s with the construction of standardised hardened aircraft shelters. Apart from political considerations, the inescapable factor of geographic location determined the degree of militarisation of the landscape and type of defence facilities created. Britain, as well as being a leading member of NATO, is an offshore island, an 'unsinkable aircraft carrier' for NATO air forces. Germany, divided by the Cold War frontline – the Iron Curtain – became one of the most militarised landscapes in the world.

Figure 7.3. Falkenhagen, Brandenburg, Germany, site of the main wartime command centre for western Warsaw Pact forces, a relief rendition of the Kremlin in its cultural centre. © W D Cocroft

Another factor determining the infrastructure found on Cold War bases may be defined as military culture – how a country's armed forces (perhaps heavily influenced by the dominant Superpower) were organised with regard to the social relationships between the different ranks and specialisms. In some instances, this might be as a foreign culture imposed on the existing military infrastructure of another country. Military culture is most visible in the domestic facilities (messes, barracks and cultural facilities) and in wall art.

The contrast between western and eastern military cultures is thrown sharply into focus when comparing the living conditions on United States bases to those of the Soviet armed forces, through, for example, the quality of interior fittings and the amount of space allocated to individuals. National culture is also revealed through technical styles and preferences, which will become more apparent as more national studies are undertaken. The application of archaeological methods to the dismantling of United States Phantom aircraft supplied to the RAF would, for example, reveal British Rolls-Royce engines and avionics components. Similarly, Soviet equipment supplied to East Germany was often modified to meet national requirements.

Many of the sites and structures found in England are just one component of wider Cold War systems. Some sites, such as the Ballistic Missile Early Warning System, at Fylindales, North Yorkshire, were, and still are, one element of a wider United States defensive system. Britain, as a leading member of NATO, also has many sites linked to and designed to operate with other sites in the NATO area. Historians have used systems analysis to study the evolution and functioning of complex technological organisations (see Bijker et al 1987; MacLeod and Johnson forthcoming). The application of systems analysis to the examination and assessment of the built legacy of the Cold War may provide one method of ensuring that the most significant elements of this global resource are recognised and recorded, and representative examples preserved. One of the attractions of systems analysis is that it may be used on a graduated series of levels, from the study of global characteristics of the entire Cold War system to those of different power blocs and the countries within them. At the lowest level, systems analysis is also vital in the understanding of the significance of individual sites. All Cold War sites were part of wider networks, for example air defence systems, structures of emergency government, or research and manufacturing organisations. Many Cold War sites exhibit a single phase of activity or function, and at a basic level may be interpreted in terms of process recording, as has been applied to analysis of many industrial complexes (Malaws 1997:75–98).

Militarily, the defining feature of this period was the possession by the Superpowers of vast arsenals of nuclear weapons and the stockpiles held by a handful of other countries. The development of nuclear technology for both peaceful and warlike purposes was also one of the most significant postwar scientific and industrial advances. Any sites associated with the development and deployment of nuclear weapons may be seen to be characteristic of the Cold War, as are structures that were designed to protect against their effects. Such is the power of nuclear weapons that complex procedures (rituals) are placed around their handling. This is reflected in the architecture of their stores surrounded by multiple layers of fencing entered through restricted gateways. Once inside, combination and remotely controlled locks protect doors with notices proclaiming 'No Lone Zone'. Elements of the complex control and command procedures governing the handling of nuclear warheads are also reflected in the storage sites. The deployment patterns of nuclear weapons by NATO reflect a defensive and reactive posture. The warheads and delivery systems were generally guarded and maintained by the units whose task it would be to use the weapons. Where United

States nuclear weapons were allocated to alliance troops, they always remained under the control of an American officer until the point of release. On late-1950s Thor missile sites, although the missiles were operated by the Royal Air Force, the maintenance of the warheads was undertaken by United States personnel in a separate fenced enclave. The launch of the missile was controlled by a dual key system, one key held by a British officer and the other by an American. In contrast, until the late 1970s the Soviet Union held most of its nuclear weapons far from the frontline on its own soil. Even after this date, with warheads moved forward to eastern Germany, such was the mistrust by the political leadership of its own armed forces that the warheads were kept separate from their delivery systems under the control of politically reliable KGB troops. In comparison, during the 1980s United States Air Force personnel lived next to fully armed ground launched cruise missiles, ready to respond at a moment's notice.

National aspirations also played an important part in defining the types of remains found in any country. Postwar Britain desired to retain her position as a world power, and to maintain an independent military

Figure 7.4. Royal Aircraft Establishment Bedford. The wind tunnel hall section of the High Speed Supersonic Tunnel built 1957–61. © English Heritage AA051180

Figure 7.5. RAF Spadeadam, Cumbria, *Blue Streak* intermediate range ballistic missile test stand, 1959. Similar stands were built at Woomera, Australia for test launches. © Crown copyright NMR AA94/02010

capability. The pattern of defence research in postwar Britain comprised a mixture of state-of-the-art government scientific research establishments, often working in close collaboration with private sector manufacturers. At a time when the country was still subject to rationing, these facilities were assigned the highest national priority. Not only were research centres set up to develop and manufacture atomic weapons, but also the characteristics of supersonic flight were investigated in world-class wind tunnels, while similarly impressive facilities were built to explore the dynamics of jet engines.

The quality of research, supporting scientific infrastructure and coordination amongst the manufacturers, visibly challenged the myth that postwar Britain was a declining technological power. The most ambitious project of the late 1950s was the development of Britain's independent intermediate range ballistic missile *Blue Streak*. This missile, with a projected range of 1,500 miles, although based on American designs, was built almost entirely by British companies. Vigorous debate still continues about why it was cancelled in 1960: was it due to the vulnerability of its silos to attack, or was this a feint for economic reasons? *Blue*

Streak was a technological success, and as a launch vehicle for the European Launcher Development Organisation's rocket *Europa I*, fulfilled its role on eleven successive occasions before this project, too, was cancelled in 1971. Today its test stands are some of the most architecturally impressive remnants of Britain's Cold War research programmes (see Wilson, this volume).

Despite their military connotations, projects such as *Blue Streak* may also be seen as iconic of their age and the optimistic and unquestioning presumption of the benefits of scientific advances that characterised the 1950s.

CHRONOLOGICAL CHARACTERISTICS

Cold War monuments may also be characterised according to chronological criteria. In England, two main building periods can be recognised. The first stretched from the outbreak of the Korean War in 1950 to the early 1960s. The second was from the late 1970s and gathered pace during the 1980s, until it was brought to an abrupt halt in late 1989 with the political repercussions of the fall of the Berlin Wall. Elsewhere, different periods of building activity may be distinguished. In eastern Germany in the early decades of the Cold War, existing ostensibly

Table 7.4. Principal Cold War building phases in the United Kingdom

First Cold War – 1946–62	
1946–50	Little new building
1950–62	Korean War, rearmament, massive building programme, era of *Mutually Assured Destruction*
Sustained balance/deterrence – 1963–79	
Late 1960s	Little new building, the United Kingdom's nuclear deterrent passes to Royal Navy
	Doctrine of *Flexible Response* replaces *MAD* and *Tripwire Response*
Late 1970s	NATO programme to harden its front-line bases and key assets begins
Second Cold War – 1980–89	
1980s	NATO hardening programme expands, increase in defence expenditure, new spending on emergency government headquarters

demolished underground military facilities were simply taken over and reused. However, from about 1970, along with the re-equipment of its army, East Germany embarked on a massive defence infrastructure programme, only mirrored in the west at the end of the decade in response to the more visible threat posed by the mobile Soviet SS20 missile system deployed from 1977.

The pattern of building in the first phase of Cold War (1946–62) construction in Britain closely followed the recent historical experiences of the Second World War. In establishing new bases speed was of the essence, as it was feared that the communist attack on South Korea in 1950 might be a prelude to an invasion of western Europe. Geographically the places from where the Cold War was to be fought were determined by the legacy of existing, or recently vacated, defence installations most of which had been built in the previous fifteen years. For pragmatic administrative and economic reasons, it was far quicker and cheaper to redevelop existing bases than acquire new land. Fortuitously, the greatest density of wartime sites was in eastern England, facing the continent and the new enemy. Technologically, many of the weapons and defence systems, such as visual aircraft reporting posts, radar stations and anti-aircraft gunsites, if not of wartime origin, represented developments of earlier systems. The geographical determinants of their sites, high ground with unimpeded views or proximity to vulnerable areas, such as docks or conurbations, remained unaltered although sometimes in conflict with postwar demands of land for housing.

One aspect of air defence technology which did mark a distinct break with the past was the introduction of the first generation of British jet fighters – the Meteor, Vampire and Venom. Their introduction did not affect the geographic spread of airfields, although the appearance of aerodromes was changed through the laying of long concrete runways and hardstandings in response to the new heavier aircraft, with nose wheels, and the backwash from their jet engines, which could quickly scorch a grass strip.

Another factor determining the geographic spread and types of defence installations was the political and intelligence assessments of the Soviet threat. In the late 1940s and early 1950s, the main danger to the United Kingdom was thought to come from manned piston-engine bombers (the Tupolev-4 'Bull', a reverse-engineered American Boeing B29) carrying atomic weapons. Intelligence assessments doubted the ability of Soviet crews to find purely military objectives and believed that the main targets would be the major cities. They also suggested that Soviet crews lacked the necessary skills and equipment to fly at night, and as a consequence, radar stations were only manned from half-an-hour before dawn to half-an-hour after sunset. However, for the first decades of the Cold War the western intelligence agencies had too few reliable sources of information to judge Soviet technical abilities (Stocker 2003). Assessments of future threats were often based on extrapolating the potential development of wartime technologies, the pace of equivalent western research, and interviews with returning German prisoners of war.

Devastating though an attack by atomic weapons might be, solidly built structures a few miles away from the detonation may survive. The greatest priority in the early 1950s was given to the renewal of Britain's early warning radar defences. Under a massive programme codenamed 'Rotor', the key radar stations and command centres down the east coast of England were placed in underground bunkers, up to three storeys in depth. The Achilles heel of this system would have been the relatively fragile radar heads, which were vulnerable to blast. Linked to the radar stations were the antiaircraft gun sites controlled by the army, and these, too, were commanded from newly constructed, heavily protected operations rooms. At the gun sites were smaller command bunkers and protected buildings for generators and ancillary equipment. In the event of war, leading perhaps to the loss of control by central government in London, it was envisaged that the country would be run by a series of regional commissioners, and they were also provided with protected accommodation for themselves and up to fifty members of staff. The bunkers built during the 1950s represented a new type of architecture in Britain. Previously, during the war, only a handful of purpose-built, heavily protected structures had been built. In contrast, East German and Soviet forces were able to make use of 1930s and wartime bunker complexes, which were often more robust than many built during the Cold War (Hofmann 1999; Kampe 1996).

If the west was to be able to retaliate, or deter, a nuclear attack by the Soviets, it needed installations from which to operate. Geographically, Britain as an offshore island was attractive to the United States Strategic Air Command, as a secure base – an 'unsinkable aircraft carrier' – and sufficiently close to eastern Europe for the aircraft of the day to reach their targets. Politically, Britain was a leading member of NATO with a stable democracy and usually sympathetic to the United States. At first, the so-called Very Heavy Bomber bases, which were being built at the end of the war, in anticipation of the deployment of B29 *Superfortresses* against Germany, were used. The stationing of long-range jet-powered bombers in the early 1950s, the B36 *Peacemaker*, and later the B47 *Stratojet*, necessitated the construction of four bases with massive 10,000-ft runways connected to new taxiways and dispersal points. Associated technical and domestic accommodation was usually built from prefabricated structures, reflecting both the need to bring these bases quickly into operation, and the temporary 90-day deployments for the squadrons. In addition, Britain was also developing her own independent nuclear capabilities, side by side with the development of the bomb and aircraft large enough to carry it. By the mid-1950s, ten main operating bases and around thirty dispersal airfields were constructed for her V-force of atomic bombers.

Advancing Soviet capabilities, often many years ahead of those predicted by western defence analysts, quickly rendered the early 1950s defensive system and its infrastructure obsolete. The detonation of the Soviet H-bomb in August 1953, the introduction of new high-flying bombers and the prospect of unstoppable missiles were the new threats. Modified wartime systems would be useless against these developments, and in 1956 the antiaircraft gun defences were stood down. Defence planning now placed the emphasis on the nuclear deterrent, the V-Force, and American Thor missiles in addition to United States Air Force units stationed in Britain. Protecting these forces were the newly introduced British Bloodhound surface-to-air missiles.

In contrast to the 1950s, very few new buildings were added to the defence estate during the 1960s. This was partly a reflection of changing defence policy as the United States placed less emphasis on manned bombers, as nuclear-armed intercontinental missiles came into service. During the early 1960s Britain's nuclear deterrent remained with the RAF, but improving Soviet air defences forced a change in strategy and

Figure 7.6. RAF Ash, Kent. A former radar station, this surreal landscape of lettered concrete ventilation cubes reveals little of the intense building activity that took place below ground during the 1980s. © Crown copyright NMR AA96/03084

two squadrons were equipped with a stand-off bomb, *Blue Steel*, which could be launched many miles from its target. The introduction of this system resulted in a small amount of building work at two bases. The adoption of the Polaris submarine-launched missiles as the country's nuclear deterrent forces represented a loss of status for the RAF and the diversion of resources to the construction of new submarine maintenance facilities, mainly in Scotland. Another factor that led to a reduction in defence construction was Britain's declining economy, which forced the cancellation of many promising defence projects.

By the late 1960s, the 1950s policy of *Mutually Assured Destruction* had given way to the doctrine of *Flexible Response*, whereby any expansionist plans of the Soviet Union would be countered by a variety of means – economic, political, and military. In the military sphere, any attack on NATO would be met by a graduated response, the resort to nuclear weapons representing the ultimate action. For this policy to represent a credible deterrent, enough doubt had to be left in the minds of the Soviet planners that sufficient numbers of NATO forces might survive a surprise attack to mount a counterstrike. This policy required that both the correct weapons were put in place, such as F-111 aircraft, but also that NATO's key assets were placed in protected, or hardened, shelters.

This new policy of *Flexible Response* is reflected in the NATO-sponsored infrastructure programme, which began in the mid-1970s and gathered pace through the 1980s.

In contrast to the 1950s, improving Soviet defence technology potentially allowed them to strike at NATO sites holding nuclear weapons – so-called counterforce targets. NATO, and to a lesser extent Warsaw Pact, bases of this date are characterised by standardised structures, in itself a reflection of central planning of both alliances, designed to offer defence against conventional, biological or chemical attack, and to offer some protection against nuclear attack. On airfields the key assets, which would ensure that the airfield was to function for at least a number of days after an attack, were placed in heavily protected reinforced concrete structures. Typically, these might include aircraft shelters, squadron headquarters, fuel installations, airfield command centres and communications centres (Figure 7.1). The threat was judged to come not only from missiles, but also from manned aircraft, which would be able to more precisely target their weapons on individual structures. For this reason most structures of this date were rendered in dark brown earthy colours, in contrast to the earlier antiflash white paint of the 1950s and 1960s. They were also given a low profile, some with earthen banks to enable them to blend into the landscape. On some sites, structures were placed in woods, or had trees planted around them, to further confuse hostile, low-flying aircraft. Bases reconstructed during the

1980s acquired a grimly functional air, with their aircraft often hidden from view in shelters. The 1980s were also characterised by the introduction of new weapons systems, most visibly at two locations in England (Greenham Common and Molesworth), where distinctive shelters were built for the ground-launched cruise missile system. For a more detailed description of Greenham Common and the issues surrounding its future management, see Fiorato this volume.

CONCLUSION

In English Heritage's assessment, key Cold War sites and structures have been identified relatively soon after their redundancy and before the agencies of loss have taken their toll. Decisions about their protection are made at national level, which has allowed Cold War structures to be placed in a national context before making judgments about which sites or structures to try to retain. In other countries, where decisions about preservation are devolved to lower regional levels, this may not be possible. The recommendations contained within English Heritage's assessment (Cocroft 2001) are beginning to be implemented, and to date a 1950s atomic bomb store, an early 1960s Royal Observer Corps Group Headquarters, and the 1980s cruise missile shelters at Greenham Common have been scheduled. Elsewhere, the report is allowing advice to be given to developers about the retention of significant structures, or to recommend recording before demolition in other cases.

The remains of Cold War installations across England have cultural and educational value in presenting a narrative of the national experience of the Cold War and the complex interactions between high-level government policy and technology. A number have already been opened as museums, and there is the potential to develop wider national networks of Cold War trails to explain the nature of this late twentieth-century confrontation.

REFERENCES

Bijker, WE, Hughes, TP and Pinch, T (1987) *The Social Construction of Technological Systems*, Cambridge, Massachusetts: The MIT Press (eighth printing 2001)

Bold, J, Donald, A and Kendall, D (2001) *Greenwich: An Architectural History of the Royal Hospital for Seamen and the Queen's House*, London: Yale University Press

Braasch, O (2002) 'Goodbye Cold War! Goodbye bureaucracy? Opening the skies to aerial archaeology in Europe', in Bewley and Rączkowski (eds), *Aerial Archaeology Developing Future Practice*, Amsterdam: IOS Press

Clark, C (2000) *Vintage Ports or Deserted Dockyards: Differing Futures for Naval Heritage across Europe*, Working Papers 57, Bristol: University of the West of England

Cocroft, WD (2000) *Dangerous Energy: The Archaeology of Gunpowder and Military Explosives Manufacture*, Swindon: English Heritage

Cocroft, WD (2001) *Cold War Monuments: An Assessment by the Monuments Protection Programme*, typescript report on CD, English Heritage

Cocroft, WD and Thomas, RJC (2003) *Cold War: Building for Nuclear Confrontation 1946–1989*, Swindon: English Heritage

Cunningham, KB (1997) *Base Closure and Redevelopment in Central and Eastern Europe*, Bonn: Bonn International Center for Conversion

Department of Defense (1994) *Coming in from the Cold: Military Heritage in the Cold War*, Washington DC: DoD

Department of the Environment (1990) *Planning Policy Guidance Note 16: Archaeology and Planning*. London: HMSO.

Dobinson, CS (1998) *Twentieth Century Fortifications in England, Vol XI: The Cold War*, CBA/English Heritage.

Dobinson, CS, Lake, J and Schofield, AJ (1997) 'Monuments of war: Defining England's 20th-century heritage', *Antiquity* 71, 272: 288–99

English Heritage (2000) *MPP 2000: A Review of the Monuments Protection Programme, 1986–2000*, London: English Heritage

Feversham, P and Schmidt, L (1999) *Die Berliner Mauer Heute: The Berlin Wall Today*, Berlin: Verlag Bauwesen

Hofmann, H (1999) *Militärische Geheimnisse 1938–1992: Das 'Seewerk' Bunker im Wald von Falkenhagen*, privately published

IABG (Industieanlagenbetreibergesellschaft mbH) (1997) *Study on the Reuse of Former Military Lands*, Bonn: Bonn International Center for Conversion

Kampe, HG (1996) *The Underground Military Command Bunkers of Zossen, Germany*, Atglen, Philadelphia: Schiffer Publishing Limited

Kippin, J (2001) *Cold War Pastoral*, London: Black Dog Publishing Limited

Macleod, R and Johnson, JA (forthcoming) *Frontline and Factory Comparative Perspectives on the Chemical Industry at War, 1914–1924*, Dordrecht: Springer

Malaws, BA (1997) 'Process recording at industrial sites', XIX *Industrial Archaeology Review* 75–98

Schjeldahl, P (1999) *Jane & Louise Wilson: Stasi City, Gamma, Parliament, Las Vegas, Graveyard Time*, London: Serpentine Gallery

Schofield, AJ (2002) 'The role of aerial photographs in national strategic programmes: Assessing recent military sites in England', in Bewley and Rączkowski (eds), *Aerial Archaeology Developing Future Practice*, Amsterdam: IOS Press

Stocker, J (2003) 'The Soviet missile threat', conference paper, British Rocketry Oral History Project, Charterhouse, April

Watson, K (2004) *The Hush House: Cold War Sites in England*. London: Hush House Publications

Greenham Common: The conservation and management of a Cold War archetype

VERONICA FIORATO

Greenham Common is internationally acknowledged as the archetypal Cold War site and focus of the peace movement and protest. In the early 1980s the air base in West Berkshire was one of six in Europe selected for the deployment of NATO Ground Launched Cruise Missiles. The Cold War occupation of the site has left behind both monumental military remains, such as the massive cruise missile shelters, and the contrasting vulnerable, painted images of the peace protestors and the fragile archaeological remains of their camps. This archaeological diversity, in addition to the emotive response of the public to the site, both then and now, presents real challenges to those managing Greenham Common today.

BACKGROUND

Greenham Common lies two miles (3.2 km) southeast of the market town of Newbury in West Berkshire. Situated on a low ridge between the Kennet and Enborne rivers, it is a large, flat site that is well served by major roads – factors which were undoubtedly of importance in the selection of the site for Cold War activity. Although the former airbase is known as *Greenham Common,* and this name will be used for the purposes of this chapter, the site actually comprises the two adjacent commons of Greenham and Crookham.

A Second World War airfield

In 1939 the common at Greenham was purchased by Newbury Borough Council, shortly before being requisitioned by the Air Ministry in May 1941 as a satellite airfield for RAF Aldermaston located 10 miles (16 km) to the east. Three concrete runways were constructed across the heathland, and glider marshalling areas, bomb stores and dispersal areas were located around the field. Two aircraft hangars and the administrative, technical and training functions were located to the south along the Newbury-Basingstoke road.

RAF Greenham Common was associated with a number of key wartime events including *Operation Torch*, the 1942 invasion of North Africa. In 1943 the airfield became a United States Army Air Force (USAAF, later to become the United States Air Force or USAF) base with two fighter groups stationed there, and was involved in preparations for the D-Day landings. On 5 June 1944, the day before D-Day, the Supreme Commander of the Allied Expeditionary Forces, General Eisenhower, gave his famous speech to the 101st Airborne Division at Greenham Common in which he told them that 'the eyes of the world' were upon them. Over 130 aircraft and 50 glider sorties from the base subsequently supported the Utah Beach landings. The airfield was also involved in the airlift for the Arnhem landings in September 1944, as well as the parachute drop for the capture of the Arnhem Bridge known as *Operation Market Garden*.

Between June 1945 and the closure of the base in June 1946, control of Greenham Common transferred back to the Royal Air Force. The airfield was decommissioned in 1947 and the Common reverted to the ownership of the Borough Council. However, the Second World War association of the base with the USAAF was to pave the way for its reoccupation of the site and the construction of the Cold War airbase whose remains bear testament to this fearful period of recent history.

Cold War occupation

During the late 1940s political tensions between east and west increased dramatically; keys events marking the deteriorating relationship included the Soviet blockade of Berlin in 1948, the detonation of the first Soviet atomic bomb and the formation of NATO in 1949, as well as the outbreak of the Korean War the following year. Against this background, in March 1951 the Air Ministry announced its intention to re-requisition land at Greenham Common. The worsening international situation prompted the USAF to deploy aircraft in Britain, and the base was reconstructed in preparation for USAF Strategic Air Command (SAC) B-47 Stratojet bombers and KC-97 tankers. The Second World War airfield had to be substantially rebuilt, the principal development being a runway capable of servicing these large aircraft. The single landing strip, at 10,000 feet (3,048 m) was one of the longest military runways in Europe.

Figure 8.1. Greenham Common, West Berkshire: the iconic cruise missile shelters of the GAMA site contrast with the restored heath. © Veronica Fiorato

New dispersal areas, known as Areas A, C and D, were located on the site of their Second World War predecessors and the administrative and accommodation centre of the base, Area E, also mirrored the former technical, training and administrative site. The line of the Newbury-Basingstoke road was retained in the new layout as *Main Street*, although for security reasons the road was closed to the public in September 1951. Other roads through the 'technical' area of the site were laid out on a grid pattern. The general layout of the base, with its single runway and large concrete apron in front of the hangars, is a classic form for many postwar airfields.

Various different units were stationed at Greenham Common in the 1950s, and from January 1958 until the closure of the base in 1964 it was part of the *Reflex Alert Scheme* whereby B-47 Stratojets, armed with nuclear weapons, were held on constant standby. The base was again deactivated and returned to the Royal Air Force in 1964 but reopened as a USAF stand-by base in 1968, in response to the French decision to leave NATO and the subsequent withdrawal of American forces from France.

In 1979, in response to the USSR's increased nuclear capability, NATO adopted a two-fold policy: negotiating for the reduction in intermediate-range weapons, while at the same time deploying its own in Europe.

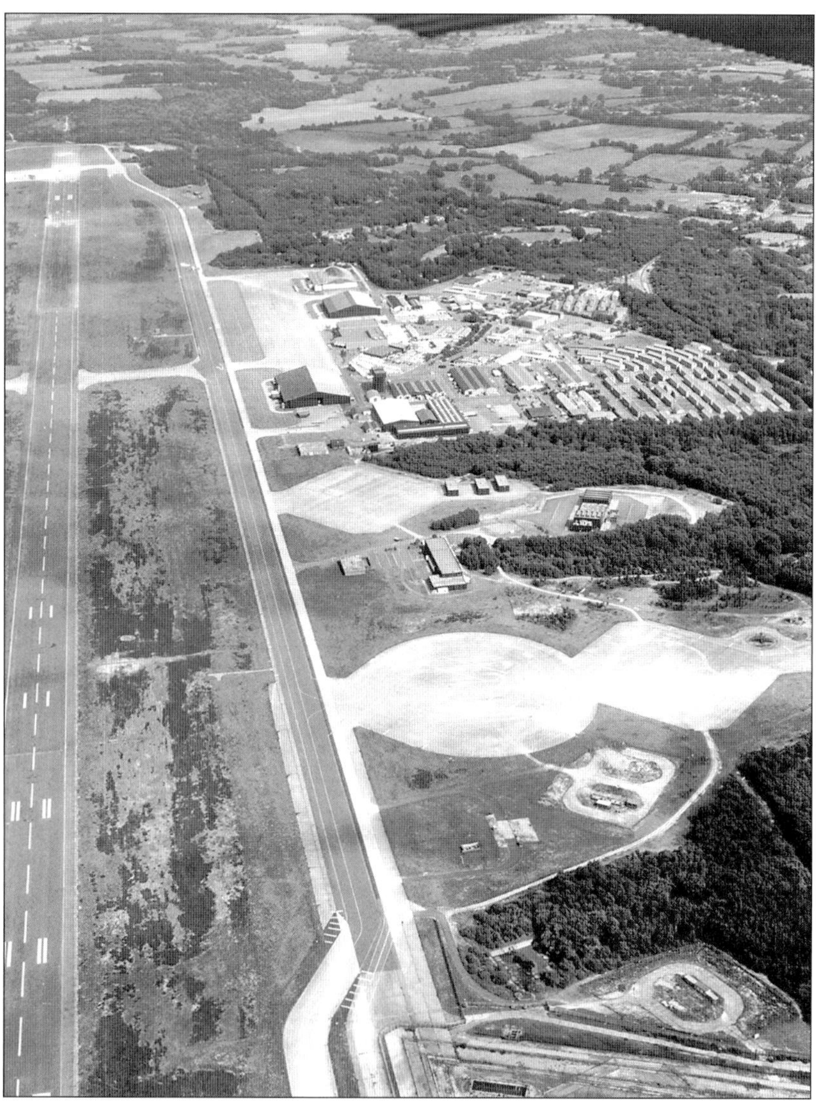

Figure 8.2. The Cold War runway, at 10,000 feet (3,048 metres), was one of the longest in Europe. This photograph, taken in 1995, shows the relationship of some elements of the base. The technical site (Area E) can be seen top right including the numerous barrack blocks for the bomber crews (laid out in curving streets to the extreme right). The Vehicle Maintenance, Wing HQ and Combat Support Buildings (Area D) are in the centre right and the northern fence of the GAMA complex (Area C) is located bottom right. The circular and diamond-shaped areas of hard standing were built in the 1950s to house bombers while on Reflex Alert. © English Heritage NMR 15288/36

In June 1980 it was announced that Tomahawk Ground Launched Cruise Missiles (GLCM) were to be located at six sites in Europe, including Greenham Common and Molesworth, Cambridgeshire. At both sites in England this necessitated the construction of a new storage and servicing facility, which at Greenham Common was known as the GLCM Alert and Maintenance Area or 'GAMA'.

The 501st Tactical Missile Wing operated and maintained GAMA from July 1982 onwards, and in November 1983 the first 16 cruise missiles were delivered to the site. The construction of GAMA continued

Figure 8.3. The GLCM Alert and Maintenance Area or 'GAMA'. The six cruise missile shelters are surrounded by a triple fence which also encloses ancillary buildings. These include a vehicle maintenance facility (bottom left), a fire team building and generator house (top left) and a guard house by the main entrance (top centre). One of the shelters (top centre) was manned 24 hours a day to provide an immediate response in an emergency. © English Heritage NMR 21863/13

until 1986 when its final capacity was 96 missiles and five spares, made up into six flights. The longest commissioned of the six bases in Europe to house cruise missiles, Greenham Common, and GAMA in particular, provided a national focus for the peace movement. Peace camps were established around the perimeter fence of the base, and the Greenham women, in opposition to the deployment of cruise missiles, used non-violent protest to bring the nuclear capability of Greenham Common airbase, and the campaign for disarmament, to the attention of the world.

Under the terms of the USSR-USA Intermediate-range Nuclear Forces (INF) Treaty, which was signed in 1987 and came into force the following year, the last ground-launched cruise missiles were withdrawn from Europe by mid-1991. Greenham Common's missiles were removed in stages and were taken to the USA to be destroyed.

After the Cold War

RAF Greenham Common was declared surplus to military requirements and closed in 1992. In 1995 much of the open area of the base passed back to Newbury District Council (the successor to Newbury Borough Council) with the intention of restoring the site to publicly accessible common land. The exception to this was those areas, such as GAMA, retained by the Ministry of Defence under the terms of the INF Treaty. This allowed representatives from Russia to visit and inspect key areas of the site to ensure that no nuclear weapons were present. The ownership of the technical site and the headquarters area buildings have subsequently passed to the Greenham Common Trust. The GAMA site is currently in private ownership.

COLD WAR ARCHAEOLOGY AT GREENHAM COMMON

The Cold War archaeological heritage at Greenham Common is generally well preserved and there are a number of reasons for this. The military structures are substantial and robust and therefore not easy to damage or remove. The archaeology of the peace protest is less robust, but the location of some of the camps within fairly densely overgrown and little visited parts of the common has aided the survival of features. In addition, as options for the future uses of parts of the site are only now being considered, a 'mothballing' approach has been applied to the interim management of some areas until such time as these decisions are made. Finally, the relative recentness of the site means that natural deterioration processes experienced at all archaeological sites have yet to take a firm hold.

At the present time large numbers of buildings survive from the former airfield, the majority of which are located along the southern site boundary including Area C (the GAMA site) and Areas D and E comprising the headquarters buildings and the technical site (the accommodation, administration and recreation buildings), respectively. On the north side of the runway, a small complex of buildings, known as Area A, includes the air traffic control tower, and at the extreme east end of the runway lies the base school (Area B).

No buildings survive from the Second World War occupation of the site, the earliest examples being from the major building phase of the 1950s. Many of these are very simply designed, prefabricated structures of rectangular or H-plan. The majority are single storey with corrugated roofs and metal-framed windows. Some are painted in the 1980s USAF colours of cream and brown. The aircraft control tower, two fire stations (one by the control tower and one on the technical site) and the base power plant are also from this period, as were the extensive (in excess of 70 structures) two-storey barrack blocks in Area E constructed to house the SAC bomber crews (see Figure 8.2). These were demolished some years ago in preparation for redevelopment.

The second construction phase followed in the 1980s with the decision to house cruise missiles at Greenham Common. A number of buildings were built or modified during this decade including the base school (Area B), the Wing Headquarters and ancillary buildings (Area D) and the GAMA complex (Area C). In Area E, the site was considerably enhanced by community facilities such as a library, fitness centre (including the 'Liberty' ballroom), bank and food mall. This area still retains something of the character of an American settlement transported to rural Berkshire, despite more recent modifications and new construction work. A combination of 1950s and 1980s US architecture (including paint schemes), street signs and furniture, such as yellow fire hydrants and distinctive street lights, all create a curiously American townscape.

In 2000, English Heritage conducted a national assessment of the monuments of the Cold War in order to identify the surviving resource, and also to identify those structures which would merit either legal protection or the instigation of management agreements with owners (Cocroft 2001). This was a timely study as owners, and indeed most of the heritage sector, did not consider such structures as being of archaeological value given their recency. Demolition was a very real threat. At Greenham Common, English Heritage identified five buildings for retention, in addition to the GAMA complex, and also commented on the importance of contemporary signage, street furniture and deliberate planting as contributors to site significance and historical integrity. The selected buildings were all associated with cruise; they were either deliberately built or modified for use during the heightened tensions of the 1980s. It is the buildings of this later occupation phase, therefore, rather than those of the 1950s, that have been identified as being of national archaeological importance.

Key buildings and structures

The Wing Headquarters Building (Figure 8.12) was the command centre for the base and the conduit for orders from High Command to the mobile cruise missile flights. It is located in close proximity to the GAMA site and adjacent to the Combat Support Building. As with many of the buildings of the period, it was designed to withstand conventional, biological and chemical attack. Of particular importance is the large decontamination suite and self-contained air filtration system at the western end of the building, enabling the structure to be sealed and continue to function even if the surrounding atmosphere became contaminated. The Battle Operations Room, which also lies in the western section of the building, is another significant survival.

The building, which is now known as *Venture West* and *The Bunker at Venture West*, is currently leased to commercial firms for office space and storage. The eastern section of the ground floor and the whole of the first floor are now office and conference suites, let to small companies or individuals on a short-term basis. *The Bunker*, which is effectively the Battle Operations Room and decontamination area, has been established as a secure data centre. Interestingly, the state-of-the-art nature of Cold War-era bunkers and the use of the former command centre's stand-by generators and back-up power supply are stressed in advertising for the facility. It is proposed that this building will either be listed or a management agreement entered into with the owner, to enable change to take place while retaining features of historical significance.

The nearby Missile Launcher Vehicle Maintenance Building, which was also recommended for listing or a management agreement, has been demolished since the publication of the English Heritage study. The owner justified this action by stating that it had no modern use and was in poor condition; its loss was mitigated by an archaeological building record commissioned prior to demolition. The structure had been situated to the south of the Wing Headquarters Building forming a group with it and the Combat Support Building. Vehicle maintenance was very important given that cruise was a mobile missile system.

Figure 8.4. The now demolished Missile Launcher Vehicle Maintenance Building. This structure illustrated the importance of the mobility of the cruise missile flights with its large garages designed to accept and service the transporter vehicles. © English Heritage AA003344

Hangar 303 was also recommended as a potential candidate for listing, but following discussion and agreement of the heritage agencies it was also agreed that demolition might take place after documentation. Located on the technical site (Area E), this 1950s USAF concrete-framed hangar was a very unusual hangar type in the United Kingdom. It was erected post-February 1958 when its predecessor was destroyed by fuel tanks jettisoned by a stricken B-47 Stratojet. In the 1980s, the hangar was modified for cruise use when it housed and maintained support vehicles for the missile flights. It contained wall and floor art by the cruise flight crews. Unfortunately the art representing the cobra of 'C-flight' was painted directly onto the concrete slab floor and it was not

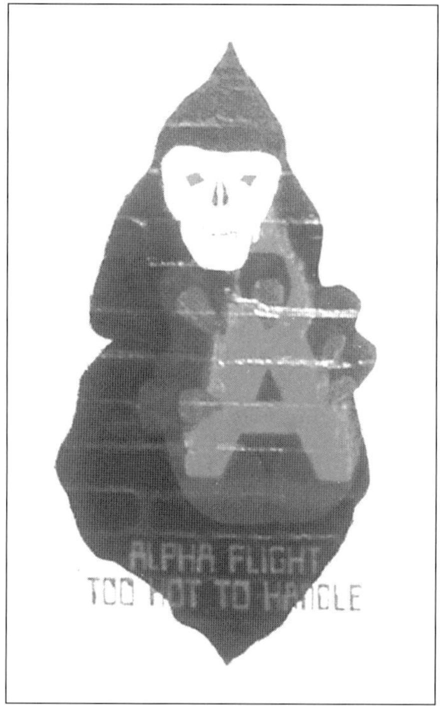

Figure 8.5. This example of wall art was removed from one of the Greenham Common hangars and after conservation was placed on display at the Ridgeway Military and Aviation Research Group's museum, RAF Welford. Each missile flight used different symbols and slogans to identify their particular areas of a building. Such art was officially endorsed to unify the flight crews and boost morale. Here we see that A- or Alpha-flight is represented by the hooded figure of Death gripping the letter A, embellished with the slogan 'Alpha Flight Too Hot To Handle'. © Veronica Fiorato

Figure 8.6. The camouflaged Combat Support Building, located adjacent to and in support of the Wing Headquarters Building, housed accommodation for troops for the protection of the base against conventional ground attack. © Veronica Fiorato

possible to remove it to safety, although it has been photographically recorded. However, some examples of wall art from hangars at Greenham Common have been carefully removed by members of the Ridgeway Military and Aviation Research Group to their nearby museum at RAF Welford.

Initially it was hoped that Hangar 303 could have been reused until it was discovered that planning permission for its demolition had been granted some years prior to the English Heritage assessment. On closer examination, the large quantity of asbestos in the structure meant that its retention would not have been feasible. This is obviously an important point when considering the preservation of relatively modern buildings; the materials used in their construction may be too dangerous for them to be retained on health and safety grounds.

The fourth structure, the Combat Support Building, adjacent to the Wing Headquarters building, is currently unoccupied and is not believed to be under threat at present. English Heritage has proposed that it should be considered for protection. Its purpose was to provide protected accommodation for around a hundred soldiers who could defend the base from hostile infiltration even after a conventional, chemical or biological attack.

The control tower (Figure 8.13), which is the fifth structure identified for retention by English Heritage, was built in 1951 and continued in use until the final closure of the base. It is a brick-built three-storey tower identical to examples erected at all the SAC main bases (Cocroft and Thomas 2003:55). Unlike the other significant buildings described above, however, it is owned by West Berkshire Council. Currently unoccupied, it has been secured against vandalism and 'mothballed' pending a decision about a future use, although not before many of the interior fittings were stolen and the windows broken. However, the control tower has seen some recent low-key use such as a sound installation by the composer and sonic artist Hywel Davis which was commissioned specifically as a new work for the building. The tower was opened to the public and visitors climbed through the three floors experiencing different Greenham-inspired sounds on each level.

The GAMA complex is the key Cold War monument at Greenham Common. Visually dominating the skyline, the six cruise missile shelters are vast structures, symbolic of the most controversial occupation of the base during the 1980s. Effectively bomb-proof garages on a monumental scale, each shelter housed a 'flight' of four Transporter Erector Launchers (with four missiles on each), and two Launch Control Centre vehicles and probably two recovery vehicles. When deployed, each flight with its 16 missiles would have been accompanied by 16 support vehicles and 69 men comprising the flight commander, a doctor, four launch officers, maintenance crew and combat soldiers (Cocroft and Thomas 2003:76–78).

The shelters are of reinforced concrete with three internal garage lanes protected at each end by steel blast doors. Two pedestrian concrete access tunnels are located on one flank of each shelter. The roofs and flanks, constructed of concrete and compacted sand and covered in turf, were designed to absorb and disperse any direct bomb blast.

One structure, the Quick Reaction Alert (QRA) shelter, is located adjacent to the main entrance of the complex and is unique in that it was designed to enable immediate retaliation to attack. Attached to the side of the QRA are accommodation rooms, which were permanently manned by a flight crew. GAMA was designed with the intention that the missiles would be deployed and fired outside the base from predetermined dispersal sites, but the QRA is a physical recognition that there may not have been time to react to a threat other than by firing either from the concrete apron of the GAMA complex or from the adjacent airfield.

The complex is surrounded by a high-security triple fence topped by razor wire, in marked contrast to the lower degree of security elsewhere on the base. The sterile strips between the fences were regularly patrolled and monitored using closed-circuit television and radar intruder alarms (Cocroft and Thomas 2003:76). Contained within the fence were ancillary buildings such as a heavily fortified guard-house control point at the main entrance, a watchtower (now demolished as it became

Figure 8.7. Examples of art within the GAMA complex QRA

Top An adhesive sign for the 11th Tactical Missile Squadron on the pedestrian entrance door. This is the squadron's badge which would have been displayed on uniforms as well as buildings. © Veronica Fiorato

Bottom A wall painting of a bomber and mushroom cloud on the first floor of the accommodation block. © Veronica Fiorato

unsafe), a group of 1950s SAC bomb stores or 'igloos' (modified and re-used in the 1980s as stores for food, conventional munitions and war-heads), as well as vehicle maintenance and inspection structures. A secondary gate, known to the protesters as Green Gate, provided access to the Newbury-Basingstoke road to the south. GAMA was deliberately designed such that it could stand alone and function even if the rest of the base was compromised or destroyed.

With the exception of the watchtower and fixtures and fittings, GAMA is remarkably complete, although the hydraulics have been removed from all of the shelter doors apart from the Quick Reaction Shelter. These have been deliberately left in place in order that educational restoration could be achieved. The accommodation rooms and plant room within the QRA provide a fascinating insight into the facility's function, and the military wall art at various locations throughout the complex add a human dimension to these monumental structures.

The expiry of the INF Treaty in June 2001 allowed the Ministry of Defence to dispose of the complex as surplus to requirements. It is now in private ownership and discussions regarding a suitable future use are currently taking place. Following English Heritage's national Cold War assessment, the GAMA site has been designated a Scheduled Monument under the Ancient Monuments and Archaeological Areas Act 1979 (as amended), which offers full legal protection.

The archaeology of the peace protest

During the military occupation of the base during the 1980s and early 1990s, a series of women's peace camps was established at Greenham Common. The first camp was established in September 1981 after a group of women marched from their homes in South Wales to protest against plans to station cruise missiles at the airbase. The Greenham Common camps were distinct from other contemporary peace camps in being exclusively female. The Greenham Women's nonviolent protest, in opposition to the occupancy of the base by the US military and the presence of cruise, resulted in worldwide publicity and led to Greenham

---

Figure 8.8. The Peace Garden on the former site of *Yellow* (or *Main Gate*) *Camp* was dedicated by the Women's Peace Movement in October 2002 as a commemorative site. The garden includes a circle of Welsh standing stones containing a steel sculpture of a campfire and a spiral water feature (foreground) inscribed with the words 'You can't kill the spirit. Women's peace camp 1981–2000. You can't kill the spirit'. The sculptures were designed by Michael Marriott in conjunction with the peace women to symbolise the camp. Part of the garden is dedicated to Helen Wyn Thomas, who lost her life at Greenham Common. © Veronica Fiorato

Common becoming a focus for the peace movement. Located at the gates to the airfield, mostly along the northern perimeter fence, each camp was distinguished by two names, one identifying the gate by a colour, such as *Blue Gate* or *Turquoise Gate*, the other identifying the make-up of its residents, for example: *Artists' Gate* or *New Age Gate*. A large camp, known as *Yellow Gate*, existed at the main entrance to the base, located south of the technical site. This had the longest occupancy, with the final peace caravan and its residents only leaving the site in the autumn of 2000. Perhaps the best known camp was that at *Green Gate* given its location at the southern entrance to the GAMA site and thus its proximity to the missiles. Each camp was individual in both layout and philosophy. Although all were opposed to the deployment of cruise and were campaigning for nuclear disarmament, they also had other diverging agendas and there was well-documented rivalry between the women of the different camps.

There is little archaeological evidence for most of the camps. Yellow Gate was destroyed by the construction of a new entrance to New Greenham Business Park, although there is now a peace garden here, designed and created by the Greenham Women in recognition and as a permanent reminder of the role of the peace movement at the base. Many of the northern perimeter camps have also been lost. In this area the protestors were confined to a narrow strip of land between the perimeter fence and the external perimeter road, known as Bury's Bank Road, but heathland restoration and road improvements have removed any traces that may have survived here. However, site reconnaissance in 2002 by the author with colleagues from English Heritage and West Berkshire Heritage Service identified good survival of features at three other campsites. In contrast to the military remains these are insubstantial, reflecting the temporary and phased occupation of the camp sites. The peace women lived largely in tents or homemade shelters (known as benders), constructions which have left little archaeological trace. In addition to this, camps were the subject of regular evictions and there are contemporary accounts of bulldozers being used to ensure that they became uninhabitable. At three of the campsites, Turquoise Gate, Green Gate and Orange Gate, surviving archaeology includes mounds of earth (presumably from such episodes although some will relate to later restoration works), pits (perhaps for campfires or latrines), deliberately cleared areas of woodland to accommodate the tents and shelters, and artefact scatters. These artefacts present a fascinating insight into the possessions and lives of the peace women and vary from consumables, such as empty cans and bottles, to personal effects. At Orange Gate items of clothing, multicoloured hair slides and jewellery can be found on the ground. Pegs, string and other fixings for tarpaulins survive in the trees. The fact that so many features and artefacts survive at these three camps

Figure 8.9. One of a number of posts decorated by the peace women at Green Gate. The use of the female symbol and the snake was common. This example deliberately used the anarchist colours of red and black. Others use the purple, green and white of the women's suffrage movement. © Veronica Fiorato

has been a surprising discovery. Clearly the final stages of occupation at these locations were not removed by bulldozing and the archaeological survival is also helped by the camps being somewhat 'off the beaten track'.

Additional evidence of the peace protest comes in the form of painted symbols and words. These can be found on the tarmack road surface (at Green and Orange Gates), on the surviving base gates (Green and Blue Gates), on low fence posts beyond the perimeter at Green Gate, and also within the GAMA site: From time to time the Greenham Women would breach the security fences by cutting through the wire, and would take their protest inside the base and indeed inside GAMA before being evicted. The cuts and patches to the fences are therefore also significant as part of the archaeological record as well as being symbolic of their protest. However, these are often difficult to distinguish from other interventions, particularly those of vandals attempting to gain entry to the site.

Painted slogans, for instance 'Women against Cruise', and the female symbol can be seen on the exterior walls of the vehicle maintenance structure, although these may postdate the closure of the base. Other commonly used motifs include snakes, flowers, spirals, the peace symbol and words such as 'Peace'. These are in danger of loss, particularly those on the tarmac surface which are fading so rapidly that the design of some is no longer discernable. All the surviving paint work needs to be photographed and recorded as a matter of urgency in order that these important visual components of the peace protest are not lost.

A FUTURE FOR THE COMMON

The open heath

The open areas of the former air base have been the subject of considerable restoration and conservation work since ownership of the land

Figure 8.10. The perimeter fence in situ with an internal road and security lighting. © West Berkshire Heritage Service 2868

reverted to the local council. It is clear that the former military land management regime has contributed to the ease with which the heath has been restored. Under the RAF and USAAF/USAF, Greenham Common was managed to ensure that the vegetation was compatible with the necessary functionality and security of the base. The restricted access during the active life of the base, maintenance of a short grass sward and scrub management has meant that the Common has not had the opportunity to become overgrown and thus has remained species rich. Much of the former airbase has been designated as a Site of Special Scientific Interest (SSSI). This provides legal protection and recognition for its nationally important ecology, as Lowland Heath is a rare habitat type supporting a number of threatened species. The restored heath is now managed for its nature conservation interest.

The restoration work also included the removal of buried fuel tanks, which were a contaminant danger to both the natural aquifer and any restored habitats, and the removal of much of the perimeter fence. This was done for a number of reasons, not least the symbolic act of restoring access to the formerly restricted common and returning it to the people, but a retained fence of several kilometres in length would also have had significant practical and financial implications for its owners. Its removal has facilitated the unrestricted movement of grazing cattle, which are crucial to the maintenance of the healthy heathland sward. Small sections of perimeter fence are still standing and it is hoped that they will be retained both as a reminder that this was once an airbase, and also as physical markers for the former divisive line between military and civilian life. In addition, a section has been removed to the Peace Museum in Bradford where it will be curated as part of the museum's collections.

The runway has also been removed and the concrete recycled. The site of the runway is still evident as differential vegetation growth with only the central crossing deliberately retained as a symbolic archaeological monument. Positive and ongoing management will be required here to ensure that weed growth is prevented; root action could rapidly result in the break-up of the surface.

The open areas of Greenham Common are once again common land. Small parking areas have been created around the perimeter and the Common is used for horse riding, cycling and walking. Open public access does occasionally cause problems for the nature conservation management regime, for example, through erosion of well-used paths or disturbance of nesting birds, but the scale of the Common is such that these are not significant issues. A Common Warden, employed by the Council, manages any necessary conservation or repair work, monitors the ecological health of the site, and has an educational role in encouraging sympathetic uses such that leisure activities and conservation can be compatible. There are clearly educational opportunities on the archaeological side which have not been fully exploited to date, and while this is true of the Common as a whole, it is particularly relevant in those areas with public access.

A business park

As mentioned above, at the current time Areas D and E to the south of the former airfield largely retain their 1980s layout with deliberate planting and American-designed street features such as picnic benches, street lights and signage. However, the buildings and street pattern in Area E, with the exception of a very small number of structures, are shortly to be demolished. Planning permission was granted several years ago to clear and redevelop the whole site as a business park. As this permission was granted prior to English Heritage's Cold War assessment, heritage agencies now have no authority to prevent the demolition.

Discussions have been held with the owner, the Greenham Common Trust, to try to retain representative buildings, as well as some of the key elements of the US streetscape. However, if this is not possible, the Trust's decision to commission a thorough archaeological building record prior to demolition is warmly endorsed and will provide an essential record of the technical site for the benefit of future generations. The redevelopment proposals at *New Greenham Park,* as the technical site is now known, should be a clear warning to all those interested in modern archaeology; it is important to identify the potential 'archaeology of tomorrow', and to ensure that it is legally designated or locally recognised as significant, as failure to do so can result in serious loss.

The Control Tower and GAMA

In anticipation of the expiry of the INF treaty and the 'liberation' of the GAMA complex, discussions as to the future use of GAMA began in the late 1990s between English Heritage, the Ministry of Defence (the owner), and West Berkshire Council (the local authority and prospective owner of the site). It was originally intended that the MOD would sell GAMA to West Berkshire Council for a nominal sum and that the Council would then manage the complex in conjunction with the rest of their holdings on the Common, integrating GAMA with a proposed interpretation/visitor centre at the control tower. It was envisaged that the tower would include multimedia displays telling the archaeological and ecological story of Greenham, as well as housing visitor facilities such as a cafe and shop. A viewing platform on the top floor would have allowed the visitor to look out over the Common before following a trail across the site, culminating with a visit to the GAMA complex.

Figure 8.11. This photograph of July 2002 shows the Common during restoration. In contrast to Figure 8.2 taken seven years earlier, the runway tarmac is in the process of being removed and the barracks in the technical site (top right) have been demolished. The control tower is located centre left (Area A) and the base school (Area B) at the extreme eastern end of the runway in the background. © English Heritage NMR 18884/17

In anticipation of the new visitor centre, a roundabout to improve site access and a visitor car park were constructed adjacent to the control tower building, but the finances to complete the project were not available, and this remains the case today. Local councils often have to make difficult choices about the allocation of limited funds and West Berkshire Council is no exception, but it is hoped that the control tower project will be revived in the future as the benefits to education and tourism in the area would be considerable. The Council has decided not to purchase the GAMA complex, however, given concerns over future liabilities from both health and safety, and repair and maintenance perspectives. The Councillors' decision is to be deeply regretted as the opportunity to manage and interpret the site holistically has now been lost. As a future use for GAMA remains uncertain, decisions need to be taken about what could be achieved at the control tower by way of interpretation and a 'whole-site' visitor experience.

The Ministry of Defence, in consultation with English Heritage, marketed and sold GAMA in 2003 after assessing a shortlist of prospective purchasers to ensure that the future owner's proposals would be sympathetic to the site's historic significance. Reuse of some or all of the GAMA structures is not out of the question, but usage must be sympathetic to the national importance of the site and not compromise its historical integrity. Access to GAMA is also very limited – on foot across the Common, or by a narrow lane from the south with neighbouring houses and this would preclude any use where large vehicle movements were necessary. Notwithstanding, there is the potential for the site to be reused in a number of ways, perhaps most obviously for secure and long-term storage, but some ideas have been more imaginative, such as the restoration of the Quick Reaction Alert shelter as part of a Cold War trail, the use of a shelter as an art gallery, the occasional use of the concrete apron for public events, and so on. There are, naturally, local public concerns about the potential proposals, many of which are unfounded given that the scheduling legislation will prohibit certain uses. Of particular concern is the possibility of a significant increase in visitors and traffic, and it is clearly important that the local community's views are considered during the decision-making process. It is to be hoped that the new owner will be sympathetic to the history and archaeology of this important site, and will work closely with West Berkshire Council and English Heritage to secure its future.

Figure 8.12. The Wing Headquarters Building was the command and control centre for the base during the deployment of cruise missiles at Greenham Common. The building contained a decontamination suite and air filtration system (in the single-storey section to the left) as well as a Battle Operations Room. It is now occupied by offices and data storage facilities. © Veronica Fiorato

Archaeological research

Following the realisation that archaeological evidence for a number of peace camps does survive at Greenham Common, a project known as Common Ground has been established. Initial work has taken place at Turquoise Gate, including a topographic survey and field collection of objects, the results of which will be used to assess the potential for further archaeological investigation both here and at other camps (Orange and Green with the possible addition of the small camp at Emerald). It is hoped that this project will ensure that the ephemeral evidence of the occupancy of the Greenham Women is recorded before it is lost and that archaeological techniques can be used in understanding the anticipated difference in material culture between the camps. Input from those involved with Greenham Common during the 1980s and 1990s, including former peace women, is bringing an invaluable dimension to the

Figure 8.13. The Control Tower (a USAF type 5222A/51 tower) dates to the early 1950s and was built during alterations to the airfield to accommodate the USAF Strategic Air Command. The structure is currently secured for its protection until a long-term use can be determined. © English Heritage AA003331

Figure 8.14. Artefacts from the peace camp lying in the undergrowth. © K Posehn

Figure 8.15. Discarded boot left by one of the peace women. © K Posehn

research. Although at a very early stage, the unusual opportunity to use scientific archaeological techniques in the study of the very recent past presents a number of challenges, but will hopefully serve to redress the balance of archaeological work at the base, which to date has concentrated almost exclusively on the military remains.

It can be difficult to engage society in the archaeology of a site as recent as Greenham Common, and particularly one that so polarised opinions. Many would wish to see the complete removal of the military architecture whilst others see no merit in recording the peace camps. In truth it is essential to study, record, and where feasible retain elements of each, as the story of Cold War Greenham cannot be told without looking at the archaeology on both sides of the fence.

REFERENCES

Cocroft, WD (2001) *Cold War Monuments: An assessment by the Monuments Protection Programme*, London: English Heritage

Cocroft, WD and Thomas, RJC (2003) *Cold War: Building for Nuclear Confrontation 1946–1989*, London: English Heritage

FURTHER READING

Croom, J (1994) *Greenham Common Airbase, Greenham, Berkshire*, unpublished historic building report, Royal Commission on the Historical Monuments of England

Kippin, J et al (2001) *Cold War Pastoral: Greenham Common,* London: Black Dog Publishing

Roseneil, S (2000) *Common Women, Uncommon Practices: The Queer Feminisms of Greenham*, London: Cassell

Schofield, J and Anderton, M (2000) 'The queer archaeology of Green Gate: Interpreting contested space at Greenham Common Airbase', in *World Archaeology* 32(2) 236–251

www.greenham-common.org.uk, a lottery-funded web site by West Berkshire Council in association with Sense of Place South-east (SOPSE), which provides a textual and pictorial introduction to the Common from its earliest history to the present day.

www.greenhamcommonground.com describes the ongoing archaeological research project to examine the peace camps at Greenham Common.

Out to the waste: Spadeadam and the Cold War

LOUISE K WILSON

Sometimes it seems that being an artist brings a strange passport of admission, allowing one relatively easy access to otherwise inaccessible or sensitive places and the apparent freedom to move around inside them. For nearly five years now I've become increasingly fascinated with a place called Spadeadam in Cumbria. This remote location has an extraordinary history of occupation: It was the rocket test site for the Cold War Intermediate Range Ballistic Missile Blue Streak in the late 1950s and '60s and is now used by the RAF as an electronic warfare tactics range.

My initial curiosity was aroused by misinformation. Originally, as part of a visual arts residency at Grizedale Forest in the Lake District, I had expressed an interest in wanting to map landscape by launching tiny video rockets over the Grizedale Valley. The director of the arts programme emailed me about an aspect of 'local' history he thought would be of interest:

> Subject: Re rockets
> Spadeadam, near Appleby, Rocket testing centre, 'Blue Dart' planned to be britains man on the moon missile cancelled in the late 50's. Bits of it are still up on the moor

Little of that information was correct apart from the name 'Spadeadam', the concept of a cancelled rocket programme and the fact that 'bits' remain. In time the correct title of the project was given and Doug Millard, the space curator at the Science Museum in London, gave me some background.

The history of Blue Streak is complex – embracing firstly military, then civilian intent. Briefly, Blue Streak was a British Intermediate Range Ballistic Missile system that was conceived in 1954 as a nuclear deterrent. If armed with a British-built nuclear warhead and fired from concrete silos within the United Kingdom, the missile would have all of the Western USSR within its range. However, a review of the programme was ordered by the government in 1959 and concluded that the launch of Blue Streak from a silo was no longer to be considered practical as the silo and its contents would be too vulnerable to nuclear attack. In April 1960 the project was cancelled as a weapon system. But it was then reborn as the first stage of the European Launcher Development Organisation's (ELDO) first satellite launcher project, *Europa 1*. France would supply the second stage, Germany the third, and it would carry an Italian satellite. Much testing took place but United Kingdom involvement was withdrawn in 1971 as the Europa system as a whole had problems. The Blue Streak continued to perform well, unlike the French and German stages. These were behind in development, and the cost of continuing was felt to be prohibitive. In 1973 the ELDO programme was abandoned.

The original Blue Streak rocket technology came from the 'States when an agreement was reached with the US government to transfer technology from the Atlas programme (the Atlas rocket had been the United States' first successful Intercontinental Ballistic Missile, initially tested in 1959). Contracts to modify and build the rocket in the United Kingdom were awarded to De Havilland (later Hawker Siddeley) for the vehicle and to Rolls Royce for the development of the engines. The companies Sperry and Marconi became involved, designing the rocket's guidance systems and radar.

Spadeadam Rocket Establishment was set up in 1956 for engine tests and static test firings of the assembled rockets. The site in Cumbria, next to the Northumbria border, was selected for its isolation and high rainfall. This was because a lot of water was needed for cooling the test stands. Spadeadam Waste was also chosen because of its bogginess, necessary to absorb the sonic fallout.

The rockets themselves were first launched from Woomera in South Australia in 1964 (where identical stands had been built) and once at Kouru in French Guyana. Eleven Blue Streaks were launched altogether.

I was curious why I hadn't heard of Blue Streak before. Personal coincidences emerged. I realised I'd been in the vicinity of the Australian launch site as a child (though quite a few years after the last Blue Streak firing). My father had been an engineer in the Ministry of Defence. I grew up with the language of ordnance and three years of my childhood were spent living in Adelaide, South Australia, with a visit to Woomera. In some ways I'm still metaphorically peering into attic cupboards like the one in which my dad hoarded manuals stamped 'Classified'.

My process for researching material is that of a magpie, loosely appropriating and sampling research methods from different observational disciplines (from journalism and anthropology, for example) and combining visual documentation, oral history and collaboration. I am interested in the way in which theory and anecdote collide. The passport of artistic admission apparently allows the right to take these liberties.

So I began to embark on an ad hoc process of piecing together Blue Streak and Spadeadam for myself – not by methodically seeking out documents at the National Archive (formerly the Public Records Office) but by building up a personal archive of images and interviews. One contact led to the next. I met museum curators and retired engineers; Dave Wright, an academic in Liverpool writing his PhD on Blue Streak; a television producer who made a TV documentary in 1994; a local radio producer who'd done the same, and so on. I heard stories about Spadeadam from all sorts of sources with various shades of reliability. Someone told me that a few episodes of Dr Who had been filmed there in the post-Blue Streak years, but that was probably unlikely, I concluded.

What was becoming really fascinating to me, in what appeared to be a resurgent interest in Blue Streak, was the intersection of the worlds of archaeology, museology, heritage and amateur testimony. At least two ex-Blue Streak engineers/designers had or were writing books about Spadeadam and the rocket and distributed their own video compilations of archive trials film of the rocket launches at Woomera, set to light classical music.

The late Charles Martin, the Blue Streak chief designer, whom I met in 2001, was surprised by all the heritage interest 30 years after the project was completely cancelled. 'It's now history', he said.

When the project finally ended, documentation was either destroyed or dispersed, driven off in the boots of people's cars. I heard stories of some larger artefacts turning up in people's gardens, and recently some turbo pumps have apparently showed up on eBay. In 1992 the Solway Aviation Museum (a small amateur-run museum at Carlisle Airport) arranged for the rescue of a number of items. Its 'Blue Streak room' contains rocket engine motors, photographs and memorabilia with 'Blue Streak' spelled out in blue neon.

With larger artefacts – the rockets themselves – fragments presumably still litter the Australian desert and in the jungle of French Guyana one rocket was famously used as a chicken coop. In the United Kingdom, three rocket vehicles are on display, with two in museums in various stages of assembly.

I began documenting the Blue Streak hardware on public and private display in this country, including the Museum of Flight at East Fortune in Scotland and the National Space Centre in Leicester which opened in 2001. The Space Centre displays the last of the fifteen Blue Streaks that were made. This was rescued off the production line by Liverpool Museum when the Blue Streak project was cancelled. Although there had been restricted access to it in the Large Object Store, it had been largely hidden from public view for nearly 30 years. The 18.5-metre-long, incredibly fragile rocket is now suspended vertically to show what it would have looked like on the launch pad. Captions provide minimal information, just a brief technical history and statistics.

Ray Hancock, who was the liaison engineer for Rolls Royce and now organises the Annual Reunion of Rocketmen, allowed me to document a Blue Streak fuel injector plate, which he had stored for 30 years under his sitting room table in a small terraced house in Carlisle.

Ray told how the plate had been mislaid and then rediscovered in an upstairs room. He and Jim Foulds, chief engineer officer for Rolls Royce at Spadeadam, went to collect it in his car.

> He didn't want it at his house so it was dumped here – it's been here ever since. We lifted it with that piece of angle iron that's bolted across the top of it. Now it's rather heavy. Jim Foulds got a hernia, and I got a double hernia lifting it in and out of his car and into here!

Ray has since had it relocated to Rolls Royce's own museum in Derby.

In 2001 and 2003 Ray allowed me to come to the Annual Reunion of Rocketmen. I didn't realise at the time but I was very privileged to be present, as these events are only open to ex-Spadeadam rocketmen and their families. They meet for lunch and drinks in the subsidised bar at RAF Spadeadam and reminisce about life on site and adventurous postings to the Australian desert and South American jungle in the 1960s.

On the handheld video footage I have of the 2001 reunion, John Salton, a jovial Scottish instrumentation engineer based at the Prior Lancy site, carefully tilts a full glass of beer to and fro to demonstrate a freak accident when a universal joint attaching the thrust chamber snapped. 'For all the firings that we did', he said, 'the problems were negligible; we had brilliant engineers working on the whole project'.

After lunch, a minibus escorted those engineers who wanted to go up to the site to view the decaying concrete rocket and engine test stands at Greymare Hill and Prior Lancy. At this point the stories and recollections became more animated. I picked up snippets such as how Spadeadam made its own 'clouds' during the rocket firings, that it was the first place in the country to have colour TV, and that Wernher von Braun visited in the 1960s (and inadvertently heard John Salton play *Scots Wha' Hae* on the bagpipes).

The strong camaraderie amongst the ex-employees is very obvious as is the bitterness and regret still felt at the cancellation of the project. Ray often quotes the pronouncement by the Minister of Technology at the time that there was 'no future in satellites'.

At lunch at the 2001 reunion it was possible to begin to gauge the effect Spadeadam had on the locale, both in developing the economics of the area and in the aftermath when it was cancelled.

I was interested in the sensorial impact of the test firings and asked how far away they would be audible.

> Ten miles – Brampton – you could hear it test firing during the day and at night the sky would light up orange … windows and doors used to rattle when both engines were firing. You could hear the firings in Carlisle with an east wind.
>
> There's a lady used to have an antique shop – it may still be there – in Brampton and she said she can clearly recall that when it fired the glassware used to rattle on the shelves and she had a crystal ball – she said her lovely crystal ball was shattered with the vibrations!

It can't have been very popular having test firings at night, surely? I asked.

> Well they didn't seem to get the complaints about things like that in those days. … Everyone accepted it I think; everyone accepted that that was what was going on anyway.

RAF SPADEADAM

The project finally ended in 1971. Five years later Spadeadam became an RAF station and the location for Western Europe's first full-scale Electronic Warfare Tactics Range, covering about 9,000 acres. The landscape is now dotted with radars acquired after the Falklands War and East German army radars and missile launchers 'procured' after the fall of the Berlin Wall and the first Gulf War – as well as clunky life-size versions made out of wood (what are called visual targets). There's a dummy airfield called Collinski – like some latter-day Cargo Cult (as in Cult adherents of the western Pacific who apparently built imitation runways to attract the cargo planes which had supplied the American Forces during the Second World War). As the RAF Spadeadam web site says,

> The Electronic Warfare Tactics Range fields a wide selection of threat systems that can generate many types of electronic signals for aircraft. These signals stimulate the aircraft's Radar Warning Receiver and jamming systems, causing the aircrew to react to the threats by employing various tactics to 'survive'.

The station's (Latin) motto means If you want peace, be prepared for war.

It is impossible to screen out the activities of the RAF if the interest is in visiting Spadeadam solely for its Blue Streak history. Various sites have been taken over and used for storage. The bunker at the engine test site at Prior Lancy is full of spare parts for East German military hardware like valves and instruction manuals in Russian, where a kind of reverse engineering is practised.

The roar of low-flying jets has now long since replaced the low-frequency rumble of the rocket firings. The pilots who fly over Spadeadam (from all over the United Kingdom and beyond) have generally never been there at ground level and so have never met the station personnel who are trying to outwit them. This land is essentially 'enemy territory' when they are flying over it.

I phoned two RAF pilots (from different bases) who had flown at low level over Spadeadam at great speed and asked them to describe the landscape from memory. Interestingly, the pilots didn't mention the Blue Streak remains, just the visual targets, masts and so on.

> The one time I did go into Spadeadam that I remember very very clearly there was a lot of low cloud there and as we were running into it at 750 ft you could just about see the treetops and stuff and the rest of it was just a layer of mist that was rolling in the hills. As far as the landscape goes – although you probably think it's quite rugged I suppose if you actually go around it on foot – because you're going at such speed I find that it tends to smooth the landscape out a little bit. And what would be fairly sharp hills whatever become more rolling hills. Spadeadam is also I think covered in trees.

I gave transcripts of these descriptions to a local amateur painter, who had been a pilot and instructor since 1949 and made paintings from memories of wartime flights over the farm he was brought up on. He produced some small watercolour paintings based solely on these verbal memories. They are a sort of Chinese Whispers reconnaissance – part remote viewing and part (imagined) landscape painting.

SPADEADAM BUS TOUR, 2002

I was finding RAF Spadeadam easier to access and document. In early visits I had to be escorted at all times, wasn't allowed to film the visual targets (even those made of wood) and had to have my videotape vetted. Now was a good time to take others along as well, so I organised a minibus trip to RAF Spadeadam in June 2002 (as a Grizedale Arts event).

It was originally scheduled for 12 September 2001 but postponed that morning because of heightened security.

The RAF was to host the afternoon, showing videos and explaining aspects of electronic warfare; Ray Hancock was to talk about Blue Streak.

Bus tourists included the then curator at the Museum of Flight in Edinburgh and an elderly artist friend who had taken part in a peace march on Spadeadam in the 1960s and was still living nearby. Her home was a cottage divided into two flats; for thirty years or so she had effectively lived in the same house as a Blue Streak engineer whom she didn't get on with.

Some months later I asked some of the bus tourists for their impressions and memories of the day at Spadeadam:

> I found myself as one of a motley crew on a bus tour of RAF Spadeadam. My fellow passengers included retired people from the local village (whose families had worked at the base, and had grown up knowing that the rocket existed but that it was not to be talked about), artists and Ray Hancock an engineer on the Blue Streak Project (so the secret really had to be true). And sure enough, parked up on a trailer at the entrance to the base, is a section of the rocket that really should be in the science museum.
>
> As we bumped along the bleak and exposed moorland we unpeeled the layers of secrecy and openness covering the site. ... We visited the fantastic rocket test beds – beautiful examples of modernist concrete architecture that may one day become a listed heritage site (much to the annoyance of the RAF who would have the responsibility of maintaining them).
>
> We also visited the control station of the EWTR – and witnessed the chaotic transition from what looked like a DOS operated computer system to windows. Spadeadam seemed like the furthest outpost of the RAF, full of eccentric officers who spend too much time in the beautiful but isolated environment. We drove past the British Gas test centre where they blow up gas cookers! and as things got curiouser and curiouser I formulated my own conspiracy theory – that the hard granite geology was in fact being tested as a site for storing radioactive waste, but who knows?

From another artist (who took GPS readings at various Blue Streak sites):

> The strangeness of a concrete support structure being made a listed building seemed apt in an environment where there was a mixture of real but ancient anti-aircraft devices with no english [*sic*] instructions, on an airbase with no runway, along side fake wooden

---

Figures 9.1–9.8. Photographs and stills from video used in filmmaking at Spadeadam. All photos in this chapter are © Louise K Wilson.

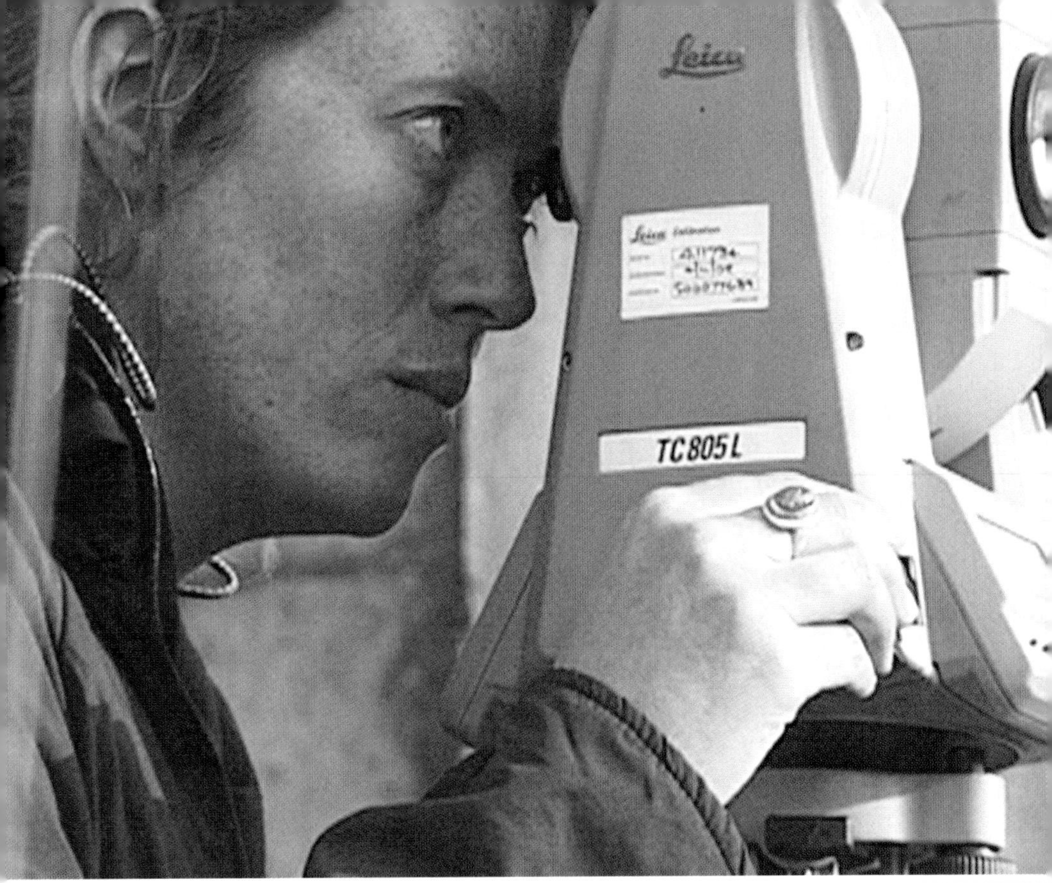

TC805L

> tanks and decoys. Somehow the whole place was a support structure and a test ground, a place to fly over rather than to land, almost making it a non-location. Feeling like I had to be furtive with my gps emphasised that, almost as if secretly it was impossible to map (incidentally I never did manage to save the gps data properly, all that is left are a few co-ordinates labelled owl or phonebox or decoy).

From a photographer:

> It's difficult to pull out a single impression from the visit and I don't want to attempt a major statement which will sound pompous. I suppose I would say that I am always amazed at the things that take place in Britain which are 'on our behalf' and all of the secrecy which surrounds them.
>
> The remoteness and closed nature of the area surrounding Spadeadam must have greatly added to the feeling of isolation and exclusivity of the whole enterprise. I'm also slightly surprised at how the real reason for making Blue Streak in the first place becomes wrapped in a kind of miasma around British craftsmanship and excellence as opposed to French incompetence. The fact is that Blue Streak was to deliver nuclear weapons to Moscow as part of a totally lunatic defence policy which institutionalises genocide as an acceptable outcome of conflict. Phew. ... That said I have very fond memories of the sandwiches which (you) brought in on a baker's tray with a gingham cloth covering them. They seemed to be reflective of an era when Spadeadam was at its height.

SPADEADAM (2003)

There were four main sites within the complex at Spadeadam during the Blue Streak days. Many of the buildings were demolished in the years following the end of the project but some buildings and rigs remain, mainly the rocket plinths at Greymare Hill, engine test plinths at Prior Lancy, the control bunkers at both sites and the Component Test Area where individual engine parts were tested and developed. The facilities at Greymare Hill (the rocket test area) were designed to carry out test firings of fully assembled tethered Blue Streak rockets before the rockets were shipped for launch. Two were built; only Greymare east was ever used. In recent years, the RAF has on occasion used the stands for abseiling practice. These selected sites were now scheduled to be designated as 'ancient monuments' by English Heritage.

Figures 9.9–9.14. Photographs and stills from video used in filmmaking at Spadeadam.

I had amassed many hours of audio and video footage and wanted to structure this material into a portrait of Spadeadam. The focus would be on the days I had spent watching English Heritage archaeologists painstakingly recording the remains at Spadeadam (mapping all the concrete in great detail with GPS equipment, electronic theodolites and so on) for a necessary survey prior to scheduling. This survey was part of a wider project called 'Cold War People and Places' in which English Heritage is investigating a number of Cold War science and technology sites, combining traditional archaeological surveys with oral testimony, all initiated by Wayne Cocroft.

This video material had been shot at different times on a number of visits but I decided to structure it around the principal Blue Streak sites. I also included footage of Berry Hill, the headquarters of electronic warfare (where, filming from the roof underneath a huge radar dish, my camera had been temporarily impaired) and Kingwater House, where the annual reunion takes place.

The intention was to provide a different sort of captioning for the site, which would cluster around ideas of memory and landscape and touch on the tensions and contradictions underlying experience of this place now. It was a documentation of visits made, rather than a documentary. But it was increasingly about investigating space, taking visual ownership, for example, by flying over Spadeadam in a small Piper aircraft on a weekend when the airspace was open.

I wanted to make some sort of sense of the surroundings through a sensorial engagement. Nearly all material was filmed with a hand-held camera to indicate my presence there as a witness or interloper. At Greymare Hill once, shortly after rainfall, I had climbed up onto a wet concrete structure. Upon descending the rusty metal ladder, a Tornado jet flew past at what seemed like only a few metres away. It was instantly invisible, save for some lasting ringing tones that quickly merged with birdsong.

Something else to make visible was the activity/inactivity at the base, how it felt particularly in the first surveying week I was there, as the attack on Iraq had started the previous week and it was quieter than usual. I was interested in the physical situation that archaeologists Cathy Tuck and Dave McOmish were in. The restrictions of access posed by radiation hazard, the physical difficulties of traversing the land, the vicissitudes of measuring but also making sure you're not falling down a shaft.

More important was the need to foreground sound (both real and imagined). The surreal atmosphere when the working archaeologists were encircled both by invisible simulated electronic warfare and springtime birdsong, at a time of deep disturbance and trouble on another continent.

The sound track on the video *Spadeadam* incorporates tracks by the band :zoviet*france: and were created from manipulated field recordings the two musicians made at Spadeadam: the edgy, metallic scraping of gate locks repeatedly opened and shut, buttons on old fuse boxes rattled, a trout leaping for flies in a concrete water tank – and studio-made low-frequency rumbles, electronic swallows and a simulated radar sound redolent of 1960s sci-fi.

Ben Ponton, of :zoviet*france:, subsequently spoke of his response to the place:

> My hook into the project was that Spadeadam was this mysterious place I'd been familiar with since I was a kid. I'd been taken on car trips along the military road and seeing in the distance and having it pointed out to me this was the British Space program testing site – it was like pure science fiction to me as a kid. The idea that Britain had a space programme and rocket engines being tested there was weird, impossible to believe.
>
> Actually going there for the project, it was strangely sad. It was melancholic. Inevitably with an abandoned place that's semi-derelict, it's inherently going to have some melancholia to it. But I think also given the fact of its location in that wilderness between Northumberland and Cumbria that only seems to be passed over by military aircraft and really disconnected from the rest of the world in a way that's rare to find in this country. ... The most overwhelming feeling I got from it was absence. There is this place [and] everything associated with it is no longer there.

I had wanted to avoid editing in too many shots of the magnificent, strange geometries of concrete structures, but to visualise the place 'inhabited'. As an outsider to the means and processes of archaeological surveying, it was becoming interesting to read what the archaeologists were doing as some strange form of performance or ritual. In order to take GPS measurements, they were physically traversing the Blue Streak sites – climbing over and around the disintegrating concrete. There was of course something very ironic about the use of sophisticated GPS kits to survey the test stand for a doomed satellite launcher.

I asked Cathy about the strategies they had adopted:

> Dave tends to do banks, dips and slopes. It looks as though he's pirouetting along in the grass when in fact he's doing exactly the same thing as me but he's actually doing it along the edge of an earthen bank or around a hollow or something like that.

Dave said,

> Being quite physically close to what we're surveying is important. ... Obviously not so much if you're surveying the edge of a piece of concrete but if we were surveying a medieval village for example the very little subtle lumps and bumps that are all that remains of a medieval village would be quite complex and it's only by standing on them, walking all over them, looking at them at different angles, in different light levels that you would get to understand ... what they are.

The notion of archaeologists surveying different time periods was also becoming interesting to me. According to Dave,

> Essentially we don't need to know anything about a place we're surveying. We apply the same techniques and the same skills to surveying a Neolithic bank barrow or a medieval village or a rocket test site. What we're doing is looking at the landscape, looking at the ground, assessing what's surviving and recording that in a way that communicates that in either plan form or written document – communicating what's surviving there.

Surveying something without being able to walk on it or touch it apparently feels quite strange, as the process demands a sensory engagement. Dave stressed that remote recording couldn't do the site any sort of justice at all. There has to be an intimacy between the physical act of surveying and the architecture to get the fullest story possible. All sorts of remote archaeology need this intuitive layer. Someone is needed on the ground if there is to be a real concern with accuracy.

This physical and intellectual engagement by the surveying archaeologists has yielded much material information. However, I believe it can also be interesting to superimpose fictions when considering a site such as Spadeadam and its histories.

Blue Streak has already been immortalised in a short story. *Prospero One* by Stephen Baxter and Simon Bradshaw, published in *Interzone* in 1996, is a speculative fiction which takes as its starting point the idea once mooted that Blue Streak rockets might be strapped together to create a bigger rocket for a manned space programme. Ultimately the story speaks of failure.

When I visited Spadeadam in late March to first document the archaeologists, I invited writer Duncan McLaren. He wrote,

> I am here to survey Louise, surveying English Heritage, surveying the surviving industrial archaeology associated with Blue Streak.

> And I, like Louise, am fascinated by the fact that we will all be doing our work side-by-side with, and no doubt under the watchful electronic eye of, the RAF.

His response, involving description and magical realism, says much about the ambiguities, complexities, and difficulties in coming to terms with the place both then and now.

I'm still grappling with notions of 'heritage' and am intrigued by the particular philosophical difficulties of preserving Cold War sites. I realise the question is in part one of what and whose stories/memories are being told. It is this that enables us to see beyond the concrete. As Cathy said,

> As far as I'm concerned archaeology … is all about people. If all you do is look at this very dramatic concrete structure, then you're kind of missing the point. It is very important to bring people into it and not only look at how they interacted with the place then [but] think it's quite relevant what people are doing now.

As an active military structure or as a Cold War ruin, Spadeadam still asserts itself. Whether resonating with the concrete strata of its physical landscape or with the more subjective layers of memory and expectation, it produces and engenders complexity. Given the apparent talent for this place to generate rumours, mythologies and narratives, I feel fortunate to have known it first-hand.

Figures 9.15–9.26. All photographs and stills from video used in filmmaking at Spadeadam, except top of p. 176 – watercolour of Spadeadam from a written description.

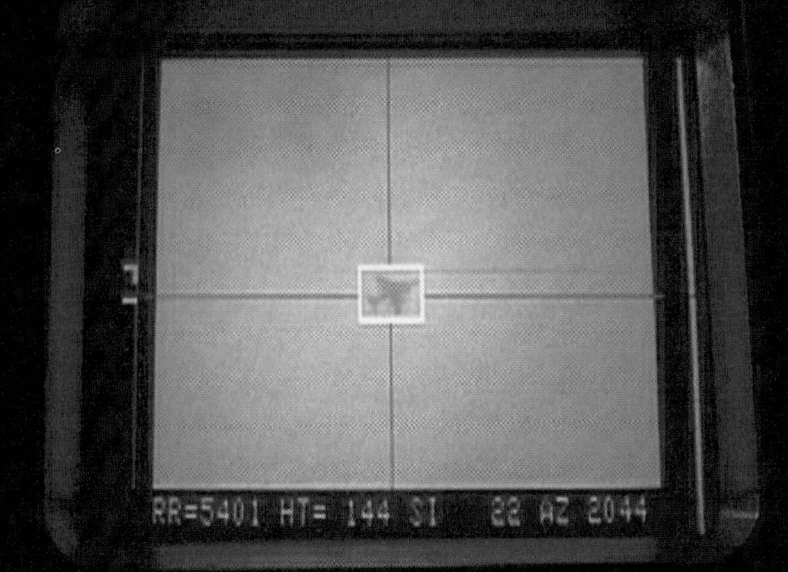

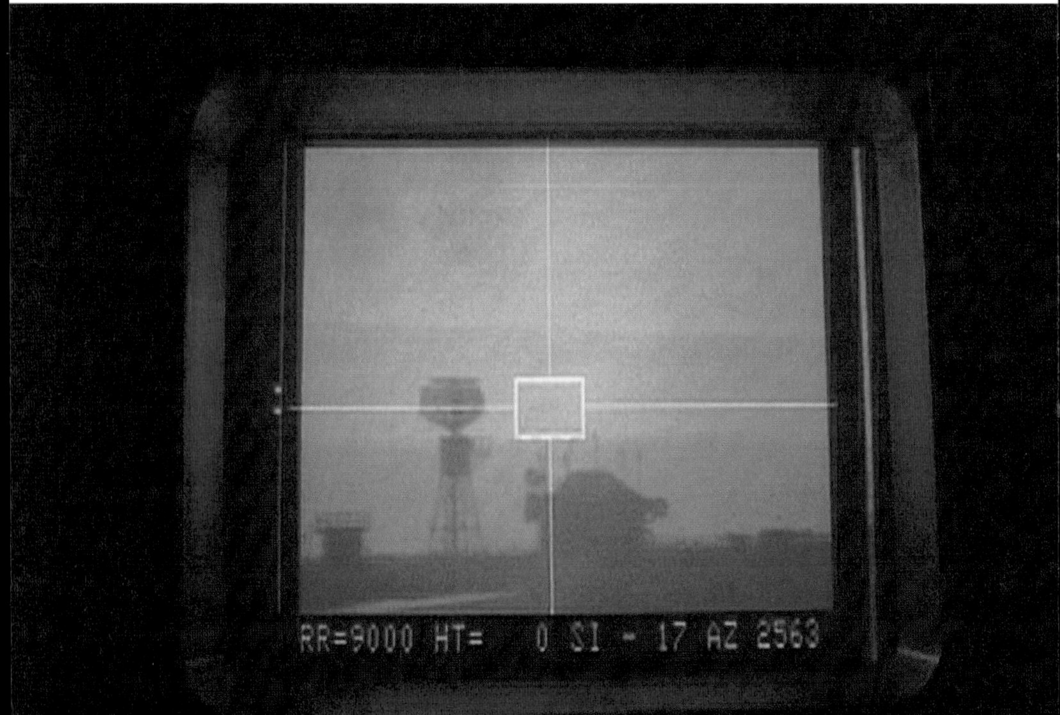

RR=9000 HT= 0 SI - 17 AZ 2563

Cood bay Forst Zinna

Angus Boulton

INTRODUCTION

Viewed from the window of a passing train, an installation momentarily becomes visible in a forest clearing. Approached on the ground, this large site, obscured by a grey concrete wall, appears abandoned, cut off from the outside world. Inside, one encounters a bewildering complex of accommodation blocks, exercise areas and assault courses. There is a neglected children's playground and forlorn fountain, a group of farm buildings and animal enclosures. Walking further, towards the perimeter wall, various sports and recreational facilities become recognisable. An empty, crumbling swimming pool with faded Olympic rings, a football pitch overgrown with silver birch saplings, assorted gymnasia with peeling murals, are all facilities that perhaps might indicate the site of a derelict sports academy. However, further exploration reveals a stranded armoured personnel carrier at the gates to a large garage and a workshop area, with curious teaching aids and murals in a Cyrillic script. Entering a vandalised room, bedecked with faded black-and-white photographs, our initial impression begins to appear misleading as the full nature and true purpose of Forst Zinna is revealed.

THE SOVIET WITHDRAWAL

On 12 October 1990 a treaty was signed between the German and Russian governments. The terms of this agreement set out a timetable for the complete withdrawal of troops from the Western Group of the Soviet Armed Forces then stationed within the former German Democratic Republic (GDR). This lengthy task was completed, relatively smoothly, with the final handover of Central Command at Wünsdorf in July 1994.

The Land of Brandenburg, which surrounds Berlin, covers approximately 250 by 150 km and contained more than half the total number of Soviet military bases inside the GDR, accommodating some 250,000 troops and additional personnel. While almost all these locations originally date from the Prussian or Nazi periods, many underwent further expansion once in Soviet hands. Indeed, over 200,000 hectares within Brandenburg were requisitioned for military use, so that by 1990 almost 9 percent of the region appeared on maps as 'restricted areas' (Brandenburgische Boden Gesellschaft mbH 1996).

Many bases, within or adjacent to towns, have undergone conversion into housing, offices or centres of light industry. Installations in more remote locations have simply been closed off and left to slowly decay. Initial development was further complicated by the absence of any form of occupation records for the barracks when finally handed over by the departing troops. The majority of sites had been in military hands for much of the last century and although the buildings are frequently of historical value, much of the outlying land remains dangerous and problematic. The vast training areas and firing ranges have been fenced off as prospective 'nature reserves', to which access may eventually be permitted along a few designated safe footpaths, once the lengthy and expensive task of munitions clearance has been thoroughly undertaken, frequently to a depth of four metres.

One such restricted area can be found south of Berlin, and formed the northern border to the complex of bases situated in and around the Prussian garrison town of Jüterbog. The main element stationed here was the 32nd 'Poltava' Armoured Division, part of the 20th Guards Army. The division, numbering around 11,600 personnel, included motor-rifle and armoured regiments along with the normal ancillary and support services, everything from missile, artillery, transport, and signals units to catering, schools, shops and a hospital. At Damm, west of Jüterbog, the 172nd and 439th Special Helicopter Regiments were situated, while a Flying Academy, a large adjoining airfield and the 833rd Fighter Regiment were located at Altes Lager in the north (Dimitriev et al 1995). At the eastern edge of this cluster of bases was the barracks at Forst Zinna, home of the 57th Construction Brigade and the 118th Armoured Training Regiment. Both units formed an integral part within the overall group, and although directly subordinate to the main headquarters in Wünsdorf, they were administered to some extent by the authorities in Jüterbog. The training regiment was responsible for instructing the new conscripts (six monthly intakes) and NCOs to operate tanks as drivers, commanders and gunners, utilising the large training area opposite the base. The construction brigade was responsible for major projects throughout the GDR, including accommodation blocks, training facilities and command bunkers, and was divided into 'project teams', which varied in size, depending on the tasks involved. All told, the combined force in this particular area was believed to be around 40,000 personnel.

Figures 10.1–10.13. Stills from the film *Cood bay Forst Zinna*.

ЖИЗНЬ
КОМАНДОВАНИЕ ШКОЛЫ ПРАПОРЩИКОВ ГСВГ
ОНИ

ФИЗИЧЕСКАЯ ПОДГОТОВКА ЯВЛЯЕТСЯ
НЕОТЪЕМЛЕМОЙ ЧАСТЬЮ ВОИНСКОГО
ВСЕГО ЛИЧНОГО СОСТАВА ВС СНГ

The tank driving school was to become infamous at 5.30 pm on Tuesday 19 January 1988. While undertaking his first night-driving exercise, a 19-year-old conscript made a tragic error en route to the training area north of the railway line. It was later reported that confusion may have arisen between the Kazakh driver and his Russian instructor, partly due to language differences, but certainly exacerbated by a broken radio communication system within the tank. In a state of panic the driver turned before the small access bridge to the training area and, attempting to cross the rails, caused the aerial to touch the overhead power cables, short-circuiting the electrics and cutting the engine. The crew exited the tank immediately, but unable to alert railway staff at the nearby signal box in time, watched in horror as the oncoming Leipzig to Stralsund express train, travelling at 120 kph, ploughed into the stranded T-72 tank. Six people were killed and over thirty injured.

GENESIS

As with many children growing up in the 1970s, the Cold War inevitably impinged on my formative years, both at school and especially at home where I found myself surrounded by an eclectic collection of military

books amassed by a father who had served in the Royal Navy. At the time, the threat of nuclear war seemed distant and difficult to comprehend. Even trips to air shows at nearby RAF Finningley, to watch the Vulcan nuclear bombers demonstrating their emergency response capabilities, were seen simply as awesome spectacles put on for the general public and impressionable children. Photographic trips to the Somme and the Ypres Salient at the beginning of the 1990s had a more profound effect on me, and led to a growing interest in these contested landscapes, and how to interpret them visually.

My own awareness of the Soviet military occupation of the Eastern Bloc countries developed gradually in the 1990s through reading newspaper articles, although I had never actually visited Germany or its neighbours. The possibility of pursuing the subject further arose in the summer of 1998 when I embarked on an art residency in Berlin. I proposed to spend the year working towards a photographic project that investigated the city ten years after the fall of the Wall, looking at how this scar had affected the urban landscape, both directly and indirectly (Boulton 1999). However, a chance reading of an article in a newspaper prior to my departure rekindled a desire to visit and photograph a Russian military base, perhaps including it within the Berlin project or undertaking a parallel body of work. The article uncovered a previously unreported story of a secret operation by Greenpeace to highlight the problem of nuclear proliferation back in 1991. Their intention was to purchase a nuclear bomb and unveil it to the world media, turning the spotlight on the dangerous situation perceived to be arising with the break-up of the Soviet Union. A Russian second lieutenant was to bring the device out of his base with two soldiers in return for $250,000 and safe passage to Sweden. Ultimately the plan failed as the officer, suspected to be under KGB surveillance, disappeared without trace. The place in question was Altengrabow (*The Independent* 1998).

Altengrabow was the first name I looked for a short while after arriving in Berlin. Once located on a map, and also noting the numerous areas shaded red and described as *Sperrgebiet* (restricted areas), I began to plan a series of trips to Potsdam to investigate an area north of the city. After days spent wandering back and forth along roads, circumnavigating perimeter fences and peering through locked gates, a chance phone call to a receptive press officer at an agency overseeing redevelopment eventually led to an appointment. Following lengthy negotiations and the signing of a contract permitting access, I found myself outside, key in hand, with a simple request to lock the gate behind me, and a Russian barrack complex all to myself. It seemed bizarre to have unhindered access to some place recently completely off limits to the public. Investigating the buildings became something of a game, a process of trying to deduce what went on within these rooms, meandering down corridors, unlocking doors unaware of what lay inside, searching for clues within the leftover detritus of army life. My intention was to undertake a photographic project that not only recorded these sites, raising awareness of the legacy and its implications, but also commented on a chapter in recent history hitherto unreported, except at a local level. I felt that the logistical nightmare of withdrawing such a large occupying army had been largely ignored, eclipsed to some extent by the unfolding situation in the Balkans.

COOD BAY FORST ZINNA

By the autumn of 2000, having visited and recorded over thirty bases in Brandenburg, a move into film appeared to be an ideal way to capture the strange atmosphere frequently encountered within these desolate places, augmenting a strictly formal photographic approach through the added dimension of sound. Forst Zinna exhibited all the major features to be found inside a medium-sized barracks, and remained surprisingly intact, probably due to its isolated setting. Following careful planning and utilising notes made during the detailed photographic survey undertaken the preceding October, filming took place during two days in March 2001. Working on a tight schedule and making use of the fortuitous contrast in weather conditions, I deliberately shot footage of the extensive sports and recreational facilities in the pleasant spring sunshine, saving the more overtly militaristic imagery for the rainy gloom of the following day. By adopting a quasi-forensic style, one that replicated my methodical process of investigation, I planned to mix carefully chosen restricted views, akin to still imagery, with short panning sequences. In this way, I could steer the viewer through a succession of particular scenes, letting each scene unfold slowly, primarily in an effort to trigger a more personal interpretation through memory and association. Although the film is initially misleading to those unfamiliar with the landscape of a Soviet military base, the final sequence and musical accompaniment reflect what actually came to my mind, while I stood alone in silence, contemplating the photos peeling from the walls of the unit's small museum.

Cood bay Forst Zinna is my impression of a particular place. The film could be seen as a comment on the death of a belief system. In many respects the Cold War can be viewed as a dangerous game played out with set rules, in secret, at certain times and specific locations. Moreover, in the light of global events today, and at a time when the rulebook appears all but torn up, witnessing such places allows us the opportunity to reflect on the recent past, perhaps with an ambiguous tinge of sadness. This feeling just might have been uppermost in the mind of the soldier who poignantly wrote 'good bye' in pencil on the bedroom wall, shortly before setting off for home and an uncertain future.

REFERENCES

Alimov, S & Atourov, T (1993) *Song of the civil war*, The Red Army Song and Dance Ensemble

Boulton, A. (1999) *Richtung Berlin*, Berlin: Vice Versa Verlag

Brandenburgische Boden Gesellschaft mbH (1996) *Geschäftsbericht 1995*

Dimitriev, S, Fadin, K, Fjodorov, V, Furs, A, Potapov, A and Timachkov, D (1994) *Sowjetische Truppen in Deutschland 1945–1994*, Moscow: Junge Garde Verlag

The Independent Newspaper (1998) London, 26 July 1998

Poggendorf, S. (2003) '*Der Panzer auf den Schienen*' – Mitteldeutscher Rundfunk

The Berlin Wall: Border, fragment, world heritage?

POLLY FEVERSHAM and LEO SCHMIDT

INTRODUCTION

Well over a decade after its fall in November 1989, the Berlin Wall hovers uneasily between memory and reality. Many celebrate the fact that it has virtually disappeared from view whilst others are critical that it was demolished too quickly and too thoroughly. But whatever their attitude, most people take it for granted that – apart from a very few well-trodden sites – the Wall no longer exists. A case in point is provided by the fact, circulated in the press during the last days of February 2003, that the Checkpoint Charlie Museum in Berlin has published an audio guide to accompany tourists to the places where the Wall once stood – not, as one might think, to explain any visible remains, but on the contrary, 'because the Wall has disappeared completely'.

By contrast, this chapter describes the unexpected wealth of extant remains and traces of the fortifications on the border between East and West Berlin, to present and discuss the manifold remains and their value as a material witness of the unique situation which existed in Berlin between 1961 and 1989, and, finally, to argue the case for adding the 155-km (96-mile) stretch of borderland around former West Berlin to the World Heritage List as the most representative and evocative monument of the Cold War era.

After more than a decade of, initially, deliberate destruction and then of general oblivion, the Berlin authorities became aware in 2001 that the remains and traces of the Wall are imbued with a significance which merits the preservation of the tangible traces that have survived. Accordingly, a semi-archaeological survey of the border area between East and West Berlin was commissioned by the Department of Urban Development of the Berlin Senate and has been carried out by the Department of Conservation at the Brandenburg University of Technology

Figure 11.1. A section of border Wall preserved in the Liesen Cemetery. Photo by L Schmidt

in Cottbus. The full documentation was handed over to the Senate in July 2003 and has since been made accessible to the public through publication as a compact guide book which appeared in both German and English editions in May 2004 (Klausmeier and Schmidt 2004). Its maps and images are also accessible over the Internet, allowing people from all over the world to browse along the border and get a visual impression of the extant remains and traces (www.tu-cottbus.de/berlinwall/).

The remnants of the border provide a highly detailed image of the complex structures known simply as 'The Wall'; they offer many fresh insights into their functions, into the intentions and motivations of their builders and into the historical background of the Wall (see also Feversham and Schmidt 1999; Harrison 2003).

EAST-WEST AMBIGUITY OF PERCEPTION

One of these insights concerns the process of destruction itself. There seems to have been a particular pattern of demolition: It was most efficient in removing those elements of the border fortifications that were

---

Figure 11.2. A section of hinterland Wall in the Nordbahnhof area. Photo by L Schmidt

easily and directly identifiable as parts of the Wall – essentially as seen from the West. Thus, not a single one of the nearly 300 standard watchtowers has survived, and very little indeed of the 'Border Wall 75', as the last version of the Wall was called by its builders.

But the Border Wall was only prominent, indeed dominant, from a Western perspective. Seen from the East, from the perspective of a potential fugitive who wanted to leave the German Democratic Republic (GDR), it was just the very last element in a long sequence of obstacles. It is part of the Orwellian character of the Wall that the 'Anti-Fascist Protection Rampart', as it was hailed in GDR propaganda, was of course only indirectly a protective barrier against the West. Its function was to keep people in, not out. Anyone trying to cross from East to West Berlin would have initially met a restricted area and various obstacles which served as a perimeter defence in front of the structure that defined the eastern face of the border area proper. This was the so-called hinterland security Wall behind which the death strip began.

The Western public has never been fully aware of the eastern-facing appearance of the Berlin border and of the hinterland Wall, indeed has never shown an interest in it even whilst the Wall was operative. And most people in the East, because of the restricted area which prevented any access to the border fortifications proper, never had a chance to become acquainted with it before most of the structures were swept

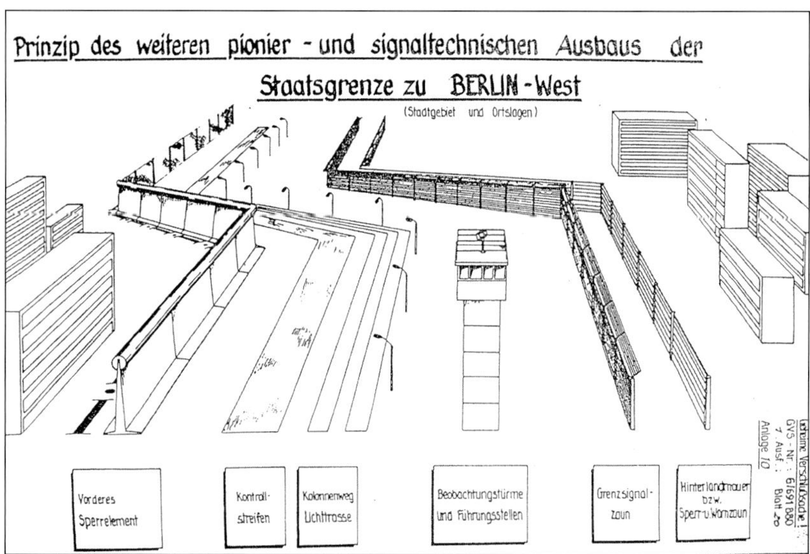

Figure 11.3. The standard layout of the border Wall in Berlin in the 1980s. Photo courtesy Berliner Mauer Archiv (Hagen Koch)

away very rapidly in 1990–1991. But in fact, if one knows where to look, significant portions of the hinterland Wall and of the eastern-facing structures of the border can still be retraced quite clearly, and they illustrate the variety of means by which GDR citizens were prevented from escaping from their country.

The standard layout of the Wall and the way it evolved in the 1960s, 1970s and 1980s have been well publicised, frequently illustrated by schematic drawings from Border Guard files. Seen from right (east) to left (west) in Figure 11.3, the 1970s standard layout of the border consisted first of the hinterland Wall; immediately behind it stood the electric signalling fence which, when touched, set off alarms in the nearest control posts. Antivehicle obstacles and 'area obstacles' came next: the latter were mats holding long, upright steel spikes which inflicted terrible injuries on people jumping down on them. The watchtowers ranging along the patrol road were placed so that their occupants could see both their neighbours. The lamps of the light strip illuminated not the patrol road but the 'control strip', an area of raked sand which would retain the footprints of any fugitive. This meant that in case of a successful flight the investigating officers were able to determine which guards had failed in vigilance and were able to discipline them. A last element, just before the border Wall proper, was the antivehicle ditch – incidentally built in such a way as to be virtually useless against any vehicles advancing from west to east and thus belying the propaganda name of 'Anti-Fascist Protection Rampart'.

Plans and written sources tend to evoke a clear and convincing image which is then taken as fact – but, as is often the case, a careful analysis of the situation produces a far more complex and sometimes an entirely different picture. It turns out that few sections of the wall actually conformed fully to the 'standard' layout. This layout may be said to have provided a kind of basic orientation, a toolbox of the main elements of the border. But the ordering and arrangement of the actual border was governed by only one consideration: to make any attempted crossing from east to west as difficult as humanly possible. To begin with, there is one significant and extensively employed category of the border fortification which has never been mentioned and which has only come to light through the semiarchaeological survey conducted in the last few years. It might be described as a cordon or glacis and consisted of various obstacles whose purpose was to impede any unauthorised approach to the border area from the East. These obstacles were many and varied. There were, for example, concrete walls, similar in shape and construction to the standard hinterland Wall, securing difficult areas where a would-be fugitive might hide before making a dash towards the border. These areas were also well lit by floodlights. In some particularly sensitive situations, such as Bernauer Strasse, there were two parallel perimeter walls. 'Flower bowl barricades' were deployed to prevent people from crashing through the border by means of heavy vehicles driven at high speed: filled with decorative plants to mask their real purpose, they were massive concrete elements, sometimes the prefabricated square elements from which watchtowers were assembled. The intercolumnia of the Brandenburg Gate were also secured in this way. In many cases, grilles were attached to windows overlooking the death strip as well as to other openings fugitives might use in their approach to the border. Spikes were added to fences as well as to gutters and other parts of buildings, forestalling any attempts at scaling them.

Unusual precautions were often necessary wherever the border followed one of the many waterways in Berlin. Where the water itself belonged to GDR territory, it was patrolled by Border Guard speedboats. But Berlin waterways were also – and still are – frequented by river freight ships. Border crossing points had to be provided for them. In some places, ingenious and complicated means had to be devised to make these water crossings secure against fugitives who might swim across them at night; there is still one extensive structure in the river Spree in the Osthafen area whose only purpose was to screen the opening into the Flutgraben canal belonging to West Berlin.

THE BORDER TROOPS

Whilst the study of the material remains provides a clearer insight than written sources of what the Berlin Wall meant when it was operational, there is a further category of information which should also be taken into account: the human sources, particularly the former border guards themselves. A fugitive saw the border as a confusing thicket of obstacles; the risks incurred in crossing it were incalculable. No statistics were available to East German citizens, but the fact that many people were killed whilst trying to cross the Wall was widely known (Hilton 2001). If anything, people overestimated the actual risks and imagined that the death strip was crowded with vigilant border guards. Former soldiers who describe the actual everyday situation at the border from their own experience tell a different story. They felt they were undermanned, harrassed and overworked: understandably so, when one analyzes the actual figures. A GDR Border Guard regiment (unlike its NATO counterpart) consisted of four companies, each of which was able to field 70 combat soldiers; one company was always off duty while the other three rotated in shifts to man the border. In the case of *Grenzregiment*-33, responsible for the stretch from the Reichstag to the northern city limit, a shift of 70 soldiers had to cover 23.4 km. As they invariably operated in pairs, this meant that the patrols were stationed on average nearly a kilometre apart. During the day some pairs were moving along the patrol road whilst others were busy testing electric fences; only at night were all the

Figure 11.4. Perimeter wall near Bernauer Strasse. Photo by L Schmidt

Figure 11.5. Flower bowl barricade made from a BT9 watchtower element. Photo by L Schmidt

Figure 11.6. Spikes on a courtyard gate next to the hinterland Wall. Photo by L Schmidt

Figure 11.7. Border Guard patrol boat in the river opposite the Reichstag building. Photo by Henryk Pastor

watchtowers manned. For the border guards themselves, it was quite clear that the Wall could be penetrated if one knew the layout. In their view, the effectiveness of the border was largely due to the secrecy surrounding it and to the constantly changing routines of the guards.

Needless to say, Border Guard commanders lived in fear that their own troops would desert to the West, or disobey the standing order to shoot any fugitive on sight. To prevent this, great care was taken in selecting soldiers for the border in Berlin, particularly those young conscripts who were doing their national service. Invariably they were from remote, often rural areas, never from Berlin itself. Many of them were either professional sailors – on the grounds that these were unlikely to escape across the Wall because they would have had better opportunities in foreign harbours if they had wanted to jump ship – or married men with children, or people who were obviously working towards a GDR career. Internally they were graded by reliability: Those who were deemed safest might even be allowed to guard a border crossing station where there was often nothing at all to prevent them from stepping into the West; less reliable ones were confined to the death strip and never let out of their patrol leader's sight. Receiving a letter from a West German relative or listening to a Western radio station would immediately result in being downgraded.

Various fairly simple psychological means were employed to ensure that the border guards would actually shoot people they detected in the death strip and who did not give themselves up immediately. The soldiers, who hardly ever left their barracks, were put into a state of artificially induced paranoia. They could all recite the names of Border Guard 'heroes' who had been killed at the Wall by the Class Enemy, and it was easy to make them believe it was a question of either shooting first or being shot by the – often only dimly seen – opponent. They were used to thinking of everything that moved in or around the border as 'provocations'; even a tourist peering into the East from one of the platforms erected on the western side was counted and registered as another case of 'conducting people to the border with provocative intent'; in 1979, no less than 845,000 such 'provocations' were recorded (Feversham and Schmidt 1999:108). With this background, anybody moving in the death strip was automatically classified as a provocateur, possibly armed and dangerous. Every former border guard tells stories of frequent alerts with soldiers about to go out on patrol being told that an armed criminal was on the loose – often adding he was a former border guard – who would no doubt try to get across the border at some unknown point. It is not difficult to imagine the effect of such information on a young man carrying an automatic rifle in a lonely place at night.

One particularly graphic example of the reality of this unique border and of the relevance of physical and human sources in connection

Figure 11.8. Colour markings on a lamppost. Photo by L Schmidt

with its history is provided by colour markings on the lampposts in the light strip. Horizontal colour bands (red-white-green-white) were painted on lampposts along the side of the patrol road that faced the 'enemy'. This colour code signalled the line separating the border guards' working area between hinterland Wall and light strip from the no-go area along the sector border. Innocuously called 'patrol limit', it was not to be crossed unannounced by a border guard. Infringement of this rule meant that the soldier would immediately be treated as a fugitive himself and consequently fired upon: a rule which contradicts the view still held publicly by former Border Guard chiefs and GDR politicians that this 'was a national border like any other'.

Figure 11.9. Turkish immigrant's building erected on no-man's land in Berlin. Photo by L Schmidt

FRAGMENTATION AND THE RUIN

There are of course many perceptions and memories of the Wall from both Easterners and Westerners – one side knew it as the Anti-Fascist Protection Rampart, the other as the Wall of Shame – but it is the physical remains of the Wall, the material witness itself, which proves the existence of the border which was carved through the heart of a populous city and which stood for 28 years. It was a structure so bizarre that unless the hard physical evidence is secured it may well be that future generations will find it hard to credit its existence. But quite apart from the physical remains, there are also secondary traces of the border whose significance should not be underrated.

Apart from memorials for people who died at the Wall, most secondary traces are buildings whose shape and position can only be explained because of the fact that the Wall existed, and because they reacted to its existence in some particular way. One example is the residential buildings in Zimmerstrasse not far from Checkpoint Charlie, part of the 1987 International Building Exhibition. Today it is hard to understand why they stand so far back from the street, unlike their prewar neighbours: The reason lies in the fact that the Wall stood right on the pavement as the line defined by the old facades was in fact the border. The new position with much more space in front of the buildings illustrates clearly that people in the West, in 1987, confidently expected the Wall to stand for at least another generation.

Another witness of the Wall is a building at the edge of the Kreuzberg district. One of the many Turkish immigrants who took over this part of West Berlin in the 1970s noticed an unused plot of land, a triangular segment legally belonging to East Berlin but abandoned to the West because of its awkward shape. He took possession of it in order to grow courgettes. Nobody from East Berlin interfered or claimed the land, so he built a garden shed on it. Beyond the reach of West Berlin planning authorities, the original hut gradually grew into a sizeable, albeit highly unusual, house without a single right angle or level floor in it. Eventually the Wall fell but the house still exists; having stood for so long, it is now legally safe from forced demolition.

There is also an emptiness created through the demolition of the fortifications, an emptiness which – in a densely built-up urban area – has its own kind of negative shape or body. This emptiness should also be seen as a constituent part of the unique memorial landscape which the Wall has left behind. A void, an absence, may constitute a place of cultural significance. On the largely empty site of an ancient ruined city one would certainly regard the shape and dimension of a place which once held a particular structure as significant, graphic information. Similarly, the border landscape holds information even in places where there are no longer material traces of the walls, towers and fences themselves.

Figure 11.10. Traces of the border Wall amongst the spontaneous vegetation in the Nordbahnhof area. Photo by L Schmidt

There are, for instance, foundations and basements of houses demolished to make room for the death strip, or windowless walls indicating where neighbouring houses were demolished and where there are impressive remains of escape tunnels deep underground. There are also places where spontaneous vegetation helps to visualise the course the Wall took, either in the shape of trees that grew on its western side and survived the demolition, such as in Bernauer Strasse, or the stunted growth of new plants over the rough concrete bed of the free-standing Wall elements, quite different from the vigorous new trees springing up on both sides of it in the largely deserted Nordbahnhof area.

All these places, whether strewn with physical remains or impressive by virtue of their emptiness, hold not only historical information but also emotional values. The experience and perception of the authentic place, the authentic fragment, can act as a reinforcement or corrective of views or imaginative projections acquired by other means. The human desire to visit significant historic places is daily illustrated by the tourists who come to Berlin from all over the world and who are keenly interested in even the most minute traces of the Wall. Memory is place-oriented; it clings to places and objects (Feversham and Schmidt 1999:134–142). Objects, buildings in particular, are identified with the memory of events and people. Many intact buildings have been destroyed because they were harbours of painful memory whilst many others, whose destruction has caused too many painful feelings, have either been recreated or have at least become the focus of highly emotional reconstruction debates (the Royal Palace in Berlin being the most obvious example in this context). Without the human factors of memory and emotion, any debate about monuments or cultural heritage is pointless; without them, no cultural significance can exist.

WORLD HERITAGE?

Indeed, significance and its relative degree can only be assessed by taking into account this human factor, by asking: to whom is a place significant, why and to what degree? The significance attached to the Berlin Wall, for instance, differs widely depending on who is asking the question. Arguably the Berlin Wall is known by more people around the world than any single site inscribed on the World Heritage List. Being universally known may not be the same as being of universal significance, but by looking at the World Heritage convention and at the criteria for selecting World Heritage sites, one can explore this question further (Operational Guidelines for the Implementation of the World Heritage Convention, § 77; http://whc.unesco.org/archive/opguide05-en.pdf).

Of the six criteria, the third, fourth and sixth might seem applicable to the Berlin Wall to some degree. The third criterion speaks of 'a unique or at least exceptional testimony to a cultural tradition or to a civilization which is living or which has disappeared': nothing could characterise state and society of the GDR, and to some extent the whole Eastern Bloc, better than the Berlin Wall. The fourth criterion fits even better, speaking of 'an outstanding example of a type of building or architectural or technological ensemble or landscape which illustrates a significant stage in human history' – the significant stage in question being the Cold War era of which no more compelling architectural symbol can be found than the Berlin Wall. The sixth criterion, referring to sites that are 'directly or tangibly associated with events ... of outstanding universal significance', can be quoted in reference both to the grief for the deaths caused by the Wall, which the world followed with great sympathy, but even more, much more, in reference to the *fall* of the Wall in 1989, that joyful and unexpected event which symbolised the end of the Cold War and heralded the liberation of the oppressed nations in Eastern Europe. According to the Operational Guidelines, § 77, 'the Committee considers that this criterion should preferably be used in conjunction with other criteria'.

The convention also lays great emphasis on the 'test of authenticity' each potential site has to meet, thus renouncing over-restored, manipulated and reconstructed sites.

Public discussion of the idea to inscribe the Wall on the World Heritage List has provoked both support and furious resistance. A frequent argument against World Heritage status of the Wall has been to point out its sheer ghastliness, stressing that it is not an example of high cultural achievement but entirely the reverse. There can indeed be little doubt, reading the convention and particularly the criteria, that the authors of this document did not have anything like the Berlin Wall in mind when they composed it in the years before its adoption in 1972. The first criterion of the convention, which refers to 'masterpieces of human creative genius', indicates the driving motivation and the predominant interest of the convention's authors in more conventional, positively charged sites.

However, times have changed and a new view of the values of historic buildings and monuments began in the 1970s – the extermination camp of Auschwitz-Birkenau being inscribed on the World Heritage List in 1979 (but not without some qualifying remarks making it clear that this was an exceptional case). Perhaps nothing illustrates this better than the Burra Charter, drawn up by ICOMOS Australia in 1979 and revised several times since, showing how developments in conservation philosophy have led to an ever-increasing awareness of values in historic places beyond any positive qualities such as beauty and architectural grandeur (www.icomos.org/australia/burra.html). Indeed, many historic places which have long been appreciated as great works of art may be shown to possess other features, other qualities on quite another level. The great palace of Versailles, for example, is obviously not just a work of art but also a monument to an absolutist and expansive, warmongering state. It may be taken, amongst other things, as a memorial to the thousands of French soldiers who died of fever during their labours in the swamps which were eventually turned into the baroque gardens admired by tourists today.

Just as some places are appreciated for their positive values and yet have a dark side to them, the Berlin Wall, which is rightly perceived as a horrible structure, has a luminous side to it: It fell, was overcome by a peaceful revolution of the people it oppressed, and the whole world took part in the joyful event.

Another argument against the World Heritage suggestion has been the fact and the extent of the Wall's fragmentation. In the words of Berlin's Advisory Council for Conservation, the Wall's 'remnants and traces are lacking in the necessary physical density and visual pithiness'. Whilst sounding reasonable enough, this argument happens not to conform to the World Heritage convention or to their Operational Guidelines. Indeed, plenty of sites on the list are ruinous and fragmentary, and the two-thousand-year-old border line of the Roman Limes on Germany's tentative list could be cited as an example of a border of enormous historic impact that is preserved today only in rather tenuous traces. What the Convention and the Guidelines demand is the 'test of authenticity' – something entirely different from a physical completeness often achieved by reconstruction of lost buildings and elements. The authenticity of the extant remnants and traces, including the urban scar showing the line of the Wall right through Berlin, can hardly be denied, and indeed the fact of fragmentation and ruination is a necessary part of the message of the Wall from the time when it was overcome and many large segments as well as millions of small fragments were sold all around the world like relics of the True Cross, tokens of 'our delivery from the Cold War' (Ladd 1997:8).

A recent report by ICOMOS on gaps in the World Heritage list clearly shows a change in perception and values and the role the Berlin Wall could play in a more systematic overview of places of universal significance (www.international.icomos.org/world_heritage/whlgaps.htm). One of its headings refers to places of the 'Post War era and Cold War' – which single site, one wonders, could fill this slot better than the Berlin Wall?

The system of compiling the list of World Heritage sites has one obvious Achilles heel: Inscription of a site can only be initiated by the state in which it is situated. In Germany's federal system, the initiative lies with the city-state of Berlin itself, and most Berliners and their politicians try not to think about the Wall if they can possibly avoid it. The memory of the incredible days of November 1989 is not lost, but buried beneath are memories both of the long separation and of the widespread disillusionment following reunification. Therefore, Berliners invariably react with incredulity to any suggestion that, to the rest of the world, the Wall today holds positive rather than negative connotations – that it is the joyful, unexpected fall of the Wall which is mainly remembered, and that it is seen as an inspiring event which heralded the collapse of the oppressive regimes in central and eastern Europe.

This attitude has produced a curious situation in which the Berlin Wall may be a monument of outstanding universal value, yet is of very little local significance. Perhaps this situation might change, particularly if an awareness of the outside view could filter through to the people and politicians of the city – but for many of the remnants of the Berlin Wall which still exist today and are gradually being destroyed in the development of the city, this will come too late.

REFERENCES

Feversham, P and Schmidt, L (1999) *The Berlin Wall Today: Cultural Significance and Conservation Issues*, Berlin: Verlag Bauwesen

Harrison, H (2003) *Driving the Soviets up the Wall*, Princeton: Princeton University Press

Hilton, C (2001) *The Wall: The People's Story*, Stroud: Sutton Publishing

Klausmeier, A and Schmidt, L (2004) *Wall Remnants, Wall Traces: The Comprehensive Guide to the Berlin Wall*, Bad Münstereifel: Westkreuz-Verlag

Ladd, B (1997) *The Ghosts of Berlin: Confronting German History in the Urban Landscape*, Chicago: University of Chicago Press

Cold War on the domestic front

VICTOR BUCHLI

This chapter examines the role of consumption and domestic space during the Cold War between the United States and the Soviet Union. Usually the Cold War is understood in terms of the military industrial complex, but the period was also one of intense and 'war-like' competition in the sphere of consumption and the pursuit of the industrialised good life: a material and ideological continuum extended from refrigerators to nuclear warheads as part of the terms of Cold War competition. Starting with the famous kitchen debate between Nixon and Khrushchev, the domestic sphere and domestic consumption will be examined as an alternate Cold War site focusing on the material culture of the home. Here the USA and USSR competed for supremacy and the material and social terms whereby the fruits of postwar modernity could be enjoyed.

+++

In Moscow on 24 July 1959, the *New York Times* reported from the opening of the American National Exhibition:

> Vice-President Richard M. Nixon and Premier Nikita S. Khrushchev debated in public today the merits of washing machines, capitalism, free exchange of ideas, summit meetings, rockets and ultimatums.

This seemingly peculiar jumble of 'washing machines' and 'rockets and ultimatums' will be considered in an attempt to understand their apparent relevance in this encounter between Nixon and Khrushchev and the impact of the Cold War on its domestic front: the home. This concatenation will be analysed with reference to two brands of Soviet appliances, namely the 'Raketa' and 'Chaika' vacuum cleaners of ca 1958 (Figure 12.1) (see Kratkaia Entsiklopedia Domashnego Khoziaistva 1959:507–508). The names of these vacuum cleaners might recall the

Soviet space programme, but more significantly they also anticipate the mission of Velentina Tereshkova who in 1963 became the first female cosmonaut and whose radio name was 'Chaika' commanding a Soyuz 6 ('raketa') rocket ship.

The improbable associations strung together by this image, of a Soviet-era housewife engaged in the undervalued and mundane activity of vacuuming, how this image is imaginatively linked through her 'raketa' vacuum cleaner with the most heroic technical feats of the twentieth century, the first man in space in 1961 and the first woman in 1963, and with this the 'rockets and ultimatums' anticipating the 1962 Cuban Missile Crisis in the intervening year, will be considered in order to gain some insight into the material culture of the Cold War.

These seemingly unrelated incidents can be best understood in terms of two competing forms of materiality embodied in the two political ideologies of these industrial societies and their competing forms of modernity (Marcuse 1958). Soviet-era materiality strove to overcome the effects of capitalist production whereby physical distinctions of gender, the segregations and geographies of capitalism, and the boundaries of time and space could all be overcome through the socialist organization of society, production and science and ultimately space with the Soviet launch of the first man and woman into space (see Emma Widdis' discussion of these themes: Widdis 2003).

The American National Exhibition in Moscow was a response to an earlier one presented by the Soviet Union in the United States (see also Colomina 1999:351–353). This was a time when the United States and the Soviet Union were engaged in the Cold War competitions of the arms and space race, which the United States was about to lose in the wake of *Sputnik* and the imminent launch of the first man in space by the Soviet Union. And as the kitchen debate was to demonstrate, it was not entirely a foregone conclusion that the United States would prevail to produce the best household appliances for the greatest numbers. This was what Herbert Marcuse called the competition for the most equitable terms for the realization of the common goods of industrialized modernity. In the pre-civil rights and pre-feminist era of 1959, it was not at all entirely certain which system could provide these goods with the greatest degree of social justice, as the Soviet observers often noted that the so-called universal prosperity of postwar American consumerism hid the realities of racial and sexual oppression, unemployment and homelessness.

At this time in the wake of Khrushchev's famous secret speech to the Twentieth Party Congress in 1956, the excesses of Stalinist totalitarianism

---

Figure 12.1. Woman vacuuming, TsGAKFFD (Tsentral'nyi Gosudarstvennyi Arkhiv Kino-Foto-Dokumentov) g. Moskvy, no. 0202719

were denounced and the Soviet Union was put again on the path of socialist construction begun by the early Soviet Leninist State of the 1920s before the rise of Stalinist totalitarianism. This meant that many of the social goals, in housing, industrial production and socialist organization of daily life and women's labour, previously derailed by Stalinism, could finally begin to be realised within a fully industrialised infrastructure and predominantly urban postwar society (Buchli 1999; Reid and Crowley 2000, 2002).

One of the cornerstones of this social programme in the 1920s was the so-called battle for socialism on the domestic front at home, where the vestiges of capitalist daily life, domestic production and gender inequality were to be fought and overcome and a new socialist basis for daily life and gender would emerge (Buchli 1999; Bliznakova 1993; Cooke 1974). The crucial element in this endeavour was the kitchen, which figured so prominently in Khrushchev and Nixon's encounter in 1959. However, at the time of the 1920s this was to be realised through the complete obliteration of the kitchen in the capitalist and patriarchal sense of the word. The capitalist kitchen enslaved women in the domestic sphere, inhibiting their consciousness though a morbid preoccupation and identification with domesticity at the expense of participating in the public realm of socialist construction alongside men. The solution was to destroy it, or rather eliminate it as much as possible. Thus it was socialised, made communal and subject to industrialised principles of production and staffed not with individual wives and mothers separated from each other and the rest of the world in individual kitchens, but by salaried workers working in an industrial enterprise like any other, be it coal mining, medical care or steel production.

The 1929 Narkomfin Communal House of the Ministry of Finance in Moscow was an early example of how this war was to be waged on the domestic front to eliminate the kitchen and the hearth of the nuclear family and free women from the traditional weight of gender and its responsibilities (Figure 12.2) (see Buchli 1999). This was a transitional structure which was designed to admit nuclear families organised according to pre-revolutionary and capitalist understandings of domestic life, production and gender and transform them into outwardly focused, sexually egalitarian communards freed from the gravitational pull of the domestic sphere and the nuclear family and engaged in the public and outwardly expanding realm of socialist construction. Here the home would not exist as such and people would live in units designed for a heterosexual egalitarian couple with children raised in communal crèches by professional staff nearby and meals taken in an industrialised communal dining room, with cleaning performed in a mechanised laundry facility.

Soon this facility suffered the same fate as the other social programmes of the Bolshevik state as they were swept away with the

Figure 12.2. Narkomfin Communal House, Moscow.

rise of Stalinism (Buchli 1999). The complex was broken up: the crèche never realised, the mechanised laundry handed over to another agency and the famous communal dining room given over to another ministry.

However, at the same time as the kitchen debate between Nixon and Khrushchev, this old social programme was revisited. In 1960 the principle of the Communal House was revived in Leningrad. In 1964, the architect Osterman built a modern version of the Narkomfin in Moscow – the Lebed Complex (Gradov), while a little earlier in 1961 the old dismembered Narkomfin was transferred from the Ministry of Soviets to the Moscow City Council and a grassroots programme for the reconsolidation of the building and social programme of the original Narkomfin complex received the blessing of the Communist Party when the Party's 22nd Congress in that year confidently announced that, 'communal dining in the course of 10–15 years [between 1971–76] will become the dominant form of eating in comparison to dining at home' (Communist Party of the Soviet Union 1961:393).

Thus the Narkomfin Complex, which had been dismantled during the Stalinist era, was being reassembled to facilitate those expansive spaces of its 1920s programme that were to break down the contradictions of capitalist life and create a unified socialist space, where nature and culture merged, and the inequalities between men and women were overcome along with the contradictions of capitalism and commodity fetishism within the uniform, free and frictionless spaces of socialism. This was particularly the case in the frictionless realm of socialist outer-space where Tereshkova proved that women were no different than men, responding similarly to weightlessness and other effects of space once free from the gravitational pull of the earth in the *Vostok-6* rocket she commanded, thus resolutely erasing capitalist patriarchal distinctions between the genders.

Back on earth the expansion of socialist space meant that the traditional distinctions between public and private, male and female, urban and rural, nature and culture would be erased and, as it was imagined later in 1968, the soviet city would result in a 'higher socialized organization of labour, daily life and recreation, a synthesis of Nature and technology, life in a natural setting – such are the main characteristics of the collectivized city' (Gradov 1968:184). This new city was illustrated by an idyllic picture of forest and lakes – perfectly integrated with nature. In the late 1970s this meant that in the home this would result in, to quote, '[the removal of] the borders between the artefactual sphere of the household from the true sphere of nature, [which] will become one of the key factors in the conception of the household in the future' (Travin 1979:112).

Theoreticians in the 1970s were predicting the advent of the post-artefactual world – when the commodity as fetish would exist no longer and artefacts would exist as need be without any concept of ownership and the enthralling fetishism of the commodity. At this time so-called 'artefactualist' orientations in the design profession were derided (Travin 1979:107). This period revealed an emphasis on process rather than the fetishistic physicality of the artefact, which is at the heart of Soviet conceptions of materiality which were radically different from established notions and – one might say – the prevalent 'artefactualist' orientation of most material culture studies today (Buchli 2002; Miller 2005).

This brave new world where the divisions of capitalist life, male and female, nature and culture/material culture would be overcome, reiterated earlier attempts in the 1920s when a new socialist geography was imagined. The boundaries of space and time that were developed within capitalist societies would be obviated by disurbanist settlements – neither urban nor rural, composed of linear cities across the soviet landscape linked by electric grids that facilitated the speedy movement of peoples – overcoming the friction of geography and time zones – where people could move as they pleased, pick-up and leave, divorce and settle down as needs demanded (see Cooke 1974; Miliutin 1930; Widdis 2003). In this geography, time and space were overcome through the communist organization of labour, industry and technology.

With this in mind, one needs to reconsider the apparent similarities between Soviet and American material culture of the postwar period at the time of Nixon and Khrushchev's encounter on 24 July 1959. The imagery of *Sputnik* and the streamlined look of household objects unified the pursuit of the domestic with the space race as part of the Cold War effort to realise the terms of the industrial good life and technological progress as all part of a unified socialist realist aesthetic project of the 1920s. This was very much in keeping with Boris Groys' analysis of the Soviet Union as a *gesamtkunstwerk*: as a modernist total art project (Groys 1992). Thus the conquest of domestic space and outer space were part of the same unified political and aesthetic project brought into focus by the Cold War. The realms of industrial production were increasingly unified through the notion of a socialist design industry and community which would coordinate, and streamline, these various industrial interests from the space and defence industry to light industry – or otherwise held separate for reasons of strategic security rather than the fragmented vicissitudes of capitalist production and industry, which in the US could only be coordinated by centralised military industry and *ad hoc* relations with private industry motivated by a common ideology of communist resistance and vested economic interests.

Thus we might consider the significance of the *New York Times* when it reported in 1959 that Nixon noted that Americans were keen to make life easier for women. 'Mr. Khrushchev rejoined that in the Soviet Union they did not have what he called "the capitalist attitude towards women"'.

Nixon took issue with this point and claimed a universal understanding of women's roles different from communist beliefs: 'I think that this attitude toward women is universal', Mr. Nixon said. 'What we want to do is to make more easy the life of our housewives'.

Khrushchev, like many Soviet theoreticians before him, understood of course that such labour-saving household appliances were mere palliatives in light of the structural inequalities between men and women enshrined within capitalism. Communist industrial production and social policy was organised specifically to overcome these inequalities between genders. The domestic sphere and all its artefacts were in fact streamlined and rationalised to become increasingly unnecessary and superfluous as the terms of a communalised and industrial daily life were realised that would gradually do away with such labour-saving devices – which feminists both Western and Soviet have always noted only further tied women down to the home.

In many respects the material culture of the two kitchens both Khrushchev and Nixon were speaking about were very similar in appearance, but radically different in terms of the social organisation of their industrial production. Here one must consider these technological achievements in light of subsequent interest in the de-artefactualization of the domestic sphere, the obliteration of the artefactual realm which later Soviet theoreticians imagined to be facilitated by the development of high technology and cybernetics (Travin 1979).

The streamlining of Soviet artefacts within the domestic sphere was unlike the streamlining of capitalist aesthetics which emphasised the aesthetics of waste, planned obsolescence and consumerism – an aesthetic antithetical to the supremely modernist endeavour of socialism as can be gleaned from the confrontation between Nixon and Khrushchev in Moscow in 1959. However, the continued rejection of the material world that planned obsolescence and consumerism required – which Ellen Lupton so eloquently discerns in the postwar aesthetics of American Cold War design (Lupton and Miller 1992) is evident to a certain but significantly different degree by the wholesale rejection of the materiality of the material world as the penultimate phase of full-blown communism and the realisation of the post-artefactual world, where the city of the future would merge through the use of high technology with nature as we saw earlier. This was a theme developed by other foreign Marxist thinkers such as the Superstudio Group in Italy alongside Soviet artists such as Bulatov.

Returning to the kitchen debate of July 1959, the *New York Times* paraphrased Richard Nixon as saying:

> American houses were built to last only twenty years, so that builders could sell new houses at the end of that time.
>
> We build firmly, Mr Khrushchev said. We build for our children and grandchildren.
>
> Mr Nixon said he thought American houses would last more than twenty years, but even so, after twenty years many Americans want a new house or a new kitchen. Their kitchen is obsolete by that time, he said. The American system is designed to take advantage of new inventions and new techniques, he explained.
>
> This theory does not hold water, Mr. Khrushchev rejoined. He said some things never get out of date—houses, for instance, furniture and furnishings, perhaps, but not houses, contradicting the logic of capitalist planned obsolescence Nixon was praising.

The seemingly indistinguishable Soviet minimalism of the period signified just the opposite of its capitalist counterpart. The materiality of the artefacts in the domestic realm were subject to the rules of modernist asceticism, where the slogan 'nichego lishnego'/ 'nothing superfluous' prevailed (Buchli 1999). The aesthetic was underpinned by a socialist ethic of resistance to the fetish of the commodity – functioning in direct opposition to its capitalist counterparts. For Soviet citizens, rather than to be increasingly implicated and subjectified according to the logic of consumerist commodity fetishism, the spirit of the slogan 'nothing superfluous' facilitated just the opposite. It released people from the fetishistic pull of objects as desirable commodities so as to move them out of the realm of the domestic and its cult of domesticity and into the realm of socialist construction where private and public would merge into a seamless whole from the inner recesses of domestic space to the outer recesses of outer space. Socialism could triumph over apparent nature and capitalism, just as it did with the magical accounting and physics of the early Bolshevik period where even the laws of nature could be overcome: the sun could be conquered by bolshevism and under the five-year plan, five-year goals could be realised in four, hence the new and miraculous arithmetic of Soviet socialism where it was proclaimed in propaganda images that 2+2=5 (Dickerman 1996:117, Figure 60).

The expanding realm of Soviet domestic space and outer space, unified within the socialist imaginary, unbounded by the capitalist divisions of public and domestic spheres and their patriarchal divisions of gender, become ever more expansive and unified. This realm was freed from these boundaries through the socialist organisation of science and industry. The world of domestic artifacts, just as the rockets and missiles of the space programme, were designed to escape the gravitational and hypnotic pull of the commodity fetish of capitalist materialism, overcoming its capitalist physicality, even the seemingly unassailable physicality of gender formed by patriarchy in the form of cosmonaut Tereshkova's own body. As Marx noted in the *Fetishism of Commodities and the Secret Thereof*, this was an attempt to reinstate a new materiality different from the traditional capitalist, one which

> forcibly asserts itself like an over-riding law of Nature that … one ton of iron and two ounces of gold appear as naturally to be of equal value as a pound of gold and a pound of iron in spite of their different physical and chemical qualities. (Marx 1983)

Such seemingly overriding rules of nature such as the earth's gravitational pull could be overcome to create this unified and ever-expanding socialist space that could reach from one's kitchen to Mars, surpassing the USSR's Cold War competitor, the United States, in its wake.

To conclude, something like the space programme, the home and the Cold War in Anglo-American scholarship tends to overemphasise these discrete realms keeping them separate conceptually, partially motivated by the ideologies of American postwar capitalism which sought to keep these realms underpinning the terms of Anglo-American social life separate. The similar physical attributes and even technical goals of the Cold War between the US and the USSR belie the fundamentally distinct terms of social life that these two profoundly divergent social programmes were intending to facilitate. These two competing regimes of materiality with apparently similar bodies of material culture – industrial, modern, and nearly identical in design – were radically different in terms of the social organisation of their production and the material worlds, the spaces and materialities they created, and their social effects. The Soviet housewife vacuuming her flat with her 'raketa' vacuum cleaner discussed at the beginning might be indistinguishable from her American counterpart, but in terms of the Cold War she could not have been doing anything more different.

REFERENCES

Bliznakova, M (1993) 'Soviet housing during the experimental years, 1918 to 1933', in Brumfield, WC and Ruble, BA (eds), *Russian Housing in the Modern Age*, Cambridge: Cambridge University Press and Woodrow Wilson Center Press

Buchli, V (1999) *An Archaeology of Socialism*, Oxford: Berg Publishers

Buchli, V (2002) 'Introduction', in Buchli, V (ed), *The Material Culture Reader*, Oxford: Berg Publishers

Colomina, B. (1999) 'The Private Site of Public Memory', *The Journal of Architecture*, vol. 4, pp. 337–360

Communist Party of the Soviet Union (1961) *Materiali XXII S"ezda KPSS*, Moscow: Gospolitizdat

Cooke, C (1974) The town of socialism, PhD Thesis, Cambridge University

Dickerman, L, ed. (1996) *Building the Collective,* Princeton: Princeton Architectural Press

Gradov, GA (1968) *Gorod i Byt,* Moscow: Literatury po Stroitel'stvu

Groys, B (1992) *The Total Art of Stalinism,* Princeton: Princeton University Press

Kratkaia Entsiklopedia Domashnego Khoziaistva (1959), vols. 1–2, First Edition, Moscow: Bol'shaia Sovetskaia Entsiklopedia

Lupton, E and Miller, JA (1992) *The Bathroom and the Kitchen and the Aesthetics of Waste*, Cambridge, Mass.: MIT Visual Arts Center

Marcuse, H (1958) *Soviet Marxism*, New York: Columbia University Press

Marx, K (1983) *Capital,* Vol. 1, London: Lawrence and Wishart

Miller, D, ed. (2005) *Materiality*, Durham: Duke University Press

Miliutin, N (1930) *Problemy Stroitel'stva Sotsialisticheskikh Gorodov*, Moscow: Gosudarstvennoe Izdatel'stvo

New York Times, 24 July 1959, p. 1

Reid, S and Crowley, D (2000) *Style and Socialism: Modernity and Material Culture in Postwar Eastern Europe*, Oxford: Berg

Reid, S and Crowley, D (2002) *Socialist Spaces: Sites of Everyday Life in the Eastern Block,* Oxford: Berg

Travin, II (1979) *Material'no-veshchnaia Sreda I Sotsialisticheskii Obraz Zhizni*, Leningrad: Nauka

Widdis, E (2003) *Visions of a New Land: Soviet Cinema from the Revolution to the Second World War,* New Haven: Yale University Press

Voices in limbo: *a conSPIracy cantata* and *The Buffer Zone*

YANNIS KYRIAKIDES

Each of the two musical works presented here deal in their own ways with the legacy of the Cold War. The material of both *a conSPIracy cantata* and *The Buffer Zone* find their resonances in current political debates around Cyprus, the former concerning the building of what are widely thought to be echelon transmitters in British military bases, and the latter the function and future of the UN in policing the divisions that exist there.

Cyprus has both the fortune and misfortune of being at the gateway to the Middle East, of being at a crossroads between three continents.

It was inevitable that at the height of the Cold War Cyprus would be involved in struggles for power in the area. What is less common knowledge is the full extent of the involvement of the superpowers in its coup and subsequent partition, and the fact that then as now Cyprus remains one of the hottest spy areas in the world.

Cyprus is one of the countries where the legacy of the Cold War has taken its toll, and the problems arising from those conflicts have yet to be resolved.

A CONSPIRACY CANTATA

a conSPIracy cantata is a 45-minute musical work for two singers (mezzo sopranos), piano, soundtrack and live electronics. It is based on recordings of number stations, transmissions by government agencies on the shortwave radio. In the summer of 2002 it was performed in the abandoned military airbase of USAF Bentwaters, in Suffolk, England, as part of the Aldeburgh Festival. Performing were Ayelet Harpaz (voice), Stephie Buttrich (voice) and Marion von Tilzer (piano).

The work, which had been previously performed in Holland and around Europe, was taken up by Jonathan Reekie, director of the festival, who had the idea to put it on at this bizarre location. The military base was renowned in the area and has a mysterious history; it was even once known as 'the British Roswell'.

Bentwaters was built during the Second World War and by the end of the decade was put in the hands of the American Air Force. It was used for Cold War defence exercises and as a base for bombers carrying nuclear weapons. These weapons were deposited in an underground bunker within the base and accounted for the fact that some of the buildings had vast concrete walls as protection.

The reason it has gained a reputation as a British 'Roswell' was because of an incident in December 1980, which occurred in the woods at the runway's western end.

> Early one morning, according to documents released by the Ministry of Defense 20 years later, 'unusual lights' were seen in the sky by American guards at Bentwaters. 'A strange glowing object ... metallic in appearance and triangular in shape' was then spotted above the trees. When it disappeared from view, the guards searched the woods and found – depending on which of their accounts you believe – either odd indentations in the ground and traces of radiation, or a landed spacecraft complete with 'life forms about four feet tall ... with big humanoid heads and dark, catlike eyes'.
>
> Five of the MOD documents about all this remain confidential on the official grounds that they contain secret briefings to ministers, relate to national security, might alter Britain's relations with America, or all three. (Andy Beckett, The Spying Game, *The Guardian* 31 May 2004)

The performance of *a conSPIracy cantata* took place at The Debrief Centre, known by the locals as 'the Star Wars building'.

Andy Beckett:

> The Debrief Centre is low and grey and windowless. A thick pebbledash wall, entirely separate from the building itself, wraps the whole block, screening it from scrutiny or attack. A pair of baffling cone-shaped towers flank the entrance. Inside, it is clammy and cold, even on a mild afternoon, the claustrophobic low ceilings and crude breezeblock walls are left as they are. The building was completely stripped when the Americans moved out in the early 1990s; your imagination is free to roam the corridors, with their silvery metal doors straight out of Dr Strangelove.

I first came across number stations by accident, as people tend to do, while scanning the nether regions of the shortwave radio late one night.

'Yankee Hotel Foxtrot - 2' a voice repeated incessantly. I imagined a salon band from the 1930s about to launch into a jazz number, or perhaps it was some variant of a ballroom dance sequence popular in New York. A few nudges on the dial was another station that seemed to be advertising an entirely different product: 'Mike India Whiskey'.

The transmissions occurred regularly just as I was going to bed every night; they found their way into my dreams.

As it turned out, this was a typical number station secret code being sent out by MOSSAD in the Middle East. The three letters probably refer to a specific agent in the field, and the number two which followed most of the three-letter phonetic alphabet call signs, meant that there was no message to be relayed.

I was fascinated by the idea that these messages could be picked up by anyone but only one listener could ever decipher the codes being sent.

Furthermore this was probably no ordinary message. There was a chance that the consequences of the message being relayed over the shortwave radio would affect what I would hear on the news broadcasts the next day, a few flicks on the tuning dial. This gave the transmissions some kind of prophetic quality.

If one could decipher these messages, it would be like tapping into the flow of cause-and-effect of global events, to have an ear on the directives being given in the dark corridors of power, overhearing the sounds of aether.

So-called 'number stations' sprang up on the short-wave radio in the early sixties at the height of the Cold War. They are used to transmit coded text messages in numbers, phonetic letters, Morse or noise. They are operated by the world's intelligence agencies (such as CIA, MI6, BND, Mossad, UDBA, and KGB) to anonymously relay messages to their agents in the field.

The messages, which are transmitted at regular times on certain short-wave radio frequencies, are encrypted with the 'one-time pad' system, making them almost impossible to decipher for anyone except the agent in the field who has the particular random set of numbers used to decipher that particular message. Although anyone in the world can receive these messages, it is impossible to deduce the destination of the messages nor anything about the content. Many different languages and forms are used depending on the agency that has sent them.

They vary from simply Morse to synthesized voices reading phonetic alphabet strings. These transmissions usually begin with an introduction such as a single letter of the alphabet in Morse or a fragment of music played for several minutes (the identity of the sender). The first numbers called are usually a three-digit number (the recipient's identity), then there is a call to attention (bells, gongs, tones or spoken 'attention', 'ready'). A 'group count' giving the number of message elements that are to be sent is then transmitted, followed by the 'groups' which are sets of numbers or phonetically spoken letters. At the end of the groups, there is sometimes a repeat; if not, there is an ending indicator, by either a spoken 'end' or a repeat of the introduction music. Though number stations continue to proliferate (despite the end of the Cold War), no government agency officially admits their existence.

What appealed to me about this phenomenon of number stations, the more I delved into them, was how they embodied basic forms of communication, in a hierarchical language which has parallels in how music functions. The bizarre variety of voices that intone the messages that are carried by the complex textures of radio waves that also interfere and modulate them, create in themselves an autonomous musical world.

In *a conSPiracy cantata*, this bizarre sound material is set against the idea of ethereal voices or communiqués from a higher power that existed in ancient Delphi. Aside from being a religious sanctuary and official divination institution, Delphi was the centre of intelligence and espionage in the ancient Greek world. For centuries the Delphic oracle was influential in many political decisions; it was even obligatory for leaders to consult the oracles before embarking on any enterprises.

The consultation itself took place in the temple of Apollo, underground. The space consisted of a room for the petitioners, an enclosed sanctuary (*adyton*) where the *Pythia* (the priestess with whom Apollo had contact) received the oracle, an *omphalos* (a stone representative of the navel of the earth) and a tripod positioned over a crack in the ground where the vapors (*pneuma*) from the centre of the earth seeped out.

Each city-state was represented by an emissary or embassy at Delphi where the important oracle pronouncements were scrutinized and their ambiguous language was deciphered and interpreted. Disinformation was rife. The unintelligible babble of the pythia, uttered in a state of ecstasy, was translated into hexameters by the prophet of Delphi. This position was often susceptible to corruption and manipulation.

The verses which are used in the cantata were given to Peisistratos by the oracle, encouraging him in his successful attempt to seize Athens and establish his third tyranny:

> The cast is made, the net is spread,
> and the tuna will leap on a moonlit night.

Figure 13.1. Exterior views of the Debrief Centre, Bentwaters. Photos by Michael Baldock

This implied that the people of Athens were ready to be caught like fish in Peisistratos's net.

The electronic sounds in *a conSPIracy cantata* are made up of layers of radio transmissions, noise textures, prerecorded voices and sampled piano sounds. The piece mixes together an archaic modal sound world with a retro radiophonic electronic atmosphere. On other levels the piece deals with ideas of reception and transmission on a human level; the images of waiting, listening, coding and decoding are prevalent in both the music and the presence of the performers in the space. The musicians are motionless and inactive until awakened by relevant signals. The two singers, at either side of the stage, have an ambiguous relation with each other; it is never clear whether they are communicating to each other or to the outside. The pianist is always facing away from us, and one never sees her face; she acts alternatively as an encoder/decoder; the sonic image of the piano, which she plays inside and out, is that of a transmitter or receiver. At the end of the piece, there is an unexpected outpouring of violence, surprising as it shatters the restrained character of the music until that point. The pianist repeatedly and rhythmically strikes the lower strings of the piano, an image of violence that is always under the surface of the act of espionage and political intrigue alluded to in the piece.

The structure of the work is in six parts which highlight different aspects of number station transmissions:

1 *Ready Ready*

The slowly changing static electronic texture acts as an introduction to the material of the piece. It is made up of what is thought to be CIA transmission.

2 *The Czech Lady*

A cut-up modal melodic line heard on the piano is juxtaposed with sung fragments of what is thought to be an old StB station (Czech Statni Bezpecnost) nicknamed 'the Czech lady'.

3 *The Lincolnshire Poacher*

The introduction and numbers used by voice 1 is based on the five number groups broadcast by MI6 nicknamed 'the Lincolnshire poacher' – known to be transmitted from Cyprus to the Gulf. Characteristically each group is repeated twice. The other voice slowly unravels the ancient Greek oracle quote.

Figure 13.2. Interior views of the Debrief Centre, Bentwaters. Photos by Michael Baldock

4 *Tango Hotel Echo*

A spoken text inspired by the three-letter phonetic alphabet stations typically used by MOSSAD (the Israeli secret service) is heard together with the hundred basic words. This is used in the work as an image of random decoding.

5 *Cuban Cut Numbers*

Morse code features in the fifth part, the inspiration behind it being the Cuban cut number messages (DGI) where Morse letter code is used as a substitution for numbers.

6 *Terminat Terminat*

The final part juxtaposes the various text materials including the Cuban cut numbers while the end quote comes again courtesy of the CIA.

THE BUFFER ZONE

The Buffer Zone, composed in 2004, is a companion piece to *a conSPIracy cantata*. It is an audiovisual work that explores boundaries of separation. It is inspired by the UN Buffer Zone in Cyprus that runs across the island and divides the two communities.

In the performance, the audience and the space is split into two halves by hanging video screens. On each side there is a musician (a pianist and a cellist) who plays imaginary duets with a virtual instrument on the other side. The central character is a UN soldier (singer/actor) who guards the buffer zone and freely crosses from side to side. The audience can only ever see one side of the performance, the side they have chosen to sit on.

The central image of the work is of the inner psychological state of the UN soldier and how that is projected into the divided space. The soldier has to deal with his own boredom and his own dislocation and relocation in a desolate no man's land where his main duty consists of reporting and turning away trespassers who stumble into the zone.

Based on interviews and recordings from UN soldiers in Cyprus, the piece explores both the undercurrents of tension and the inner and outer landscapes of the peculiar state of being 'in limbo', between two physical and mental states.

Background to the UN buffer zone in Cyprus

UNFICYP (the United Nations Peacekeeping Force in Cyprus) was established in March 1964. It was the eighth UN peacekeeping operation to be founded, and is currently the fourth-oldest UN peacekeeping operation in the world.

Cyprus became independent in 1960 with a constitution that was intended to balance the interests of both Greek Cypriot and Turkish Cypriot communities. Cyprus, Greece, Turkey, and the United Kingdom entered into a treaty to guarantee the basic provisions of the constitution and the territorial integrity and sovereignty of Cyprus. A series of constitutional crises resulted, however, in the outbreak of intercommunal violence in December 1963. After all attempts to restore peace had failed, the UN Security Council unanimously adopted resolution 186 (in 1964), which recommended the establishment of UNFICYP.

UNFICYP's mandate, as given in resolution 186, is to use its best efforts to (1) prevent a recurrence of fighting; (2) contribute to the maintenance and restoration of law and order; and (3) contribute to a return to normal conditions. In order to fulfill this mandate, 1,230 military personnel from 12 different countries currently work alongside 35 police officers and 146 locally and internationally recruited civilians.

Figure 13.3. Graffitti on barrels around the buffer zone in Nicosia. Image by Aris Kyriakides

It is UNFICYP's task to maintain peace and stability in the Buffer Zone, and to ensure that there is no alteration of the status quo along the two ceasefire lines drawn on 16 August 1974. The Buffer Zone is 180 kilometres long and covers around 3 percent of the island's surface area. It varies in width from less than four metres in Nicosia to some seven kilometres near Athienou. There are five inhabited villages, and around 8,000 people who live and work in the Buffer Zone.

For operational purposes, the military component is divided into three sectors. There are 152 UN observation posts in and near the Buffer Zone, which are used for surveillance. In addition, the military conduct patrols by air and vehicle as well as on foot and – in central Nicosia – bicycles.

The three sectors are as follows:

Sector 1: On the western side, the Kokkina pocket and from Kato Pyrgos to just east of Mammari. The responsibility of the Argentinean contingent.

Sector 2: In the central part of the Buffer Zone and including Nicosia. The responsibility of the United Kingdom.

Sector 4: On the eastern side, from the eastern outskirts of Nicosia to the east coast near Dherinia. The responsibility of the Slovakian/Hungarian contingents.

Note: There is no longer a Sector 3; this ceased to exist when Canada withdrew from UNFICYP in 1993. Sectors 2 and 4 took over the territory previously patrolled by Sector 3. (from the UNFICYP Information Technology Unit)

The motivation behind this piece is a personal one. I was born in Cyprus in 1969, part of the post-colonial generation that still had memories of a unified island. Unaware of the tensions that had been building up throughout the 1960s, one early memory was of the bombing of Famagusta in the summer of 1974, of hiding in the cellar of a hotel, collecting plaster, shells and other bits of debris that had been dislodged by the air attack. On 15 July there was an attempted coup to overthrow Archbishop Makarios, by the Greek right wing militia known as EOKA, supported in part by Henry Kissinger (recent US government documents confirm this fact). Five days later, as expected, the Turkish army bombed and then invaded the island.

The advance of the Turkish soldiers came to a halt on what is known as the Green Line. A buffer zone was created to keep the ceasefire, which has been policed since then by the United Nations.

Famagusta itself lies within the eastern end of the Buffer Zone. The old medieval part is now inhabited solely by Turkish Cypriots, while the modern part is a 'ghost town' uninhabited since the summer of 1974.

My mother's village, Petra, is also completely abandoned, lying in the middle of the Buffer Zone west of Nicosia; it is more 'ghost' than town. I am told that nothing remains other than the old school which was used as a military post.

We emigrated to England in 1975, having lost the family businesses to the new borders that were created.

Looking back on this, I think I had a sense of the past consisting of a line that could no longer be crossed: a mental wall that was reflected in the political stalemate that has grown to be, and still is at the time of writing, as artificial as it is unsolvable.

In 2003, due to mounting pressure from grassroots demonstrations, mainly from the northern part, the borders were relaxed to allow restricted access on day trips across the Green Line. People were confronted for the first time with the reality of their imagined other. Memories of

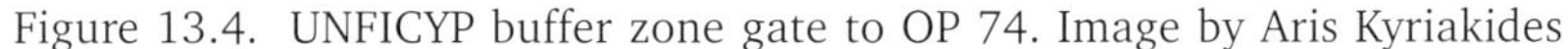

Figure 13.4. UNFICYP buffer zone gate to OP 74. Image by Aris Kyriakides

the 'other side' which had been fixed in the past or completely imagined could be once again revisited.

I also took the opportunity to visit the north of Nicosia, mentally another world away, but physically just the same town surrounded by the same medieval walls. There was something uncanny about just crossing into this other 'time' – the same city, perhaps even the same inhabitants, but another branch of time had caused it to develop in a parallel reality.

On the other hand, the UN Buffer Zone itself is still an area that is off-limits to most civilians. This is partially because there are still land mines in certain areas, but also because any relaxation of the UN mandate before a political resolution had been reached could threaten the stability. There is a paradox here, as in most enforced separations of this kind, that the very mechanism used to create peace also reinforces the divisions, and prohibits peace from breaking through at grassroots level.

A situation similar to the fall of the Berlin Wall almost happened in the spring of 2003 in Nicosia, when the queue of people wanting to cross over to the other side nearly overwhelmed the border guards. The UN was effective in imposing order and maintaining the validity of the Buffer Zone.

+++

In researching the piece, I travelled along the southern border of the Buffer Zone, collecting sound material, trying to catch a glimpse of the landscapes, and the atmosphere of the area. I ventured as far as I could go along roads that crossed into the UN area, up to the point were I would be very politely turned away.

The first impression I had of the Buffer Zone is of a tranquility and wildness one doesn't encounter in the civilian areas. The Greek name for the Buffer Zone is 'nekri zoni' (dead zone), and in this sense it is not dissimilar to the atmosphere of an unkempt cemetery. Wildflowers, birds, and insects thrive. Time has stood still to a certain extent, while entropy is clearly visible on abandoned buildings – abandoned twice, once by the inhabitants and then by the soldiers who used them as makeshift shelters.

The soldiers here were themselves in some state of limbo, having to keep watch over an area where nothing much happens. This dislocation of time, dealing with the effects of a war that happened before most of these soldiers were born, and of place, being far from one's own environment, must have some kind of effect on the soul of the soldier.

These elements drew me further away from the political questions to the internal world of the soldier dealing with his own inner state, while on guard duty miles from anywhere:

> I have been an observer at OP 96. To reach this OP, I have to drive along a very bad track which winds upwards. When the track is wet, it's too dangerous to drive uphill. This means I have to walk, but I don't mind. It's good exercise. My OP lies at about 260 metres above sea level. It's not the highest point in the vicinity. On top of this mountain there is a church easily visible from the highway.
>
> During my four-hour shift, I enjoy the fantastic view. To the west, I can see the road, many fields, and highway. Whenever I see a convoy of more than four military vehicles on the highway, or more than two on the Lymbia-Dali road, I have to report this immediately. That's considered a 'move forward'. Other incidents I sometimes have to deal with are hunters intruding the buffer zone.
>
> We have to check regularly to see if the farmers are carrying their farming permits. I am told that this area is known for its many fires, when the farmers clear their land after the harvest. We have to help fight the fires when things get out of hand. To the south, I can see the village of Lymbia. In winter time, working conditions can be unpleasant at OP 96. Sometimes it is very cold, and when there is a strong wind blowing, the tower swings a bit. You need a strong stomach not to be sick. (from Blue Beret interview with UN soldier)

The sound world of the Buffer Zone consists of UN interviews, nature field recordings, electronic sounds of military technology, piano, cello and voices, from straight to highly processed.

Throughout the piece the pianist and cellist, who inhabit different areas of the space, rarely have eye contact. They are not so much playing together, but playing with imaginary projections of their own instruments on the other side of the space. These are prerecorded parts which are spatially positioned and tuned to give the impression of a great

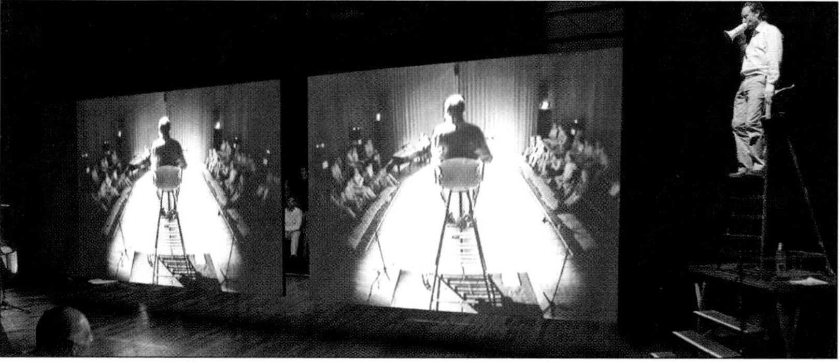

Figure 13.5. From the performance of *The Buffer Zone* (May 2004). Photo: pk@beeld.nu

Figure 13.6. From the performance of *The Buffer Zone* (May 2004). Photo: pk@beeld.nu

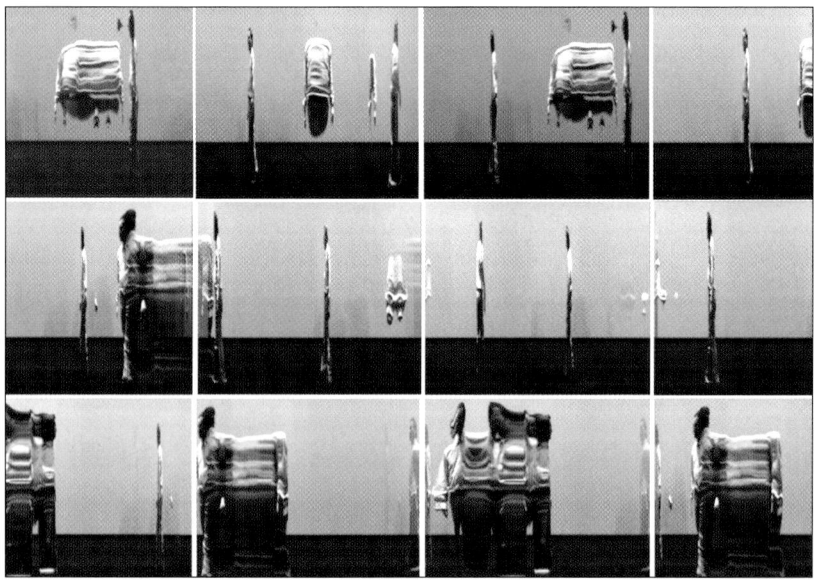

Figure 13.7. Stills from HC Gilje – live image manipulations from *The Buffer Zone*.

distance between the source of the sound and its imaginary other – like an echo that answers the caller.

The pianist – in the original performance, Marc Reichow – is a specialist in inside piano technique, so that the landscape of the piano strings is used to full effect in the music. The strings themselves become lines drawn across a resonant body, or landscape. Likewise, the cellist in the production, Nikos Veliotis, has a special technique of playing with a curved bow, enabling him to play all strings on the cello at the same time, giving the piece a rich sound world of drones that enhances the feeling of suspended time.

The electronic sounds in the piece make much use of birds and insect sounds. This is not only because it comes close to the physical sound world of the Buffer Zone, but because birds, like radio waves, emphasise the space above ground where the political divisions on land do not hold sway.

Sound carries, and Nicosia residents are accustomed to the daily counterpoint of Muslim prayer calls, mixed together with Christian church bells from the respective parts.

The main character in the piece is a UN soldier, moving between his watch tower and the two spaces created on stage.

The baritone, Tido Visser, portrays the inner world of the soldier on guard duty. There is no real storyline in this music theatre work. The first part of the work is a contemplation of the space through the bizarre actions of the soldier as he battles with his own alienation.

He subtly begins to adopt animal, bird, and insect mannerisms as a way of connecting with his environment and of passing the time. This was developed with director/choreographer Andre Gingras, who created a bizarre movement language that the soldier gradually begins to fall into. Towards the middle of the piece, he commits the classic military offence, which is to fall asleep on duty, then to be woken up by a radio voice which alerts him to the fact that there is a trespasser in the zone.

He manages to deal awkwardly with this incident and the audience is not really sure if this is just a figment of his imagination. From this point on reality begins to lose its holding, as the bird sounds become more abstract and the sound world increases in intensity; the inner world of the soldier becomes the landscape itself we are confronted with.

The visual material in the piece is created by the video artist HC Gilje using live surveillance cameras set around the space and prerecorded and manipulated images of the actions of the performer.

The concept was to turn the reality that we see in the theatre space into an inner landscape that symbolizes the buffer zone, rather than representing it by using images of the Cypriot landscape itself.

These kinds of images are too well worn; we are too used to seeing images of devastated areas in the media to consider them with fresh eyes. Furthermore, the inner world of the soldier is heightened by seeing the environment around himself as a reflection of his states of mind.

His body is transformed in slowly scanning video projections, into numerous landscapes; there is a flow of image from left to right moving at a slow, hypnotic pace.

The texts used in the piece range from interviews with UN soldiers, reread by various voices and digitally manipulated, to refrains of the opening words of UN resolutions on Cyprus of which there have been over one hundred. These texts have a distinct repetitive character which heightens the absurdity and impotence of the context for which they were used.

> *Noting – Considering – Having in mind – Calls upon – Asks – Calls upon – Recommends – Recommends – Recommends – Recommends further – requests. Having heard – Reaffirming – Being deeply concerned – Noting – Noting – Reaffirms – Requests. Noting – Expressing – Expressing its deep appreciation – Reaffirms – Calls upon – Takes note – extends.*
> *Concerned – Reaffirming – Anticipating – Reaffirms – Calls for – Calls upon – Calls upon. Taking note – Noting – Renewing – Renewing – Paying tribute – Expressing satisfaction – Reaffirms – Calls upon – Extends – Requests.*
> *Noting – Noting – Noting with satisfaction - Renewing – Renewing.*
> *Having considered – Having heard – Having considered – Deeply deploring – Gravely concerned – Equally concerned – Recalling – Conscious – Calls upon – Calls upon – Demands – Requests – Calls upon – Calls upon – Decides – Reaffirming – Demands – Deeply deplores – Demands – Urges - Demands further – Emphasizes – Recalling – Noting – Gravely concerned – Records its formal disappointment – Urges – Urges – Requests – Decides – Conscious – Recalling – Noting - Mindful – Noting also – Having Considered – Expresses its appreciation – Warmly welcomes – Calls upon – Expresses its grave concern – Requests – Further requests – Calls upon – Reiterates – Expresses the conviction – Noting – Noting – Noting – Noting also – Noting further – Reaffirms – Reaffirms also – Urges – Extends – appeals again. Reaffirming – Reiterating – Welcoming – Commends – Further commends – Regrets – Gives its full support – Stresses – Decides to remain actively seized of the matter – Welcoming – noting – Welcoming – Encouraging – Reaffirms – Decides – Endorses – Notes – Expresses concern – Requests – Decides to remain actively seized of the matter – Welcoming – Noting – Welcoming – Encouraging – Reaffirms – Decides – Urges – Expresses – Requests – Decides to remain actively seized of the matter.*

LINK

Note that a link has been created to accompany this contribution, containing musical compositions referred to and discussed in the chapter. The link is available at: www.kyriakides.com/fearsome.html.

The noise of war, the silence of the photograph

FRANK WATSON

An inherent attribute of the photograph is its capacity to speak through its very muteness. This short essay, and the photographs that are an integral part of it, examines the experience of photographing Cold War sites after they have been abandoned.

The silence of these empty sites now enables a particular kind of retrospective analysis of the way the backwaters of rural England concealed nuclear armaments, whilst the military dissonance that pervaded the peace of the countryside also threatened nuclear annihilation. The relationship between sound and silence is inherently a signifying factor of the photograph. This relationship is explored through some images from my book *The Hush House: Cold War Sites in England* (2004).

At the same time that photography emerged as a form of mechanical reproduction, other industrial inventions brought about what could be seen as a culture of noise; machines had their own rhythms, their own cacophonies. Ironically, the arrival of photography as a technology of recording, omitted the sound of this modern culture. Photography, like its counterpart, film (pre-sound), began to observe modernity yet was handicapped by its inability to hear it. Unlike cinema which developed by synchronising sound and vision, photography's arrested development meant that it continued to view the world mute and still.

Yet rather than seeing this as a deprivation, in many ways this is the photograph's strength. To represent the world in a still and silent way creates a contemplative space for the viewer to observe and reflect on the transient nature of time and the notion of history.

For those old enough to remember the Cold War era, it seemed in some respects to be a war of psychology, threat and counterthreat, a culture of spying and subterfuge. The fact that the war was never fully played out meant that its legacy lurks still within the collective mind. The sense of underlying threat made the Cold War an ominous period of history, lived under a cloud of unconscious tension. The nuclear threat still seems beyond full representation.

It is these issues that embody the photographs that make up the book *The Hush House*: how to make the Cold War tangible, how to reflect upon an event that is situated in the past, yet, like a repressed memory, may surface at any time. The past is always alive in the present; it just has to be activated.

To wander amongst the Cold War sites in England is to become acquainted with the idea of military menace, the arrival of highly advanced technology that had evolved slowly from the days of the stone axe, seen at places like Grimes Graves, a prehistoric flint-mining site in Norfolk. Yet these sites now lie dormant, many of them in Norfolk and generally within East Anglia obscured behind the camouflage of pine forests, deep within the idea of the rural idyll. The contrast between the concept of nuclear destruction and the pervasive notion of the English countryside, in which it is located, is palpable.

Yet to travel along country roads was to be oblivious to the fact that just metres away, bunkers stored nuclear armaments on airfields which cannot be located on any sign post. Local communities were often oblivious to the purpose of these sites, as Official Secrets Acts maintained a shroud around military activity. However, American airbases in England were often more prominent with the importation of mid-twentieth-century American popular culture which stood out in stark relief from the more sombre, English rural way of life.

To enter these sites was often to be literally off the map and to acknowledge that the Cold War was about secrecy. A culture of secrecy breeds fear and paranoia; the coded language of the Cold War would make for an interesting dictionary. The ciphers used then often had an amusing and occasionally poetic sensibility (see Kyriakides, this volume). The elusive title of the book *The Hush House* is derived from one of many architectural references and in this case was used to describe an aircraft hangar designed to muffle the testing of jet engines on the ground. The photographs in this chapter focus on the airbases and the storage of nuclear armaments (deliberately not identified here, to emphasise the point about secrecy, and the standard design of structures throughout NATO) at a time during the Cold War when the transportation of military weapons was very reliant upon aircraft before the arms race shifted towards sea-based launches and the increasing use of submarines around 1969.

Figures 14.1–14.20. Photographs from *The Hush House*.

To view these sites now, accompanied by the occasional skylark or bumblebee, is to walk amongst the late twentieth-century ruins (even Brutalist-styled architecture softens in time) and reflect upon the sheer solitude and silence of these sites which still evoke the terrifying noise of warfare.

It is this contrast that was important to somehow capture in the photographs, as well as the bleached appearance of the landscape in high summer that somehow gave the impression of scorched earth – the aftermath of a nuclear catastrophe.

NOTE

All photographs are by and copyright of the author. More details about this project and the book can be found at www.thehushhouse.com.

REFERENCE

Watson, F (2004) *The Hush House: Cold War Sites in England*, London: Hush House Publications

Filming the end of the Cold War

REINHILD STEINGRÖVER

GOOD BYE LENIN!

A giant Lenin statue is dangling from a helicopter as it is carried across Berlin. A bewildered woman stares at this surreal apparition, as Lenin's bronze face gazes at her, his hand stretched out for a final farewell; then the helicopter and its strange freight disappear into the sunset. No dialogue accompanies this remarkable scene from Wolfgang Becker's 2003 hit film *Good Bye Lenin!*, only Yann Thiersen's urgent score and Becker's careful lighting which emphasise this most vivid manifestation of system change in Germany. In the film, the bewildered woman is Christiane Kerner, who as a result of a stroke and nine months of coma is unaware that the German Democratic Republic (GDR) has vanished and been replaced by a unified Germany. When her children find her on the street in a state of confusion, they refuse to explain. Instead, they simply return her to the safe haven of her apartment, where they had done their best to maintain the fiction of a continued GDR in order to spare her the discovery that her beloved socialist system had expired.

Her confusion may have echoed the puzzling experiences of many former GDR citizens in the initial years after German unification in 1990. At first sight, the film seemingly refuses to answer this question. But a closer look reveals Becker's critical agenda. Christiane's short walk of a few hundred yards into unified Germany is marked by numerous signs of the new ideology. Lenin's monument is lifted, the scene's editing suggests, in order to make room for the new law of market economy, represented here by 'Go West' cigarettes, Ikea bookshelves, used BMW cars and billboards featuring seductive underwear all advertising the new capitalist identity that rules unified Germany.

While this critical drift is not explicitly commented on in the film's dialogue, the visual markers of ideological change did not go unnoticed in East Germany during the early unification years. Specifically, the dismantling of the old communist monuments caused tremendous controversies in Berlin. The Lenin bust in the film, for example, bears a stunning resemblance to the famous 21m tall Lenin statue that Walter Ulbricht dedicated on Lenin's one-hundredth birthday in East Berlin in 1970. The monumental statue was to be abolished by the new West German government in 1991 because, as Berlin mayor Diepgen stated, 'it was simply unacceptable for Berlin to honor a "despot and murderer"' (Ladd 1997:197). However, public protests against the demolition plans emanated from groups of mostly East Germans, who regarded the idea as further manifestation of the West's attempt to erase all traces of East German identity. As Brian Ladd puts it:

> The Lenin statue and soon after the Palace of the Republic became touchstones of Ossi [East German] resentment because they appeared to be clear cases of Wessis [West Germans] trying to claim that only the Federal Republic had represented postwar Germany. (Ladd 1997:198)

The dramatic symbolism of the statue's removal turned comical when the construction company hired by the government to discard Lenin for the fee of DM 100,000 found its concrete core too heavy to move and grudgingly gave up. Several months and DM 500,000 later, a more heavy-duty approach by another company worked and Lenin Square became United Nations Square.

Efforts by Afro-German activist groups, who tried to change public monuments that celebrate the 'heroes' of Germany's colonial history, have shown that the West German government can be very reluctant to 'edit' its own history while it acted swiftly to sanitize its cities from any traces of the socialist past. Clearly, the Cold War victory manifested itself in the right to erase from national consciousness the historical narrative of forty years of socialism. Wolfgang Becker's film *Good Bye Lenin!* is aware of such powers and offers a West German critique of unification that projects the ambivalent feelings of East and West Germans from 14 years after the fall of the Wall onto the very moment of the fall itself. In the film, the 1990 event, when most East Germans were jubilant at the prospect of the new promised freedoms and prosperity, is depicted as one in which East Germans lost their unique cultural and national identity. Indeed, a 1995 opinion poll found that 53 percent of East Germans declared that things had developed far worse than expected at the time of unification while 80 percent of East Germans felt treated as second-class citizens (Naughton 2000:242). The film's central point, namely that the lost East German identity needs to be revalidated and appreciated as equal to its Western counterpart, is clearly informed by hindsight and is laudable as it seeks to return agency to the losers of the Cold War. But Becker's metaphors are nevertheless clearly tinted by his West German experience in their dominant focus on the idea that consumer goods constitute everyday culture, which in turn constitutes a unique East German identity. *Good Bye Lenin!'s* central joke, the unsuccessful quest for East German gherkins, thus assigns Proustian weightiness to the consumption of a local GDR pickle.

More importantly, the temporal and geographical distance to the events depicted finds expression in the defence of an idealized and abstract socialism in a central scene of the film. The scene is staged as a fake newscast and filmed with distancing techniques that attempt to undermine the possibility of uncritical nostalgia for the past. At the same time it represents the melodramatic culmination of the mother-son conflict and creates a highly charged emotional moment of reconciliation. The speech's subtext of breaking down walls between mother and son also powerfully reminds viewers of socialism's utopian potential, as it was once propagated by prominent East and West German intellectuals. The scene has a taxi driver, who resembles East German superhero cosmonaut Sigmund Jähn, read the following description:

> We know that our country is not perfect. But the ideals that we believe in continue to inspire people from all over the world. Perhaps we have lost sight of our goals at times but we have come to our senses. Socialism does not mean building walls around ourselves. Socialism means taking steps towards our fellow citizens, and living with them. Not just to dream of a better world but to realize it.

Had the film been made around 1990 by an East German team, this heartfelt speech would have been unthinkable in the face of decades of artistic stagnation, economic collapse and environmental disasters in the old GDR. Indeed, even a cursory comparative glance at the final production of feature films by the East German studio DEFA in 1990/91 shows that films by East German directors at that historical point focused instead on digesting the devastating social and personal effects of censorship and the secret police, the Stasi, examining the validity of the founding myth of socialism-antifascism, or venting the frustrations over lost chances, creative restrictions and bureaucratic red tape in the studio. Films such as Roland Gräf's *Tangospieler* ('Tangoplayer'), Herwig Kipping's *Land hinter dem Regenbogen* ('Land behind the Rainbow') and Jörg Foth's *Letztes aus der DaDaeR* ('Last things from the GDR') all powerfully describe the mostly negative experiences of their directors with 'real existing socialism' and leave little room for abstract musings over the utopian ideal of breaking down barriers and building humanitarian communities, as it is put in *Good Bye Lenin!* Director Jörg Foth commented representatively for his generation of directors in 1999:

> The collapse of DEFA was a relief for me, as was the collapse of the GDR. It was too much, too long, too idiotic, too aggravating how we waited for the slightest improvements that never happened. (Foth 1999:107)

Unlike the East German filmmakers who looked back at the GDR in 1989 in order to document the failure of a socialist dream they had once shared, *Good Bye Lenin!* focuses on the aftermath of unification, which created such problems as economic inequalities between East and West Germans, the devaluation of East German experiences and memories, and of course the vanishing of East German consumer goods of all kinds. The resulting loss of a distinct East German identity, which East Germans were all too willing to shed in 1989, is the prime concern for *Good Bye Lenin!* Critic Michael Töteberg described the reasons for this focus on validating remembrance:

> ... and especially those people, who fought against the system and ushered in the political changes were given the feeling that they were losing their own history, a feeling of a complete devaluation of their experiences. Wolfgang Becker did not intend to take away the feeling of the dignity of their personal life stories. Therefore, he did not make a movie about the dictatorship GDR – 'That type of satirical arrogance does not interest me', he said. 'I show people as people, who even in a different political system are not that different from myself'. (Töteberg 2003:168)

Delivering a critique of the capitalist West unites Becker's own skeptical position with the disillusioned experiences of East Germans years after unification. The film utilizes the melodramatic mother-son story to remind audiences of the importance of everyday culture in the shaping of personal memories and identities. In its efforts to emphasize the sameness of all humans across political systems, Becker downplays the more difficult differences between them. Eric Rentschler wrote in his study on Nazi cinema: 'Films can maintain memories and serve as bearers of history. They can also become a medium of forgetting, a medium of stylizing, distorting or obliterating the past' (Rentschler 1996:222). *Good Bye Lenin!* intentionally stylizes and distorts the past for the audience to consider how history is written, as well as modeling an idealized coming together of East and West Germans. As the West German filmmakers are unencumbered by the actual experience of the GDR, they are more easily disposed towards evoking the continued longing for the utopian potential that socialism once held.

FILMMAKING AT THE TIME OF THE CHANGE

As the debate surrounding ownership of the historical narrative and authenticity of memory continues 17 years after the fall of the wall, it is worth returning to the remarkable films produced by East German directors around the time of the historic event itself in search of lesser known but more immediate historical and artistic documents. With the end of the GDR came the end of the state-owned film studio DEFA. The renowned 'Hollywood of the East' in Babelsberg, former location of UFA, was sold in 1992 to a French real estate corporation, with the stipulation to develop it into a European media center. More than ten years later it has become clear that these dreams have not come true. In 2006 the studio remained in a financially precarious state despite attracting several big budget productions such as *The Pianist* (2002), *The Bourne Supremacy* (2004), *V for Vendetta* (2005) and *Casino Royal* (2006).

However, while the question of what to do with the physical studio complex, the film workers' jobs and expertise, and the legacy of East German film stock was being discussed in 1990, approximately 30 final feature films were being produced by DEFA. These films were commissioned to a very diverse group of directors, spanning several generations. Many of their final films dealt with the end of the GDR and its legacy. In the remainder of this essay I will discuss two of the most remarkable feature films made in this last crop.

Jörg Foth's film *Letztes aus der DaDaeR* ('Last things from the GDR') and Herwig Kipping's *Land hinter dem Regenbogen* ('Land behind the Rainbow') both won critical praise and awards when they were released in 1990–1991 but quickly faded from the public radar screen. East German audiences were disinterested in looking back at the socialist past during the time of great upheaval, while West German audiences had little patience for the cryptic film essays containing an abundance of veiled allusions to the specific East German experience. At the time, audiences were surprised at the manner in which these two films depicted the end of the Cold War. Instead of giving viewers a handle on the disorienting process of unification itself, the filmmakers focused their gaze on the past in what was to be the first opportunity to produce a feature film independent of stifling studio structures. Many of the filmmakers, who had their first, and often last, chance to finally direct a film for the DEFA studio, were artists with a strong commitment to producing politically engaged films that dealt with issues of relevance for their audiences. Filmmaker Andreas Dresen has stated such a commitment in his acceptance speech for the German film critics' prize in 1993:

> Making films means accepting social responsibility. We have to give images to the nation, stories to the people; we have to make films

> that cover the entire spectrum of conflicts and emotions and that must not be boring. Art is entertaining and more than anything else should be fun! (Dresen 1993:57)

Jörg Foth himself stated the conviction typical for his generation that films could be an active force of social change in the GDR: 'Everybody wanted to make films that could change our country' (Hochmuth 1993:33). But the increasingly mistrustful DEFA studio administration had made it nearly impossible for its youngest generation of filmmakers to produce their own films, attempt aesthetic innovations or select the themes of interest to them. Not surprisingly, then, these directors felt the urge to digest filmically what they had been unsuccessfully trying to express throughout the 1980s. While Foth and his colleagues were clearly aware and concerned about the consequences of a rushed unification with capitalist West Germany, their primary focus was not the concern of losing a specific East German cultural identity, as *Good Bye Lenin!* emphasised over a decade later. Quite to the contrary, Foth was clearly relieved over the collapse of 'real existing socialism', as illustrated in the above quotation. Foth's and Kipping's 1990–1991 films present a view of the GDR in ruins, physically, emotionally and spiritually. While Foth's film *Last things from the GDR* takes a kind of survey of what was and casts an uneasy look ahead to what will be, Kipping's film *Land behind the Rainbow* returns to the origins of the utopia GDR and investigates its roots in order to understand the present. Kipping's surreal film echoes the ideological battles of the height of the Cold War in 1953, the year of Stalin's death, emphasizing the quest for power over the specific ideological contents of socialism, capitalism and even remnants of national socialism. At the poignant moment of 1990 he chose to return to the GDR's beginnings to depict the various discourses of the Cold War in images of destruction, cruelty, exploitation and chaos. This undoing of the official socialist rhetoric of freedom and prosperity for all erupts in surreal images of grotesque violence, where Nazis, socialists, Stalinists and opportunists of all kinds battle each other.

In Foth's film *Last things from the GDR*, the popular GDR clown duo Meh and Weh roam the desolate land performing their swan song at historically significant locations and emphasize the destruction of the GDR and its creative energies through boredom and stagnation. Foth's topics are ideological rigidity, stagnation, intimidation by the secret police, lack of artistic freedom and opportunity, and pollution as well as criticism of various social elites such as politicians and intellectuals. In sum, Foth's and Kipping's films explore the topography of the GDR's failure of realizing socialism's utopian goals on specific historical locations. By depicting landscapes of pollution, fortified borders, failed agricultural collectives, and decrepit manufacturing sites, the films underscore the crucial difference between utopia and experience as a warning against the exploitation of abstract ideologies. While both directors maintain their critical positions toward the West, their films give little indication that socialism as a political system can succeed.

LAST THINGS FROM THE GDR

Jörg Foth (Figure 15.1), born in 1949, belongs to the generation of DEFA film workers for whom he himself had once famously declared: 'Our wave was none' (Foth 1989:7). Foth complained that despite long years of training his generation could not direct independently before reaching the age of forty and even then had little choice among available scripts. Moreover, they were forced to work with established teams of cameramen, set designers and other personnel, instead of finding their own. Many film workers around Foth have voiced frustration over being a well-educated but superfluous work force in the studio. *Last things from the GDR* reflects the weariness of being strung along with empty promises, most pointedly in a scene when the clowns are carried off to

Figure 15.1. Jörg Foth with his cameraman at the time of his previous film *Biologie*. Printed with kind permission of Defa-Dieter Jaeger

Figure 15.2. Well-known writer Christoph Hein in an appearance as garbage collector in *Letztes aus der DaDaeR*. Printed with kind permission by DEFA-Pelikan and thanks to Filmmuseum Potsdam

the dump in a garbage truck. It is driven by one of East Germany's most prominent writers, Christoph Hein, who comments on the end of the GDR in a melancholic-ironic tone. As the writer takes out the trash (his fellow artists), he appears surplus himself, outside the general move towards unification but also self-conscious about his privileged past role:

> The general stupidity is drowning me. When I saw my country croak, I felt that I loved it. I feel the sadness, which the Roman patricians sensed in the fourth century. I anticipate a hopeless barbarism swelling up'. (Script, *Last things from the GDR*: 24)

This scene is emblematic for the film's position on both the end of the old and the coming of the new regime. Hein's monologue pokes fun at his own cast of artists who were too removed from 'real existing socialism,' as the GDR government called it, to offer true resistance but it also condemns the new consumerism. Staging the scene on a vast dump but filming it in gorgeous wide-angle shots, with large flocks of seagulls swooping around the clowns, lends a serene beauty to an otherwise bleak moment.

Foth's film repeatedly combines upbeat monologues with unsettling footage and vice versa. His film consists of a series of loosely strung together vignettes in which the clowns Meh and Weh move around the former GDR and perform their songs at the former prison in Potsdam, the lime works at Rüdersdorf where the cement for the building of the Berlin Wall was manufactured by prisoners, a slaughterhouse in Potsdam, the infamous chemical factory at Leuna, the Potsdamer Platz subway station in West Berlin that had been closed off during the Cold War, and the Brocken mountain where Germans celebrate an annual Faustian Walpurgis night. Each of these locations highlights a different topic, which the clowns explore in satirical songs, such as the theme of waiting for nothing and aging without the hope for change. Foth's programmatic critique of DEFA's treatment of its last generation of directors and critical artists in general is expressed by several of Mensching's and Wenzel's songs, for example:

> Time and money are vanishing goods
> Here on earth
> He who does not yet lie in his grave
> Will soon die as well
> Before you know it, my friend
> Time has run out
> And you have not had your share
> In this world's wealth …
> If one steals your time
> Do not worry
> Only the future does not age
> It belongs to all (Script, *Last things*: 32)

As the clowns perform the song they explore a deserted chemical factory. The camera's focus is on the decrepit industrial wasteland, which audience members from the former GDR might recognize as the Rüdersdorfer lime works, a place where prisoners produced the concrete to build the Berlin Wall. The film's return to this historic location in the context of the falling of the Wall adds poignancy to the clowns' song about the hopes for a better future that were never fulfilled. Image and text act as mutual reinforcement for the scene's ironic commentary. Taking stock of the caved-in ceilings, one clown asks: 'Which way of the many is the fastest?' – to which the other clown replies: 'The left path is the right one. … The furthest one on the left is the fastest but also the most dangerous' (Script, *Last things*: 31). As the scene moves around the factory, the clowns age visibly and reminisce about the past only to discover that there are few positive memories, ending with the resigned statement: 'I think there was nothing going on in the 1980s' (Script, *Last things*: 33). Foth's film is in part documentary. Unlike many later (n)ostalgic depictions of the GDR as the protected *Leseland*, ie the country of readers, where life was slower but somehow more wholesome, Foth's film records his generation's frustration over many wasted years of stagnation and illustrates his stated motivation to document the tragicomic realities of life in the former GDR: 'Because the GDR reality was sometimes more bizarre and tragic than could be reflected by traditional cinematic narratives, we wanted to adapt the clowns' programme to film' (Junghänel 1990:n.p.). This scene is also one of several that allude to the constant presence of Stasi officers, the infamous secret police who censored and intimidated artists, environmentalists and all citizens suspected of antisocialist sensibilities.

The theme of pollution is equally omnipresent but most prominently addressed in a scene entitled 'Acheron'. The boat man, Charon, steers his raft across a polluted river with the clowns aboard, and sings a melancholic song on the baroque vanitas theme, 'All is vain, all is vain, one generation vanishes and another one arrives' (Script, *Last things*: 27). The clowns chime in with a popular folk tune. Its lyrics have been modified to reflect on East Germans moving to West Germany in order to begin a new life, discarding their former identities like the polluted land. The melodies of the two songs blend cleverly and echo eerily across the poisoned landscape where dead fish swim belly up and a baby doll floats aimlessly on an abandoned suitcase. Again, Foth successfully blends the clowns' cabaret programme with carefully composed visuals to convey a Beckettian sense of endgame. The utopian dream has failed, as manifest in polluted landscapes and grotesquely deformed social behavior, where political conformity is being rewarded with literally deadly honours. This is illustrated by the two clowns killing each other off by piercing one another with ever bigger medals of honour.

But the starkest scene is reserved for the concept of the slow death of utopian idealism killed by ideological rigidity and bureaucratic inflexibility. The film stages a scene in a slaughterhouse. Initially, we see only the two clowns sitting on a bloody, tiled floor and performing a parody of Faust's monologue:

> Weh: Alas, I have studied philosophy,
> The law as well as ideology for many years
> Yet here I am, a wretched fool,
> No wiser than I was before (closes a toilet seat he is holding).
> And with a grim face build
> At home a shower stall.

Figure 15.3. The clowns Meh and Weh are dumped in a landfill, where they perform their swan song. Printed with kind permission by DEFA-Pelikan and thanks to Filmmuseum Potsdam

> Meh: That is what I cannot comprehend
> First they strive to know
> The essence of the world
> Then they reach for their house shoes and build miserable shower stalls. (quoted from the film, not in script)

The camera then follows the clowns into the slaughterhouse and presents an extreme close-up of dead cow parts before launching into a three-minute sequence documenting the slaughter of three cows, the last of which requires additional gunshots before she finally succumbs. The sequence is meant to graphically symbolize the slaughter of utopian aspirations by literally pushing back the curtains and exposing the ugly reality behind them. Like the cows, some idealists' faith in the socialist project died a slow and painful death but it succumbed nevertheless. To leave no doubt about the scene's intentions, Meh and Weh muse about the clowns' and philosophers' inability to change the world.

Mensching's and Wenzel's clown programme looks back critically at the possibilities of the socialist utopia and examines the role of artistic opposition in the GDR. They end on a melancholic note as the crowds chase them away and demand money instead. Foth emphasises his futile efforts of working within the official film studio, hoping for reforms. What the film might lack in overarching conclusive conception it makes up for in its immediacy and irreverence which derives its energy from the skillful combination of the clowns' musical cabaret programme and surprising visuals in historic locations. As such, the film resembles an archaeological unearthing of the ruins of the socialist dream at the moment of crisis. In its immediacy the film remains free from false nostalgia for the past as well as exuberant and unrealistic hopes for the future. Of course, such a critical project by its very nature also re-asserts the continued need for artistic intervention, very much in the spirit of Wolfgang Emmerich's recent challenge to German writers of younger generations to 'continue to warn about the devastating consequences of the utopian project' (Emmerich 2003:54) in the form of new ideologies without abandoning all idealist hopes for the enlightening potential of art itself.

LAND BEHIND THE RAINBOW

Director Herwig Kipping (Figure 15.4) seems to have anticipated such a challenge when he directed his 1991 film *Land behind the Rainbow*. DEFA scholar Rolf Richter described the cathartic nature of Kipping's work and prophetically summed up the film's importance:

> This film stands at the end of a film historic period and asks questions about the new beginning. I sensed that the film might one

Figure 15.4. Herwig Kipping, from the set of *Land behind the Rainbow*. Printed with kind permission of Defa-Dieter Jaeger

> day become a document for the turmoil of the times, for the tension, the liberation, the involvement, the distortions, and especially for the newly awakened desire for creative opposition, for eye opening art, which we wanted to pursue from now on because we had to make do without it and had fought for it for so long. (Richter 1991:10)

Herwig Kipping was born in 1948 and grew up in a small village in rural East Germany, an experience that he reworked in the film, in which the landscape of his childhood is transformed into the nightmarish fictional town of 'Stalina' with its bizarre inhabitants of former Nazis, aspiring socialists, anarchists and Stalinists. Kipping was regarded as the *enfant terrible* at the DEFA studio because of his uncompromising aesthetics, which caused his student diploma film on the Romantic poet Hölderlin to be rejected in 1982. (It has since received prizes at several film festivals.) *Land behind the Rainbow* was begun around 1986 under the title 'Hobbyhorse in the Rain' but would have never found backing in the studio. Only after the collapse of the GDR regime was Kipping able to use funding from the newly established group 'DaDaeR', a small

Figure 15.5. Kipping's outrageous iconography combines phallic and political imagery for his surreal scenarios. Printed with kind permission by DEFA-Jaeger and thanks to Filmmuseum Potsdam

group of younger directors within the DEFA studio, to realize his script. Without interference by studio officials, and based on his childhood memories, research in his native village and interviews with family and friends, Kipping set out to explore the roots of the socialist society in which he grew up. He provides a glimpse of his intentions through the selections of texts by authors such as Bunuel, Nietzsche, Dostojewski, Hölderlin, Tarkowskij and Rilke for the film's press kit. In an excerpt from Luis Bunuel's autobiographical *My last sigh*, for example, we read: 'We deny our history and invent, make up a new one. We are afraid of what we have done. Subconsciously we sense our guilt and deny it' (Bunuel 1991:12). In this spirit Kipping creates nightmarish scenarios of violence and destruction, exploitation and corruption in and around the small town of Stalina right around the time of Stalin's death in 1953.

Figure 15.6. The Stalinist grandfather and major of Stalina is crucified on a manure pile. Printed with kind permission by DEFA-Jaeger and thanks to Filmmuseum Potsdam

Like Foth's film, *Land behind the Rainbow* does not tell a chronological story but offers little vignettes with recurring characters, such as the Stalinist grandfather, who is trying to reform the local farms into a communist agrarian society. As the mayor of the village he holds a powerful position, which he uses to line up the village children in a daily ritual of reaffirming their loyalty to Stalinism and quizzing them about potential acts of rebellion among their parents. Hinting that loyalty to communism has greater weight than duty to one's parents, children are encouraged at a young age to prioritise ideology over family relations. Among the adults, the battles between representatives of the socialist reformers, the conservative forces, the secret Nazis and the hard line communists erupt repeatedly in violent outbursts that result in arson, rape and murder. The constant and arbitrary violence is mirrored in the interactions between the children: Hans, who is brutally beaten by his father, stomps on a young chicken, squashing it. Later, he throws a hand grenade into a fishpond in order to kill another child's pet fish. These random acts of cruelty are unsettling enough but Kipping goes a step further, suggesting that the forces of desire for domination and sexual exploitation form the core of human nature and are only temporarily covered up by the ideological justification.

Throughout the film, the men appear driven by desire for instant sexual gratification regardless of their age and of their relation to the woman in question. The Stalinist grandfather, for example, pursues his daughter-in-law, the socialist Heinrich offers his adolescent daughter to ingratiate himself with the county party official, while two hooligan brothers of uncertain political affiliation rape a mentally handicapped girl. Ironically, an outhouse in the village square serves as the political powerhouse for the activities of the party secretary and local brothel at the same time. Similarly, Kipping stages the daily meetings of the farming collective on a manure pile to emphasize the link between the protagonists' power cravings and base instincts. The cruel reality of this Stalinist scenario does not change after the dictator's death in 1953. The film depicts soviet soldiers restoring order after a rebellion by the townspeople reminiscent of the 1957 workers' uprising in the GDR, but conditions remain the same for the villagers. Kipping associates the hollow ideologies with religious overtones by linking the visual iconography of first Stalinism and then socialism with Christian symbols. Stalin's oversized portraits are centrally placed in the square (but next to the manure pile), red banners with Cold War slogans are found everywhere. Finally,

---

Figure 15.7. Kipping's film was originally entitled *Hobbyhorse in the Rain*. Marie and the rainbow maker 'play' children's games in front of the burning village. Printed with kind permission by DEFA-Jaeger and thanks to Filmmuseum Potsdam

the Stalinist grandfather is crucified on a signpost, which becomes his cross in a Christ-like sacrifice. As he gazes across the land he cries (supposedly to Stalin), 'Father, Father, why have you forsaken me?' (Script, *Land behind the Rainbow*: 63).

In stark contrast to the power-hungry machinations among adults and children, the core values of the socialist utopia have been reduced to empty slogans and meaningless rhetoric. While the communist star is placed on the tip of an extraordinarily phallic-looking monument, the bust of Karl Marx is discarded to the eerie, desert-like landscape that surrounds the village. The overturned desolate soil, photographed in an aerial wide-angle view, lends the opening sequence a surreal, apocalyptic quality and clashes with the optimistic socialist slogans that the party officials in the film offer in response to any given crisis. Exposing the hypocrisy of the official socialist language, indicting the refusal to face the grim reality of the workers' collective and accusing officials of theft, bribery and corruption, Kipping does not seem to find many bright spots in his country's forty-year history. While the allusions to the specific GDR history and the language of the Cold War are unmistakable, the director creates a visual language that goes beyond the German context. The archaic images of destroyed landscapes, violent power struggles and sexual exploitation have a universal quality that indicts humanity's destructive impulses and questions the viability of large-scale utopian models. Taking the example of the failed socialist experiment in the GDR, Kipping's film suggests that humanist ideologies, such as Marxism, are all too easily parked in the desert, ignored in their essence but abused for oppressive purposes. The resulting violence is imitated and continued throughout the generations, visualized through repeated close-up shots of a lonely hobbyhorse in the rain, and accompanied by the dramatic music of Gustav Mahler after yet another violent episode.

Nevertheless, *Land behind the Rainbow* offers a glimmer of hope in the figure of a small child, the 'rainbow maker' who promises to make a rainbow for the girl he loves. In one brief scene of peaceful harmony among the otherwise combative villagers, the rainbow maker beckons Marie, the girl, and his parents to join him in a large water barrel, where they all admire the colours of a rainbow, ironically produced by an oil spot. Such is the extent of the 'magical idealism' in the film, a concept that Kipping developed from his reading of the German Romantics, especially the poet Novalis. The final shot of Marx's bust in the desert reminds viewers of the lost utopian ideals and contrasts starkly with the abusiveness of socialist reality. But for Kipping, the exposure of the absurdities of the failed experiment, the exploration of the roots of the betrayal, can be chance. On a societal scale, *Land behind the Rainbow* suggests that greed and power hunger will prevail. But in the individual, exemplified by the rainbow maker figure in the film, lies the hope for gradual change: 'Everyone has to start with himself. In the end each person can only be redeemed by himself' (Kipping 1991:12). While Foth's film uses satire, Kipping employs archaic, surrealist images to lay the GDR to rest. *Land behind the Rainbow* challenges viewers with grotesque visuals that attempt a cathartic cleansing of the stifling past. Its poetic and apocalyptic visions suggest little faith in the betterment of humanity through enlightening ideologies on the one hand and persistent yearning for meaningful communication on the other. Whichever impulse will gain the upper hand in this existential struggle remains open but is captured perfectly in the ambivalent image of Marx's bust in the desert in the film's final frame.

Unlike *Good Bye Lenin!* Kipping and Foth are too close to the immediate historical events of 1989 to evoke even playfully a more positive concept of utopia. Whereas the West German film of 2003 uses the form of family melodrama to critique the dominance of capitalism in shaping not only the new East German landscape but also the way history is mediated, *Last things from the GDR* and *Land behind the Rainbow* express their deep-seated skepticism of all ideologies in their disjointed cinematic formats. As such, they remain as historical witnesses of a moment of crisis that seems far from over.

REFERENCES

Films discussed

Good Bye Lenin! (2003) Directed by Wolfgang Becker, Germany

Letztes aus der DDR (1990) Directed by Jörg Foth

Land hinter dem Regenbogen (1991) Directed by Herwig Kipping

Quotes are taken from the film scripts available at the library of the Hochschule für Film und Fernsehen, Babelsberg, Berlin, or from the film directly as indicated in the essay.

Literature

Bunuel, L (1983) '*My last Sigh*', here quoted from 1991, *Pressemappe für Land hinter dem Regenbogen*, Berlin: Basis Filmverleih

Dresen, A (1993) 'Von Dingen sprechen, die auf der Seele brennen, Rede anlässlich der Verleihung des Kritiker Preises 1992', *Film und Fernsehen* 2, 56–57

Emmerich, W (2003) 'German writers as intellectuals: Strategies and aporias of engagement in East and West from 1945 until today', *New German Critique* 88 (Winter), 37–54

Foth, J (1989) 'Rede auf dem V. Kongress des Verbands der Film und Fernsehschaffenden der DDR', *Filmspiegel* 19, 7

Foth, J (1999) 'Meine Töchter hatte hier ihren Mittelpunkt aber jetzt ist es vorbei', in Felsmann, B and Gröschner A, eds., *Durchgangszimmer Prenzlauer Berg*, Berlin: Lukas Verlag, 92–112

Hochmuth, D (1993) 'Interview mit Jörg Foth', *DEFA NOVA – nach wie vor?* Berlin: Freunde der deutschen Kinemathek, 82 (12), 8–54

Junghänel, F (1990) 'Odyssee mit Meh und Weh', *Märkische Volksstimme*, October 2, n.p.

Kipping, H (1991) 'Ein Akt der Liebe', *Film und Fernsehen* 6/7, 74–77

Ladd, B (1997) *The Ghosts of Berlin, Confronting German History in the Urban Landscape*, Chicago: University of Chicago Press

Naughton, L (2000) 'Wiedervereinigung als Siegergeschichte, Betrachtungen einer Australierin', in Schenk, R and Richter, E, eds., *Apropos Film 2000, Das Jahrbuch der DEFA Stiftung*, Berlin: Das Neue Berlin, 242–253

Rentschler, E (1996) *Ministry of Illusion*, Cambridge: Harvard University Press

Richter, R (1991) 'Pressemappe Basis Film Verleih', *Basis Film Verleih*, 10

Töteberg, M (ed.) (2003) *Good Bye Lenin!*, Berlin: Schwarzkopf und Schwarzkopf

Reflections on nuclear submarines in the Cold War: Putting military technology in context for a history museum exhibit

BARTON C HACKER

In April 2000 an exhibition called Fast Attacks & Boomers: Submarines in the Cold War opened in the Smithsonian Institution's National Museum of American History. Both submarines and the Cold War were firsts for a major exhibition in the museum, and how that came about is one of the two central concerns of this chapter. The second is how we structured the exhibit to attract visitors and teach them something about history and technology. Although the exhibition closed in June 2003, plans to reinstall it at the US Navy's historical museum in the Washington Navy Yard are well under way. In late 2006 the necessary funding has been secured and planning proceeds, but no opening date has yet been set.

WHY SUBMARINES? WHY THE COLD WAR?

The first questions most people will ask are likely to be, why submarines? and, why the Cold War? As for submarines, their intrinsic fascination to the public played a part, no doubt, but the proximate cause was the Naval Submarine League, representatives of which approached the museum administration early in 1998 about mounting an exhibit to commemorate the centennial of the US Submarine Force in 2000. An association of naval officers – mostly retired submariners – and officials of companies that do business with the navy, the Naval Submarine League actively promotes the interests of the submarine force. The museum accepted the league's proposal and, in a most unusual arrangement, allowed the league to become effectively a partner in organising the exhibition. Not only did the Submarine League commit itself to raising all the necessary funds, it also assumed responsibility for administering the main design and production contract. Two league members joined the museum's project team, attending all the meetings as an invaluable source of technical expertise and advice. They also provided unusual access to the active navy, which cooperated enthusiastically with the museum. We shall return to this aspect of the exhibit later.

Why the Cold War, on the other hand, owed something to the museum and something to me. The basic military history exhibit had remained largely unchanged since its original installation for the museum's opening in the mid-1960s. Some staff members thought it needed updating. At least that's what they told me during my interview for the job of curator of armed forces history. When I arrived at the museum in May 1998 to take up my new duties, the Submarine League proposal had already been accepted in principle and I was immediately drawn into the team already busy organizing the project. It was most definitely a team project. In addition to the two retired navy captains from the Naval Submarine League, the core team at the museum included a manager, a director, two co-curators, a collections manager, a graphics manager, a conservationist, a loans manager, and an audiovisual specialist. We also worked closely with the outside company contracted through the Naval Submarine League to design and construct the exhibit.

I entered the discussions about what shape the exhibit should take with only a casual knowledge of submarine history – what I had picked up along the way as a historian of military technology – but a solid background in nuclear history, including particularly relevant work on nuclear propulsion. I argued forcefully against trying to cover all of submarine history in a relatively modest 400 square meters (3,600 square feet). In the end, my personal inclinations and expertise may have been the least compelling argument in favour of an exhibit centered on submarines after World War II. For one thing, such an exhibit would move the museum in a new direction, something management much desired. With the single major exception of the Nautilus Museum in Connecticut, organised around the first US nuclear-powered submarine, all other submarine exhibits we knew about ended with World War II. Then there was America's remarkable reliance on nuclear submarines – alone among the countries that deployed them, the United States scrapped all its conventional submarines. Submarines became one of the main props of strategic nuclear deterrence, and of course the members of the Naval Submarine League that we were working with had themselves captained nuclear submarines. For all these reasons, it was not a hard sell.

The exhibit of 'Submarines in the Cold War' comprised ten sections divided among three major themes, one primarily technological – how submarines work and fight – and two less technologically specific: how

Figure 16.1. 1946 Baker test at Bikini. This photo from the second test in Operation Crossroad appeared on the Cold War timeline as one of the iconic images.

nuclear subs interacted with US foreign and military policy and how men and women interacted with submarines.

THE COLD WAR CONTEXT

The exhibit began with a sweeping photomontage of the Cold War years that featured a video introduction by Walter Cronkite, himself something of a Cold War icon. The largest and most striking images recalled iconic Cold War events such as the Berlin airlift and nuclear weapons tests. Below these images were two photo timelines, one devoted to American cultural events of the Cold War years, the other to milestones related specifically to submarine activities. Interspersed among the images, several text blocks addressed such broad topics as Cold War origins, the Vietnam wars, and the cost of nuclear submarines. This curved 12m wall provided the context for the exhibit while at the same time leading visitors in. The wall visually displayed the consequences of new technology for the military roles of submarines, at every level from tactics through operations to national strategy and foreign policy.

Figure 16.2. This photo of a nuclear missile detonated over the Pacific Ocean in the 1962 Frigate Bird test, included in the submarine timeline, was taken through a periscope. It shows the culmination of the only complete flight test of an American nuclear missile from launch to detonation.

Figure 16.3. The brain of a submarine is its attack centre. Into this critical location flow data from the boat's sensors and status reports for evaluation; from it issue the commands that direct the submarine and its weapons. The commanding officer normally stands near the periscopes, one of which is purely optical, while the other includes electronics that allow it to function as a video camera. The commanding officer's orders are relayed to sailors seated at the twin wheels of the ship control station, watching depth gauges and other indicators as they adjust the submarine's depth and heading. Other sailors man the fire control system for launching torpedoes and steering them toward their targets.

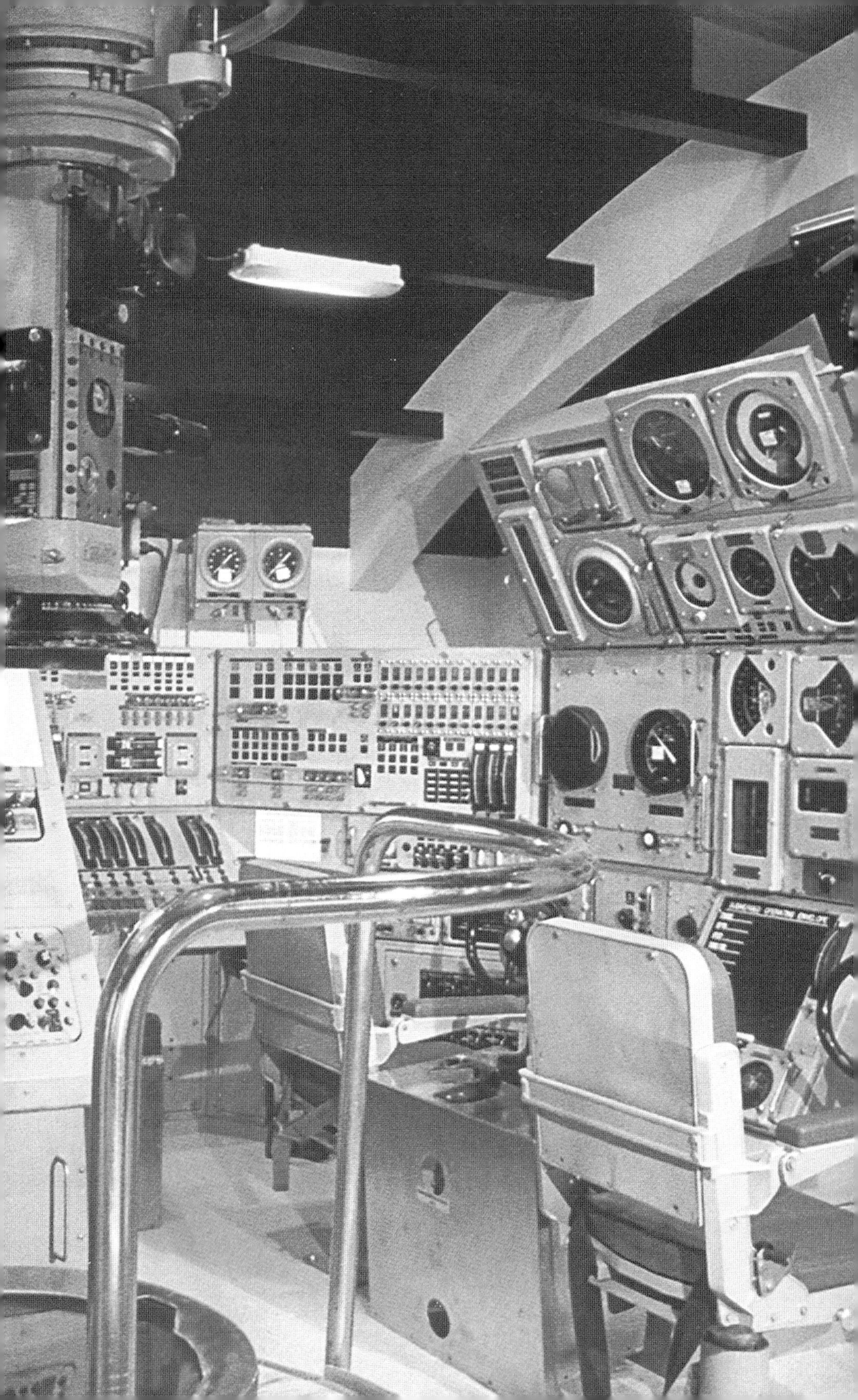

Further into the exhibit, other sections elaborated aspects of the varied roles of nuclear submarines in underwater research and exploration and their primary Cold War missions – nuclear deterrence, antisubmarine warfare, and special operations. A reconstruction of the attack centre – the submarine's equivalent of a surface ship's bridge – gave visitors a glimpse of the submarine's nerve center. It also included video displays of three types of missions based on material that the Navy declassified for this exhibit: (1) tracking a Soviet submarine in the Atlantic (re-enactment of a 1978 mission with animation); (2) observing a foreign surface-to-air missile test (re-enactment of historic mission with authentic periscope photography); and (3) under-hull survey of a US surface ship (modern-day training exercise with animation and periscope photography).

SUBMARINE TECHNOLOGY AND WEAPONRY

Dramatically positioned in tense apposition to the Cold War wall was a three-quarter-scale model of a nuclear submarine's sail positioned as if diving. Situated behind this large model were the first of several displays introducing visitors to the prenuclear history of submarines, and to the new technology of undersea warfare deployed by the United States from the 1960s through the 1980s, including weaponry and ballistic missiles. Subsequent displays expounded submarine electronic systems, including sonar, radar, and radio, and submarine power and propulsion.

Particularly striking were the control panels for power systems, the so-called manoeuvering room consoles. Displaying consoles like these in public – even most crewmembers have never seen them – required modifications to protect sensitive classified information about the design and operation of nuclear-powered submarines. Where necessary, scales on instrument faces were modified, instrument labels altered, or instruments repositioned, and some classified nuclear instrumentation was removed. The navy worked closely with us to keep such changes to a minimum and to preserve overall appearances. These consoles look much as they did during their active life aboard the USS *Sand Lance*.

One object not in the show, physically speaking, was nonetheless a compelling presence – the submarine itself. Our space was not big enough for an entire submarine and because of regulatory restrictions, we were not able to reproduce to the extent we would have liked the cramped interior of even a large nuclear submarine. Even if these options had been available, we had objectives beyond the technological. The exhibit appears, after all, in a museum of American history, not a museum of science.

LIVING WITH SUBMARINES

One of our concerns about this exhibit in a history museum was to move beyond the machines themselves to the social systems in which they are embedded. This accounts, at least in part, for the Cold War setting and for our attention to training and maintenance, limited though it had to be in this relatively small exhibit. We also wanted to address crew life aboard a submarine on patrol and strongly believed the families of the submariners were no less important. About a third of the exhibit portrayed the human impact of technological change on the lives and activities of those who built and maintained submarines, the sailors who crewed them, and the families who awaited their return.

Nuclear submarines challenged conventional ideas of life at sea. No longer surface boats that could hide temporarily underwater, nuclear-powered submarines had become true denizens of the deep. Operating entirely underwater for weeks and months on end, their communication with the outside world remained extremely limited. Sailors had to learn

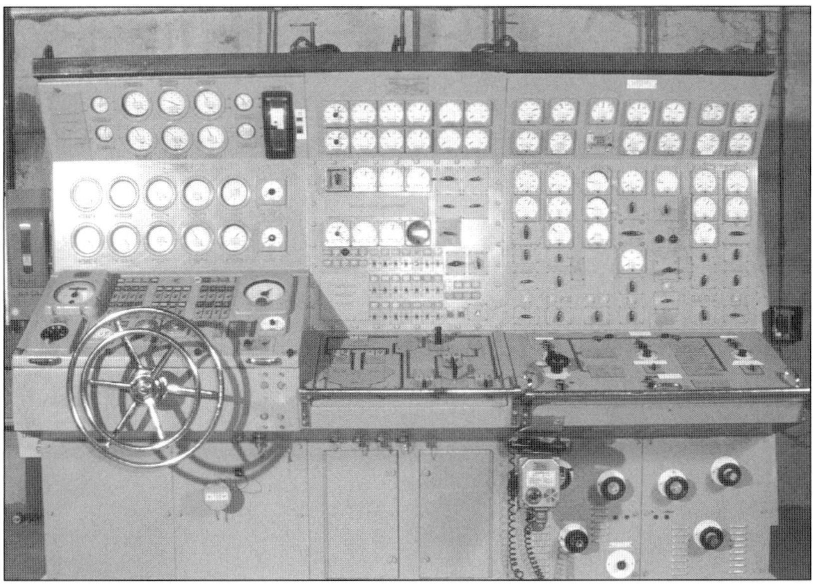

Figure 16.4. Supervised by the engineering officer of the watch, one petty officer mans each of three consoles to monitor and control the submarine's entire nuclear power plant. Shown here to the left is the console that controls the steam turbine, in the centre the nuclear reactor control panel, to the right the console that controls the electrical system. These consoles look much as they did during their active life aboard the USS *Sand Lance* (SSN-660).

Figure 16.5. The personal space for the crew on a nuclear-powered submarine is extremely tight, as shown by these stacked bunks from the USS *Trepang* (SSN-674). The bins underneath the berths represent the only space a sailor has to store his clothing and other personal items for the duration of a patrol.

new skills and adapt themselves to living in a radically confined environment for prolonged tours of duty. The changes to life aboard ship were profound. Because a submarine's weight equals its displacement (its volume), minor changes in equipment weight or volume cannot be so easily compensated aboard a submarine as a surface vessel, where deck space can be adjusted or draft slightly altered. Everything has to fit within a submarine's pressure hull and that is why a submarine is so inherently cramped. For the same tonnage, a submarine has roughly one-third the interior volume of a surface ship. Cramped quarters are the hallmark of life aboard a submarine.

The small display of crew berthing offered visitors a glimpse into the tight little world of the submariner. Just how tight was shown by the stacked bunks from the USS *Trepang* (Figure 16.5) on display. The sailor's personal space was limited to his bunk. The bin beneath the mattress was the sailor's only storage space for all his clothing and any other personal items for the duration of a patrol. On a fast attack boat such as *Trepang*, the crowding could be so great that even one bunk might be more than a sailor can call his own. Three men may 'hot bunk', or share two bunks between them, so that when one is on duty another is asleep.

Getting the families of submariners into the exhibit ran into considerable opposition from those who felt they really weren't part of the navy. We strongly disagreed, and a brown grocery bag was one of our arguments. It bears the slogan, 'Navy Wife (It's the Toughest Job in the Navy)'. To attract, train, and retain people in the all-volunteer military with skills in modern technology, the armed forces by the mid-1970s began to acknowledge the contributions of spouses and families to the military mission. These efforts included slogans on commissary shopping bags, as well as more substantial action.

SUBMARINES IN THE COLD WAR

Historically, the development of nuclear-powered submarines aroused controversy both within the military establishment and in the public arena, though for very different reasons. Internally, the issues were money and questions about the feasibility of both nuclear propulsion and submarine-launched ballistic missiles. External opposition derived in part from fears of nuclear power, which applied to all nuclear-powered ships. Opposition to ballistic missile submarines, which led to demonstrations and picketing outside submarine bases at home and abroad, stemmed from concerns by some members of the public about the morality of nuclear deterrence as national policy.

Preparing our exhibit was not so contentious. Most issues were relatively minor. Someone from the navy objected to the label about the cost of submarines, admittedly a complex issue to address in 200 words

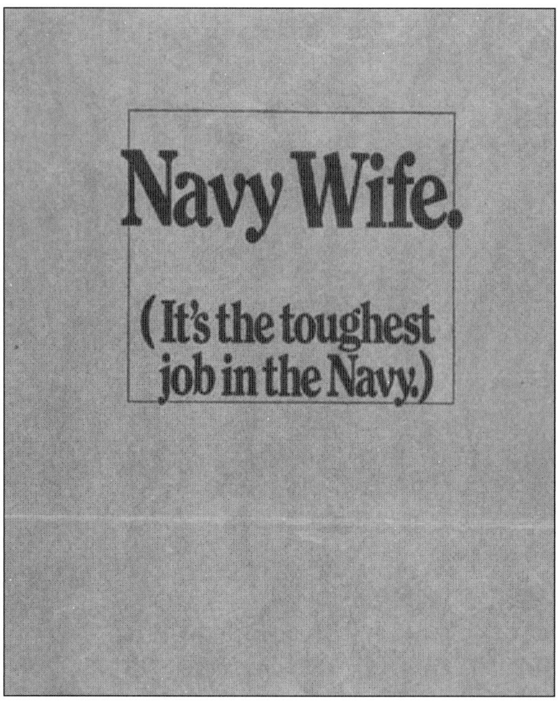

Figure 16.6. To attract, train, and retain people in the all-volunteer military with skills in modern technology, the armed forces by the mid-1970s began to acknowledge the contributions of spouses and families to the military mission. These efforts included slogans on commissary shopping bags.

or less. That was worked out. A protective suit required for repairing high-pressure steam lines reminded someone else too much of a radiation protection suit, but that too was resolved. The biggest issue involved the place of women in the story, which centered on the wives of submariners in the section on life ashore. Here the results were less satisfactory.

The problem seemed to be chiefly one of perspective. We wanted to tell that part of the story from the women's viewpoint. The Naval Submarine League representatives saw it from the perspective of the men at sea. They kept trying to make it a tale of wives longing for their husbands to return. That women, even navy wives, might have lives of their own was almost literally unimaginable. Since ex-navy people ran the production company, we achieved only limited success in imposing our version of the story. If you looked closely at the exhibit, you would have seen that the section on life ashore got short shrift compared to the rest of the exhibit. Our attempt to include in the epilogue some discussion of the prospect of women serving aboard submarines likewise met concerted opposition. This issue we didn't press, accepting the argument that this was not, properly speaking, a Cold War matter.

Overall, given the potential problems of exhibiting a topic still fresh in many minds and of much concern to many people still active, we had a remarkably trouble-free exhibit process. The appendix to this paper uses four sections from the exhibit to describe it more fully. It outlines the objects and graphics used, and reproduces the exhibit's main and secondary labels in full at their appropriate positions. The appendix concludes with a brief bibliography of the major works consulted in preparing the script.

Although we did not count visitors or formally evaluate visitor response to this exhibit, the exhibit area seemed much trafficked, the brochure pockets required daily restocking, the published reviews and web notices were good, and such visitor comments as we did receive ranged from favorable to enthusiastic. Submariners and other sailors, both active and veteran, were particularly delighted with the exhibit, inviting us to several get-togethers after the exhibit opened. Foreign submariners (British, German, Russian) who visited the exhibit were also highly complimentary. Interestingly enough, they seemed particularly taken with our attempt to depict the experience of families ashore, something they found both unexpected and admirable. So pleased was the navy with the exhibit that the Naval Historical Museum took it entire, intending to reinstall it in a new exhibit area in the not-too-distant future. Meanwhile, interested readers can take a virtual tour of the exhibit at: http://americanhistory.si.edu/subs/.

ACKNOWLEDGEMENTS

Figures 16.1 and 16.2 are reproduced courtesy of the US Navy. All other figures are courtesy of the National Museum of American History, Smithsonian Institution, Washington DC.

REFERENCES

Main books and articles used in preparing the exhibit script:

Anon (1998) 'Breaking the surface: Today's missions are drawing submarines out of the deep', *U.S. News & World Report*, 6 April 1998, 28–36, 40, 42

Duncan, F (1990) *Rickover and the Nuclear Navy: The Discipline of Technology*, Annapolis, Maryland: Naval Institute Press

Friedman, N (1984) *Submarine Design and Development*, Annapolis, Maryland: Naval Institute Press

Friedman, N (1994) *U.S. Submarines since 1945: An Illustrated Design History*, Annapolis, Maryland: Naval Institute Press

Friedman, N (1995) *U.S. Submarines through 1945: An Illustrated Design History*, Annapolis, Maryland: Naval Institute Press

Hansen, C (1988) *U.S. Nuclear Weapons: The Secret History*, Arlington, Texas: Aerofax

Harris, B (1997) *The Navy Times Book of Submarines: A Political, Social, and Military History*, Edited by Walter J. Boyne, New York: Berkley Books

Hewlett, RG and Francis, D (1974) *Nuclear Navy, 1946–1962*, Chicago: University of Chicago Press

Kaufman, Y and Stillwell, P (1993) *Sharks of Steel*, Annapolis, Maryland: Naval Institute Press

King, RW ed. (nd) *Naval Engineering and American Sea Power*, Baltimore, Maryland: Naval & Aviation

Kort, M (1998) *The Columbia Guide to the Cold War*, New York: Columbia University Press

Laur, TM and Llanso, SL (1995) *The Army Times, Navy Times, Air Force Times Encyclopedia of Modern U.S. Military Weapons*, Edited by Walter J. Boyne, New York: Berkley Books

Lawliss, C (1991) *The Submarine Book: A Portrait of Nuclear Submarines and the Men Who Sail Them*, New York: Thames & Hudson

Lightbody, A and Poyer, J (1990) *Submarines: Hunter/Killers and Boomers*, New York: Beekman House

Luttwak, E and Koehl, SL (1991) *The Dictionary of Modern War*, New York: Harper Collins

Miller, D (1991) *Submarines of the World: A Complete Illustrated History, 1888 to the Present*, New York: Orion Books

Moore, J ed. (1991) *Jane's American Fighting Ships of the 20th Century*, New York: Mallard Press

Polmar, N (1981) *The American Submarine*, Cambridge, Massachusetts: Patrick Stephens

Rodengen, JL (1994) *The Legend of Electric Boat: Serving the Silent Service*, Ft. Lauderdale, Florida: Write Stuff Syndicate

Sapolsky, HM (1972) *The Polaris System Development*, Cambridge, Massachusetts: Harvard University Press

Schwartz, SI ed. (1998) *Atomic Audit: The Costs and Consequences of U.S. Nuclear Weapons since 1940*, Washington: Brookings Institution

Weir, GE (1991) *Building American Submarines, 1914–1940*, Contributions to Naval History 3, Washington: Naval Historical Center

Weir, GE (1993) *Forged in War: The Naval-Industrial Complex and American Submarine Construction, 1940–1961*, Washington: Naval Historical Center

APPENDIX: EXHIBIT OUTLINE (PARTIAL)

Selected main and secondary labels with objects and images listed

Section (04) Nuclear submarines and their armament

Main label. IV. Anatomy of Nuclear Submarines. In the 1950s, the U.S. Navy developed two distinct types of submarine to take advantage of the new capabilities of nuclear power: fast attacks and boomers. The Navy officially designated fast attacks as SSN, for submarine (nuclear propulsion). The official designation for boomer is SSBN, for ballistic missile submarine (nuclear propulsion). Boomers are also known as fleet ballistic missile submarines. Despite significant differences, fast attacks and boomers have many basic features in common. All submarines must enclose much more of their machinery and equipment within their hulls than surface ships. That is why they are so cramped. A submarine has only about one-third the living space per person that a destroyer of the same tonnage has.

Artifacts. Pressure hull steel sample; Watertight door.

Graphics. Sub cutaway from *US News & World Report*; Sub silhouettes from Electric Boat.

Secondary label. IV.A. Nuclear-powered Attack Submarines. During the Cold War, one of the main tasks of fast attack submarines (SSNs) became finding and tracking Soviet submarines. They also carried out a variety of other covert missions related to intelligence gathering and special operations. Attack submarines have always relied chiefly on torpedoes as weapons. During the Cold War, they might also have been armed with several kinds of short- or medium-range missiles that allow them to engage surface ships or other submarines beyond torpedo range. With cruise missiles, the only type of tactical missile now in service, they can pinpoint land targets several hundred miles away.

Artifact. Model of USS *Sturgeon* (SSN-637) nuclear-powered fast attack submarine.

Graphics. USS *Los Angeles* (SSN-688) in 1976 sea trials; Photo of *Birmingham* blowing.

Secondary label. IV.B. Nuclear-powered Ballistic Missile Submarines. From 1960 to 1966 the U.S. Navy launched a total of 41 ballistic missile submarines, called the '41 for Freedom.' Every SSBN had two full crews, Blue and Gold, rotating at approximately 100-day intervals so that the ship might remain more continuously on patrol. Each SSBN carried 16 Polaris nuclear missiles. Conversion to more accurate Poseidon missiles, starting in 1972, required only modification of the existing SSBNs. And even more advanced Trident I missiles, from 1979 onward, could be accommodated on the last 12 of the original 41 SSBNs. The first of the much larger Ohio-class boats, which entered service in 1981, was designed specifically for the new and much larger Trident II missiles. Until Trident II became available in 1990, however, the new submarines were equipped with Trident I. Well over twice the displacement of their predecessors, each of the 18 Ohio-class SSBNs carried 24 missiles.

Artifacts. Model of USS *George Washington* Polaris ballistic missile submarine; Model of USS *Ohio* Trident ballistic missile submarine.

Graphics. Photo of *Robert E. Lee*; Photo of *John Marshall*; Photo of *Ulysses S. Grant*; Photo of *George Washington Carver*; Poster '41 for Freedom.'

Secondary label. IV.C. SOVIET SUBMARINES. Like the U.S. Navy, the Soviet Navy found German submarine innovations of compelling interest. It rapidly built a fleet of fast, modern ocean-going submarines based on German models and continued to build and deploy diesel-electric attack submarines throughout the Cold War. The first Soviet ballistic missile submarines in the late 1950s were also diesel-electric. By 1960, however, the Soviet Navy had launched its first nuclear-powered attack and ballistic missile submarines. It also developed a third type of nuclear-powered submarine (called SSGNs) designed specifically to launch cruise missiles against American aircraft carrier task forces. At its peak in 1980, the Soviet submarine force numbered 480 boats, including 71 fast attacks and 94 cruise and ballistic missile submarines. Because the names of individual Soviet submarines are seldom known abroad, the usual practice is to refer to them only as a member of a submarine class. The most widely known class names are those assigned as code names by NATO, such as Alfa, Charlie, and Kilo.

Artifacts. Model of Soviet Alfa-Class nuclear-powered attack submarine; Model of Soviet Typhoon-Class nuclear-powered ballistic missile submarine.

Graphics. Photo of Soviet Charlie-Class nuclear-powered cruise missile submarine; Photo of Soviet Kilo-Class diesel-electric attack submarine.

MAIN LABEL. V. SUBMARINE ARMAMENT. Submarines are combat ships that rely on stealth and their ability to pinpoint targets and threats. An array of weapons enables submarines to engage their targets and defend themselves against attack. Both boomers and fast attacks carry torpedoes; for SSBNs they provide self-defense, for SSNs they serve as primary weapons. Fast attacks can also lay mines. Both types of submarine carry acoustic countermeasure devices, such as noisy decoys, to help confuse enemy sonar and homing torpedoes. SSBNs carry strategic missiles tipped by nuclear warheads that can obliterate cities several thousand miles away. Of quite a different order were the missiles carried by SSNs during the Cold War. Whether armed with nuclear or high-explosive warheads, they were limited in range to a few hundred miles at most, and were chiefly intended for attacking individual surface ships or submarines beyond torpedo range. All such tactical missiles have now been phased out, with one exception. In recent years, fast attacks may carry land-attack cruise missiles – small, jet-propelled, pilotless aircraft with high-explosive warheads accurate enough to target individual buildings in a city.

Secondary label. V.A. TORPEDOES. A torpedo is a long metal cylinder with an explosive warhead, propelled through the water by an internal combustion engine or batteries. Modern torpedoes are wire-guided: a thin wire spooling from the torpedo links it to the submarine's fire control computer, from which guidance commands in the form of digital electronic signals flow. Although torpedoes might still be targeted against surface ships, U.S. submarines during the Cold War usually focused on other submarines.

Artifacts. Mark 48 torpedo; Torpedo fire control relay panel; Torpedo tube status board.

Graphic. Diagram of torpedo.

Secondary label. V.B. CRUISE MISSILES. Cruise missiles are jet-propelled pilotless aircraft designed to strike distant targets with great accuracy. Travelling at hundreds of miles an hour, cruise missiles use the global positioning system, inertial guidance, optical scenery correlation, and terrain comparing radar to find their targets. Their accuracy makes them especially useful in attacking military targets in urban areas with limited damage to nearby civilian facilities. Naval interest in cruise missiles during the 1940s and 1950s produced results, but the concept was shelved in favor of the much more promising Polaris ballistic missile program. Improving technology and changing missions in the 1970s revived the earlier idea. The Tomahawk cruise missile joined the fleet in 1983 and has played a particularly important role in the Persian Gulf War and in actions since the end of the Cold War.

Artifact. Tomahawk cruise missile.

Graphics. Post-war cruise missiles; Flight profile of Tomahawk missile.

Secondary label. V.C. OTHER SUBMARINE ARMAMENT. In addition to torpedoes and land-attack Tomahawk missiles, submarine armament includes mines. During the Cold War, U.S. submarines also carried several weapons no longer in service: Harpoon and Tomahawk anti-ship missiles and Subroc (*sub*marine *roc*ket) anti-submarine missiles.

Graphics. Harpoon anti-ship missile; Harpoon flight profile; Photo of subroc launch; Subroc rocket-propelled anti-submarine nuclear depth charge; Line drawing of mobile mine.

Main label. VI. Ballistic Missiles. Long-range ballistic missiles entered American military service during the late 1950s. They are called ballistic because, like the shell from a gun, they receive a brief but powerful initial impetus (from a rocket motor), then follow an unpowered ballistic trajectory after launching. Polaris was the first U.S. Navy ballistic missile system – a nuclear-powered submarine with 16 guided missiles, each armed with a nuclear warhead many times more powerful than those used in World War II. The first model of the missile, Polaris A-1, went to sea in late 1960. Polaris A-2 became operational in 1962 and A-3 in 1964. The Poseidon missile succeeded Polaris beginning in 1972, followed by Trident I in 1979, and Trident II in 1990. Each step brought major advances in warheads and accuracy.

Artifacts. Models of submarine-launched ballistic missiles (SLBMs); Weapons shipping hatch; Missile guidance access door, watertight closure, and portable crane; Attack center indicator panel (ACIP) and missile-firing key; Reentry vehicle (RV) protective cover; Trident I missile nose fairing and aerospike.

Graphics. Comparative diagram of sub-launched ballistic missiles; Launch profile of Polaris missile; Photo of Trident launch; Photo of nuclear test.

Section (07) Manoeuvering room

Main label. XI. Submarine Power and Propulsion. U.S. submarines rely on nuclear power for both propulsion and life support. The nuclear reactor heats water to make steam that drives a turbine to turn the propeller. The same system also provides steam for the boat's turbine generators, the source of electricity for all submarine systems, including oxygen makers.

Artifact: Manoeuvering room consoles.

Secondary label. XI.A. Nuclear Reactors. Nuclear reactors are basically heat engines. As uranium fissions, the breaking apart of atoms releases energy, much of it in the form of heat, which can then be used to do work. In a nuclear-powered submarine, reactor heat produces steam to drive the turbines that provide the submarine's actual power. The development of compact, safe, and highly reliable pressurized water reactors for naval use in the early 1950s was the major technological achievement that made nuclear-powered submarines possible.

Graphics: How Reactors Work.

Secondary label. XI.B. SUBMARINE PROPULSION. Steam turbines propel nuclear-powered submarines. Heat from the nuclear reactor, regulated from consoles in the manoeuvering room, generates the steam that drives the turbines, which are geared to a propeller shaft. The rotating propeller drives the submarine through the water.

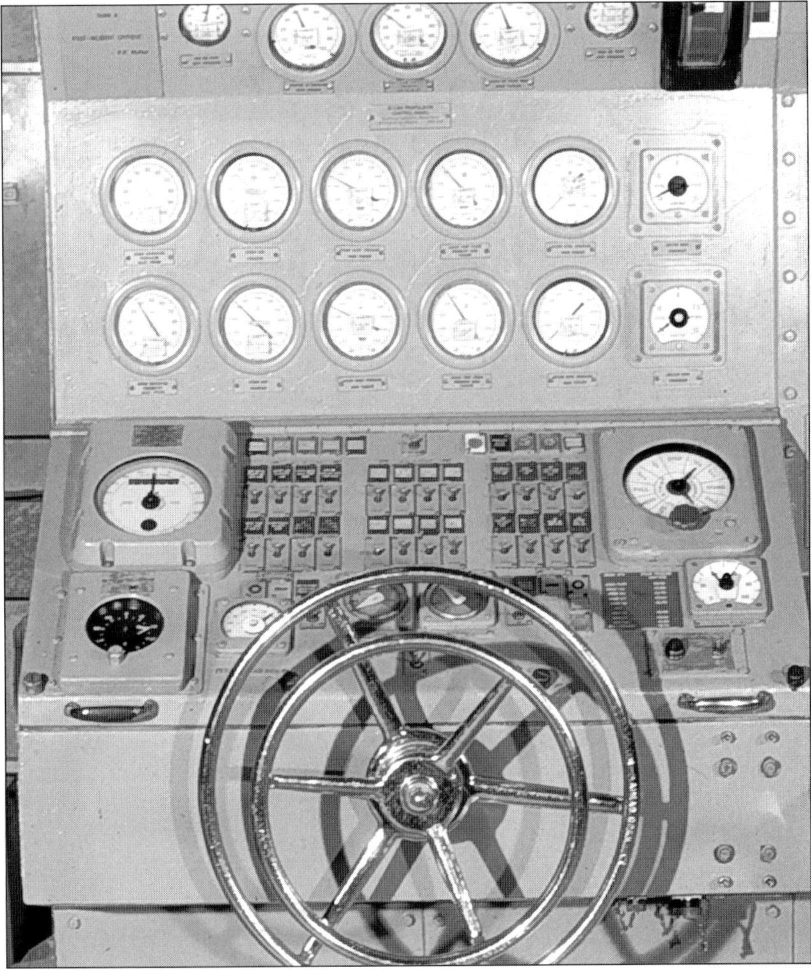

Figure 16.7. The console, the leftmost of the three manoeuvering room consoles as they line up in the submarine, controls the steam turbine that propels nuclear-powered submarines. Heat from the nuclear reactor generates the steam that drives the turbine, which is geared to a propeller shaft. The rotating propeller drives the submarine through the water.

Artifact: Model of Propeller from Sturgeon-Class Nuclear Submarine.

Figure 16.8. Because propeller design is so important to both speed and noise levels, it remains one of the most secret aspects of submarine technology. Used in design tests, this declassified model of the propeller from a 1960s Sturgeon-class fast attack submarine is the first ever put on public display.

Graphics: Photo of *Los Angeles*-class propeller; Diving and Surfacing; The Loss of the *Thresher*.

Secondary label. XI.C. Auxiliary Systems. Reactor-generated steam drives not only the propulsion system but also the turbine generators that provide the electricity submarines require for their auxiliary systems. These systems furnish power for equipment cooling and the operation of weapon systems, for lighting and cooking, for climate control and water distillation. Air must be purified and oxygen generated as well, because the submerged submarine is a closed system and must maintain its own atmosphere.

Section (08) Life aboard a nuclear submarine

Main label. XII. Life Aboard a Nuclear Submarine. Nuclear-powered submarines can operate submerged for months at a time. Submariners are all volunteers rigorously tested before acceptance. Even more than in conventional submarines, the physical and psychological stamina of the crew on nuclear-powered submarines becomes a crucial factor. They must also deal, while on patrol, with being largely cut off from the outside world, including their families, for long periods of time. Crew members live inside a pressure hull filled with the machinery required to keep them alive and allow the ship to function. They must make do with the cramped spaces between the machines, enjoying little stowage space or privacy. The submariner's day lasts 18 hours, three 6-hour watch cycles, one on and two off. He stands a duty watch, then has the next 12 hours for everything else: repair and maintenance tasks, study, relaxation, eating, and sleeping. Then it's back to the duty watch.

Secondary label. XII.A. Habitability. Essentially unlimited power allows a nuclear-powered submarine to maintain a far more comfortable environment than was ever possible in conventional submarines. But close quarters, especially in attack submarines, still make for such hardships as restricted storage space, little opportunity for exercise, and lack of privacy.

Artifacts. Crew berthing, bunk curtains with *Trepang* logo and wall speaker with grill; Commode from crew's head and crew's head gauge board; Submarine uniform (poopie suit); Clothes washer and dryer.

Graphic. Photo of potatoes over crewman in bunk.

Secondary label. XII.B. Damage Control. The greatest threats to a submerged submarine are fire and flooding. Although the threats rarely materialise, submariners have a wide range of equipment to combat them and conduct regular drills.

Artifact. Steam suit; OBA (oxygen breathing apparatus); Damage control tool roll, bolt cutter, and spill kit (red).

Secondary label. XII.C. Eating and Leisure. Nuclear power means virtually unlimited endurance; a submarine could stay at sea for years at a time, if power were all that mattered. But it is not. How long the crew can endure is a significant limit, as is how much food can be carried. Food for the crew is the bulkiest commodity in a submarine and becomes the limiting factor for patrol duration. Fresh food lasts about two weeks, then canned, dried, and frozen food is used for the rest of the patrol. When a submarine leaves on patrol, food fills every available corner. Eating takes place in the crew's mess. Despite the tight galley space, good meals are the rule, with the same menu for officers and enlisted men. Extra funding for food makes submarines the best

Figure 16.9. These are two of the five mess tables and benches from the mess deck of an attack submarine, the USS *Trepang* (SSN-674).

'feeders' in the Navy. But the mess deck also is virtually the only common space aboard a submarine for training and study, or where off-duty sailors can unwind by watching video tapes, playing games, or talking. Volunteer 'lay leaders' may also conduct religious services on the mess deck; submarines do not carry chaplains.

Artifacts. Crew mess tables and benches; Trash disposal unit, garbage bags and weights; Dolphin qualification status board, with dolphins; Coffee brewer and juice dispenser.

Graphics. Photo of crewman exercising; Photo of pizza night; Photo of North Pole baseball; Photo of religious service on *Will Rogers*; Photo of crew enjoying good eating; Photo of senior noncom telling sea stories.

Secondary label. XII.D. FAMILY CONTACT. Isolation and restricted communication posed potentially severe morale problems for married submariners – about half the enlisted men and two-thirds of the officers – and their families during the Cold War. SSBN patrols typically lasted 60 to 80 days, while SSNs normally deployed for six months. During the height of the Cold War, communications between ship and shore were extremely limited for security reasons. Periodically, submarines received a single message called a 'familygram' with family news for all crew

Figure 16.10. Disposing of trash, like many other activities that are relatively easy ashore, requires special equipment in a submarine. Trash is tightly compacted in bags and a cylindrical steel mesh container. To lessen the risk of detection, a 7-lb (3.2 kg) weight insures that it will sink to the bottom of the sea. Dirty laundry was handled much more conventionally, as shown by this photo of a washer and dryer from a 1960 submarine.

members. Each family had space for only a few words, and it was strictly one-way; no one on board could be allowed to respond. When operations permit, e-mail may now provide some relief for divided families, but long separations remain one of the hardships of submarine life.

Artifact. Familygrams.

Section (09) Life ashore

Main label. XIII. Life Ashore. Submariners and their families lived mostly on base or near their boats' home ports during the Cold War. At submarine bases, life was generally structured, protected, and insular. For both married and single submariners, social life was closely tied to the submariner's professional life. The sweeping changes in American society that marked the 1960s and 1970s also affected the submarine community. As more and more wives began to work outside the home and children adopted the trappings, or sometimes the substance, of the counter culture, the once-sharp boundaries between military and civilian communities began to erode.

Graphic. Photo of sub base housing area.

Secondary label. XIII.A. Family Support, Supporting Families. Following a long tradition of volunteerism in military communities, the Navy relied heavily upon wives' social networks as liaisons between commands and the families, especially during deployment. When the submariners were away, their families helped each other to meet the problems and crises of everyday life without husbands and fathers. The wife of the chief of boat (COB), a senior or master chief, usually became ombudsman – someone to assist in emergencies and to help resolve complaints equitably – and the reference point for enlisted submarine wives. The wife of the submarine's commanding officer or executive officer was usually the information link between the command and officers' families, informing them of missions, homecomings, and departures.

Artifact. Dolphin Scholarship Foundation calendar, 1969.

Graphics. Photo of family watching submarine leave on patrol; Photo of submariner's wife in kitchen 1965; Photo of families socializing 1965.

Secondary label. XIII.B. 'Dependents.' By the late 1970s more wives of submarine crew members than ever before held dual jobs – maintaining the household and working outside their homes, often in professional careers. Although women never served aboard American submarines, conventional or nuclear, they had provided many of the volunteer services that formed the framework of military communities. That role became less common as other demands on their time increased. Whether a military wife worked at home, as a community volunteer, or at a paying job, she and her children were called 'dependents.'

Artifacts. Book, *Making a Home in the Navy*, 31 July 1980; Panel exhibit board from decommissioning ceremony for *Trepang*; Mimeographed telephone tree; Brown grocery bag: 'Navy Wife (It's the Toughest Job in the Navy)'; Poem; Invitation and program.

Graphics. Photo of wives receiving citation; Photo of bake sale; Photo of pregnant baby shower.

Secondary label. XIII.C. THE SUBMARINE FAMILY. When submariners were away, family celebrations and activities – birthdays, anniversaries, visiting relatives – were minimized or put on hold until they returned. The COB often held postdated cards, messages, and presents given him by family members for delivery at the appropriate time. Soon-to-be-absent husbands, too, might arrange anniversary and birthday deliveries of flowers and gifts.

Artifacts. Familygram; Coupon book.

Graphics. Photo of family posting familygram; Photo of 'halfway night'; Photo of homecoming; Photo of child making posters; Photo of submarine homecoming; Photo of welcome to Norfolk; Photo of birthday party.

Archaeology of dissent: Landscape and symbolism at the Nevada Peace Camp

COLLEEN M BECK, HAROLD DROLLINGER, and JOHN SCHOFIELD

INTRODUCTION

Competing ideologies and the threat of nuclear war were central to the Cold War as the former Soviet Union and the United States engaged in a stalemate for military superiority (Halle 1967). The world lived under the specter of a Doomsday Clock showing the minutes to midnight, the hour of nuclear war. Governments sought to protect their countries and citizenry through alliances and the development of increasingly sophisticated nuclear weaponry and delivery systems (Angelo and Buden 1985; Baker 1996).

These military efforts and the built environment associated with them are dominant in Cold War heritage. For example, the history of a United States nuclear weapons complex explains the roles of various, interrelated facilities in the design, development, production, and testing of nuclear weapons (Loeber 2002), while on the other side of the Atlantic, a historic survey of the Atomic Weapons Research Establishment buildings and structures documents Great Britain's nuclear weapons development and design facility (Cocroft 2003). Others have focused on particular aspects of the nuclear weapons story, such as the Hanford plutonium production facilities (Marceau et al 2003) and nuclear testing remains at the Nevada Test Site (Beck 2002). Even structures whose purpose was to study the Cold War sky through radar systems have been systematically recorded (Whorton 2002), and the civilian aspect has not been overlooked with the architectural designs of this era interpreted as reflecting the nuclear threat and Cold War politics (Johnson 2002). The publication of a broad overview of nuclear testing buildings and structures throughout the United States captures the nature of the Cold War era and shows that such topics have become mainstream (Vanderbilt 2002).

During the Cold War, however, there was some visible dissent with the dominant government actions and policies by pacifists and antinuclear activists. Some of the notable pacifists, such as Lillian Willoughby, Albert Bigelow, and Ammon Hennacy, had protested against wars before the dawn of the nuclear age and their activism was only heightened by the emergence of nuclear weapons into the world's battlefields. Some others, in response to the devastation in Japan with its attendant visual impacts, protested the new weapon and its magnitude. Ultimately, as the years passed, the belief that the Superpowers would eventually fall into war, annihilating populations on the earth, with survivors facing a nuclear winter, produced antinuclear activists throughout the world.

One avenue for expressing alternative views was to conduct protests at icons of the Cold War. These government facilities included missile silo arrays, air bases with bombers on 24-hour alert, laboratories developing new nuclear weapons, plutonium processing plants, a white train carrying nuclear materials across the United States, and nuclear testing facilities. However, most protests in the United States and other countries have taken place in the paved world, on streets and in parks and parking lots, leaving little if any material remains of the protesters' activities. These centralised locations provide ease of access for the protesters and news media as well as being highly visible to people in the community. Following such actions is the inevitable cleanup and a return to the normality of daily activities. An exception to this scenario is the situation where protesters established a semipermanent camp just outside the entry to the Nevada Test Site. On a reduced scale, a similar situation also existed at Greenham Common Airbase in England, where protesters' vigils also led them to camp at the location (Schofield and Anderton 2000; Fiorato, this volume). The protests at the Nevada Test Site differ from most protest circumstances because they occur in a desert landscape, remote, and without facilities common in an urban setting. This chapter discusses the archaeological study of this place, known as the Peace Camp. The research focuses on exploring the materiality of the occupation and the use of landscape and space in order to understand the nature of protest occupations.

THE CONTEXT

The Peace Camp is in southern Nevada adjacent to the Nevada Test Site, a limited access, government-controlled facility, covering approximately 3,600 sq km. The camp and the Nevada Test Site are reached by traveling a multilane highway northwest from Las Vegas for a distance of about

100 km. The Test Site served as the United States primary nuclear weapons testing facility from 1951 to 1992, with the government testing more than 900 above- and below-ground nuclear devices there and where some form of nuclear testing research continues today. The town of Mercury is located on the Test Site a short distance inside the main entrance and serves the needs of the workers, supplying housing, a cafeteria, offices, workplaces, warehouses, a post office, and recreation. The Test Site facility was first operated and managed by the United States Atomic Energy Commission and currently by the Department of Energy National Security Administration. From its inception, activities at the Test Site were a focus for antinuclear sentiment and within a few years of its establishment, antinuclear and propeace demonstrations began taking place along the highway route from Las Vegas and at the entrance to the facility itself.

For several decades, protesters from the United States and other countries have come to this place in the Nevada desert. They congregate and camp on undeveloped and barren public land south of the main entrance, across the highway from the facility. This land, owned and managed by another federal agency, is rock-strewn and rough, a desert, with small and narrow flat ridges interspersed by shallow drainages. Vegetation is sparse, primarily limited to the ridges, and consists mostly of sage brush, yucca, cactus, and the odd shrub and forb. No trees are present for shade, other than the Joshua Tree yucca; and there are no sustainable resources such as water within 30 km other than on the Test Site itself which was of course out-of-bounds.

Initially this gathering area was known as the Protesters' Camp and then, in the 1980s, the protesters officially named their site the Peace Camp. This location has been a meeting place and base camp for individuals and for over 200 groups with different and coeval environmental and social interests, including pacifists, antiwar groups, antinuclear coalitions, environmentalists, and the Western Shoshone tribe – the traditional owners in this area. The individual protesters as well as the group participants come from all walks of life, convening at the camp to present their views and feelings in opposition to local and world events. When they come together at the camp they form a short-term, loosely organized social group for periods of limited duration with the unifying focus of expressing themselves by public actions at the entrance to the Test Site and by symbolic gestures in support of peace and protesting against nuclear testing and nuclear arms in the world. The nature of the camp reflects their short-term social activities, and to some extent their marginalized relationship to society as a whole.

THE ARCHAEOLOGY

Prior to our archaeological research, there was little information available about the camp itself. Tents and vehicles could be seen in the area during protest events, but news reports and other records focused on the events and not the nature of the encampment. During a brief visit to the camp by the archaeological team, the desert appeared undisturbed except near a 1960s gravel pit where one could see evidence of recent occupations, such as sweat lodges, camping areas and several stone hearths. A few peace symbols made out of rocks were observed on a slope above a drainage gully, and stone piles could be seen on top of a hill in the distance. The archaeological team estimated they would find 50 or so features at the site and some associated debris over an area of 40 to 50 ha. However, the desert environment can be deceptive and the predictions of the types and frequency of cultural materials in this setting were erroneous (Figure 17.1).

The methodology for the archaeological research was straightforward. Systematic survey was conducted with each feature or artifact numbered, measured, photographed, and the location recorded with a global positioning system. Two field sessions were conducted revealing that Peace Camp covered about 240 ha, stretching some 2,000 m east-west along the highway and about 1,000 m south from the highway. The site is not a small area with some campsites and a few pieces of art; instead, it is extensive and very complex with 771 cultural features recorded by the end of the 2002 fieldwork.

Features and Artifacts

The features at the Peace Camp are reflective of the environment and the nature of the occupation. Most features are built with stones taken from the surrounding terrain or, in a few cases, certain types of rock were brought by someone for the creation of a specific piece of art. Stone features include rock cairns (piles), rock caches, rock circles, rock foundations for statuary or sculptures, geoglyphs (symbols made of stone), rock lines along paths, rock lines enclosing an area containing desert plants (creating 'gardens'), hearths, and stacks of rocks usually three to five stones tall. Sometimes in conjunction with the stone features and other times not, a flat area in the desert was scraped clean of rocks, even small ones, to create a clearing for a tent pad or for sleeping under the stars. Wood items are sparse and were imported. Logs were brought for fires and tree limbs to build structures and crates and tables for camping-related activities. Wood artifacts were scarce with most notably a

---

Figure 17.1. Overview of the peace camp.

wooden peace symbol and a wooden ankh. Metal artifacts were rare with most found at campsites; hearth grates with a few metal artistic objects were found at other locations on the landscape. Other features are concrete statuary foundations, barbed wire and field fencing, prayer poles, graffiti, dirt paths, dirt roads, various sculptures and symbols, sweat lodges, masks, statues, willow branch structures, and a porta-loo.

There are artifacts at many locations throughout the Peace Camp. The types of artifacts and their locations, such as at a memorial garden, a ceremonial fire pit, and stone cairns, indicate that most have been purposefully placed at features or at special places on the landscape, as offerings or an intentional statement. Examples are crystals, a dream catcher, knives, sea shells, ceramic masks, and a watch. Discarded items are rare with only a bottle or two, and small items, such as nails, a cigarette lighter, and a child's toy, all probably overlooked and left by mistake. The almost total absence of trash is striking. Walking for hours throughout the desert, the cleanliness of the area is noticeable, especially with the knowledge that thousands of people have visited or camped there. The fact that trash was collected and removed from the camp in an organised manner is an indication that a set of unwritten rules or expectations existed for the protesters.

The Site

There are five focal areas at the site: an old camp, a new camp, Pagoda Hill, the highway drainage tunnels, and the entrance to the Nevada Test Site (Figure 17.2). The old camp is just south of the highway drainage tunnels and west of the new camp and the name, Peace Camp, written with aligned stones, greets anyone entering the old camp (Figure 17.3). The camp was easily accessed by two dirt roads parallel to the highway. In the area closest to the highway, tent pads, sleeping areas (Figure 17.4), hearths (Figure 17.5), stacked rocks and rock cairns are common and scattered across the landscape. Of interest is a rock memorial garden (Figure 17.6) dedicated to Ben Linder, an engineer and activist killed by the Contras in Nicaragua in 1987 (Kruckewitt 2001). People have placed small objects at the garden, probably as a tribute to him and his sacrifice.

Heading south near the Ben Linder garden is a very distinct path, its sides defined by lines of rocks. To the side at the beginning of the path is a small rock circle with lines oriented in the cardinal directions and in its center is a posthole that once held the prayer or flagpole for the old camp. Small offerings also were left here in the stones. Alongside the path are several rock symbols including a snake. As the path ends, it climbs onto a low ridge and one encounters a rock ring and hearth that are not habitation features. Instead, in this setting where there are no campsites, the hearth and rock ring appear to be for ceremonial use.

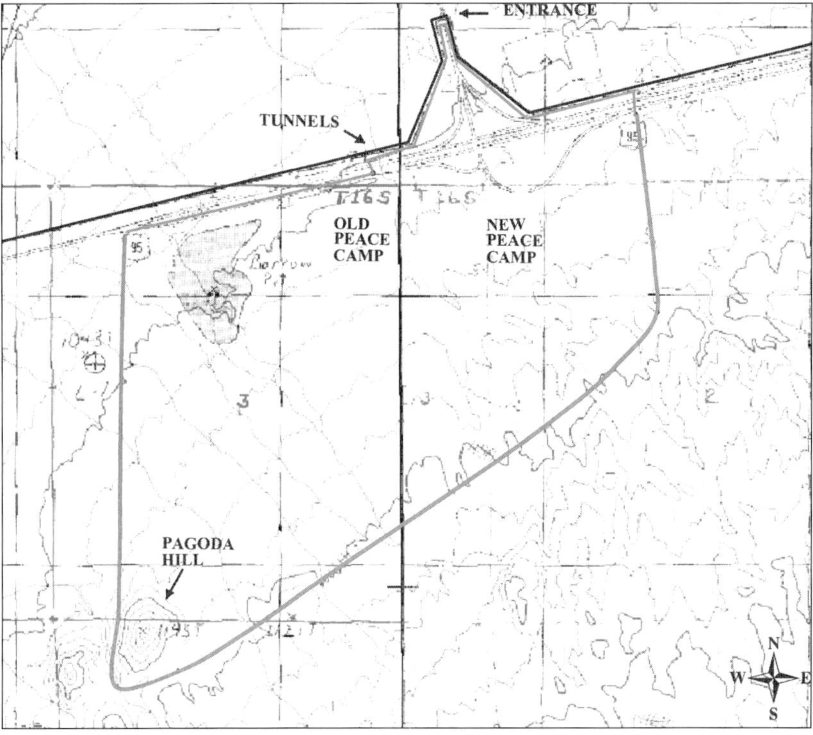

Figure 17.2. Map of the Peace Camp.

Further north along the ridge, outlined with stones, are a heart, peace signs, a dove, and the initials TTW. At first the TTW seemed enigmatic and out of place, but as research progressed, the initials made sense as a tribute to the prominent environmentalist writer and activist, Terry Tempest Williams. She has been a participant in demonstrations at the Test Site and her concerns for the environment have been expressed in a strong voice heard by many. As a citizen of Utah, she is also a member of a group of people known as the 'downwinders', people who lived downwind of the Test Site and were in the path of fallout from some of the atmospheric tests (Williams 1990).

During the mid- to late 1980s, this camp took on a different aspect when at least two residential trailers were hauled into the area. The protesters had decided to make their presence here a permanent feature of the landscape and at least one person lived permanently in one of the

Figure 17.3. Old 'Peace Camp' sign in the desert.

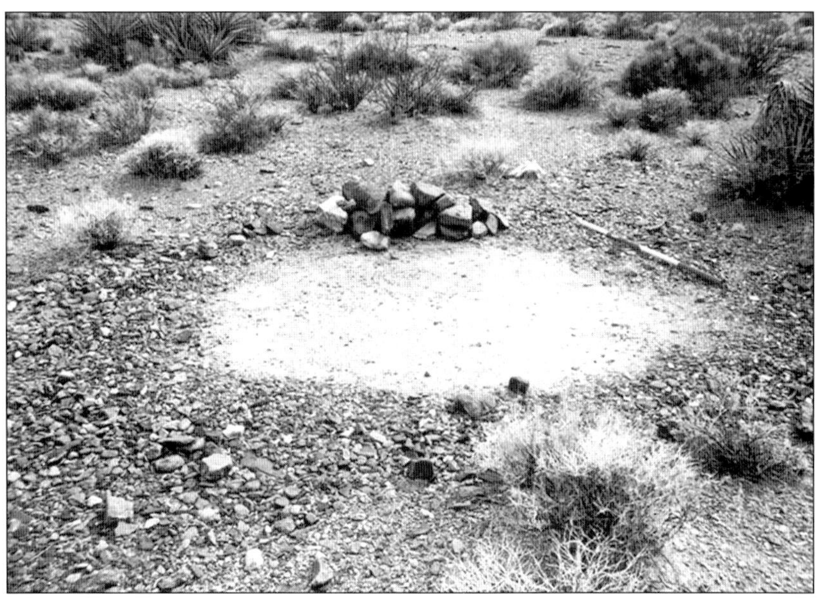

Figure 17.4. Sleeping area.

Figure 17.5. Hearth.

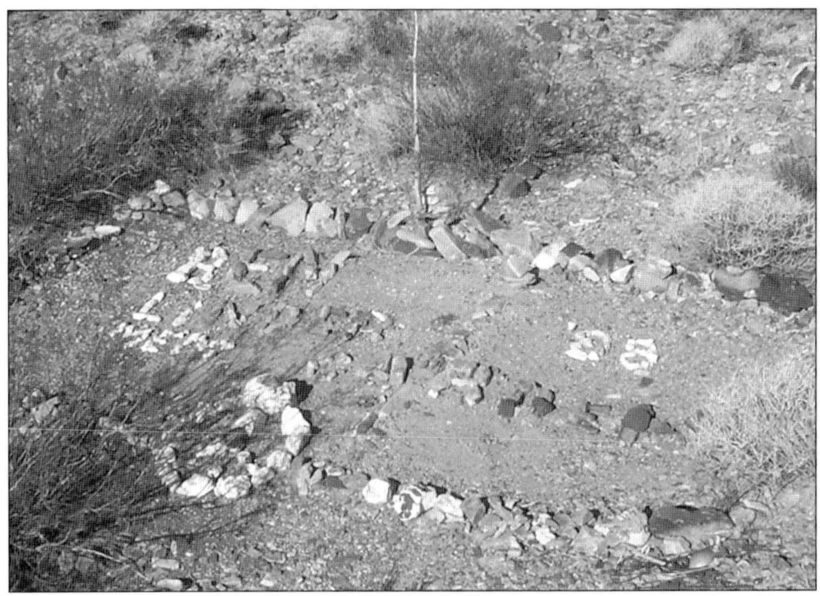

Figure 17.6. Ben Linder memorial garden.

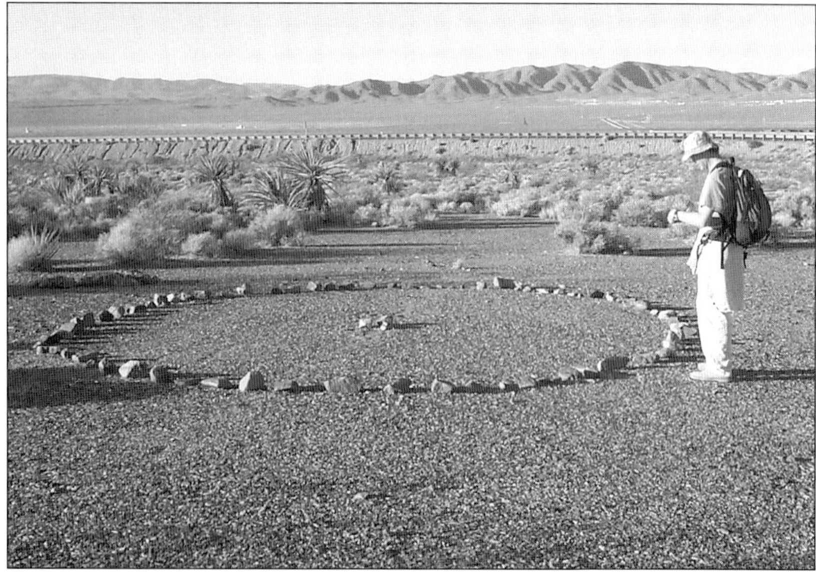

Figure 17.7. Rock ring.

trailers with others staying for shorter intervals. In 1989, the government evicted and arrested some of the residents and removed the trailers from the old camp because of the illegality of residing on this type of government land on a permanent basis. Protesters promptly moved the camp eastward to the public rally area adjacent to the main entrance of the Test Site (Cohen-Joppa 1990). Today, the only indication of this occupation is an area of disturbed soil southwest of the old camp.

After the forced abandonment of the old camp, activity shifted to the east and the protesters began using the new camp as their primary activity area. One advantage of this new location was that it had direct access by way of a highway slip-road and underpass to the entrance of the Test Site. This made the new camp more visible on the landscape to Test Site workers and those driving by on the highway.

A dirt road leads from the slip-road through a fence, then south through most of the camp. East of this dirt road, individual campsites are common and there are a number of rock rings (Figure 17.7), hearths and tent pads. Standing out on the landscape is a porta-loo, donated by the Department of Energy for the new camp as a good-will gesture. It

Figure 17.8. Sweat lodges and fire pit.

was perceived, however, as 'something of the enemy' and vandalized by filling it with large rocks and trash, making it unusable. In this condition the porta-loo, located toward the middle of the camp, took on a new role and became a symbol of action against the federal government.

At the south end of the road is a ceremonial area dominated by two sweat lodges and a large, stone fire pit (Figure 17.8). Also present are materials to repair and rebuild the sweat lodges, rock symbols of a flower and cross, and structures made of willow branches. Between the ceremonial area and the fenced entrance, directly west of the road, is another and relatively smaller ceremonial area with a large geoglyph of a circle with rock lines pointing in the cardinal directions like a compass. Nearby is a prayer pole that is used as a central feature in the Western Shoshone sunrise services. The area probably was used for this and other ceremonial activities (Figures 17.9 and 17.10). Adjacent to these is a sweat lodge centre hole, the sweat lodge itself having been removed.

From the old and new camps, paths lead to the southwest corner of the site, and a hill, called Pagoda Hill by the protesters. The main path to the top of Pagoda Hill is on its north side, and stacked rocks are frequent along the route, guiding the traveler to the top. Protesters have journeyed to the top of this hill for years. Dominating its crest are three rock cairns; two are over two metres tall (Figure 17.11). These cairns or stone piles were created by protesters carrying a rock to the top on each of their visits. Offerings placed on and inside the cairns include yarn, sea shells, white quartz rocks, sandstone rocks, a Jamaican dollar, clay cherub, green stone, sage bundle, bell, white-handled pen knife, pebbles, cactus branches, an amulet, silk scarf, necklaces, tarot cards, model of a dolphin, Zia Pueblo sign, tortoise shell, and notes in containers. Also, atop one of the cairns is a large quartz crystal. Between the cairns is a pole with arrow designs on its east and west sides and engraved with the words 'Healing Global Wounds,' and 'May Dignity and Peace Prevail'. There is a scatter of small pieces of white quartz in this area and nearby on the crest is an arrangement of white rocks arranged as a compass. Also on top of the hill is a basalt peace symbol. On the west side of the hilltop is a red clay sculpture of a female, lying on her back on the ground (Figure 17.12). She appears pregnant and her body is covered with radioactive symbols. Hanging around her neck is an amulet with the words, 'DOE Nuke Waste Dump'. Pagoda Hill is the highest location within the Peace Camp, and from the top of the hill is a commanding overview of the surrounding terrain including the south end of the Nevada Test Site and the town of Mercury. All indications are that Pagoda Hill is a ceremonial location with the journey to the top an act of pilgrimage.

Figure 17.9. Prayer pole and circular geoglyph (compass).

Figure 17.10. Western Shoshone sunrise service with Corbin Harney, the Western Shoshone spiritual leader, playing the drum.

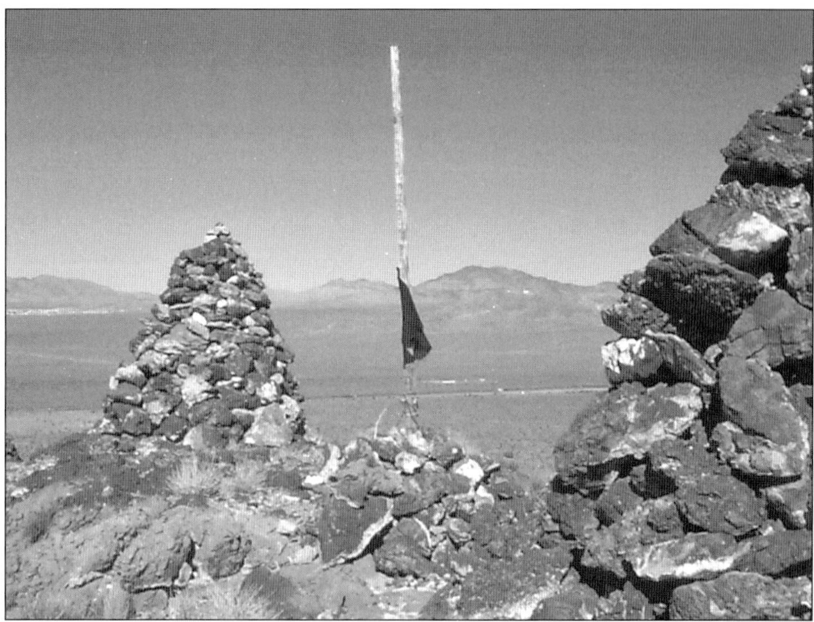

Figure 17.11. Rock cairns on crest of Pagoda Hill.

Figure 17.12. Red clay sculpture.

In contrast to the top of Pagoda Hill and the openness of that setting, are the tunnels that were built under the highway for drainage. Concrete-lined, they provide respite from the sun, an access route from the old Peace Camp to the Test Site boundary, and more significantly, a place for protesters to express their feelings artistically (Figure 17.13). The interiors of the tunnels are covered with graffiti – literary quotes, images, abstract designs, protest sayings or chants – that illustrate their viewpoints or signify who they are or what organisation they represent (Figures 17.14 and 17.15). These graffiti represent the people at the site; they identify them, just like the rock-aligned symbols left on the surface of the surrounding desert.

For most protesters, their destination point is the Test Site boundary and worker's entrance to the facility. During the protests, the participants walk north from the Peace Camp, passing under the highway, and then onward to the boundary of the Nevada Test Site. Placards portray their concerns and occasionally they obstruct the flow of traffic. At times, they walk onto the restricted facility, resulting in their arrest. The Test Site boundary line used to be delineated by a cattle guard that recently was replaced with pavement and a wide white line across it.

North of the entrance and inside the Test Site is a trailer for security personnel and fenced holding-yards for the protesters detained by the sheriff's department. A public area immediately south of the gate and boundary line contains hearths, rock cairns, stacked rocks, and ephemeral rings in the ground, the result of dancing at sunrise ceremonies.

Figure 17.13. Tunnels under the highway.

Figure 17.14. Graffiti in the tunnels.

Figure 17.15. Graffiti in the tunnels.

Still tied to the wire on the fence line that demarcates the Test Site boundary are remnants of cloth placed there by the protesters during the demonstrations.

These five focal areas of the camp are only a part of the site. At first glance, the rest of the Peace Camp looks as if it has not been used by the protesters, but in reality the desert contains hundreds of features carefully placed throughout the area and which are visible only when one walks carefully across the landscape. Stacked rocks and rock cairns are most common, and there is an abundance of symbolic art. This art most often is on flat land surfaces and ridges between the small drainages that cross the site. As with most of the features, this symbolic art is usually placed on the surface with a few slightly embedded into the soil; rock materials obtained locally are the predominant artistic medium. Some of the symbols are recognisable, such as peace symbols (Figure 17.16) and spirals (Figure 17.17); others are enigmatic, such as stone platforms or floors. There even are large stone circles with ceramic and metal masks placed in the cardinal directions. Several are so different they are of special interest, including a relatively large flower abstract (Figure 17.18) and sculptures of children, known as the shadow children (Figure 17.19). On one small ridge, and within an oval

Figure 17.16. Peace symbol.

Figure 17.17. Spiral.

Figure 17.18. Large flower geoglyph.

Figure 17.19. Shadow children, created in relation to a visit to Peace Camp by Hiroshima survivors.

configuration, the word 'peace' is written in English, French, Russian and Chinese, the languages of the countries with nuclear weapons in the 1980s.

DISCUSSION

The archaeology of the Peace Camp is the archaeology of mostly nonviolent dissent and activism. The campsites provide documentation of the intermittent aspect of the occupation, but the symbols throughout the desert portray the purpose of the protesters. The predominance of peace symbols, flowers, doves and hearts created on the desert landscape reflect the protesters' goals of world peace and healing 'Mother Earth'. The offerings at various locales are other visible expressions of the protesters' personal commitments. The graffiti in the tunnels are different from the symbols and artifacts in the desert. The graffiti contain statements of peace and harmony, but the writings and scenes also portray the anger and frustration of some of the participants, aptly placed inside the tunnels and not out in the open on the earth.

The camp itself is material evidence of social reaction to nuclear testing that has grown to encompass broader environmental and cultural issues, such as Western Shoshone rights and views. The Western Shoshone, under the agreements in the nineteenth-century Ruby Treaty between the Western Shoshone and the United States government, continue to lay claim to the Nevada Test Site land and are concerned with healing the test effects on Mother Earth. Their influence and involvement is shown by the sweat lodges and prayer poles.

However, much of the symbolism at the Peace Camp reflects other traditions, modern and ancient, and the varied constituency of the Peace Camp. The thousands of protesters from all walks of life and different countries presented a solid front against the testing of nuclear weapons. Their reason for being at the Peace Camp was a commonly held objective, the desire to bring about a nuclear-free world. For many, this goal was expressed through civil disobedience.

Protesters talk and write about crossing the boundary line as a rite of passage. Their willingness to be arrested is often a spiritual experience (Butigan 2003) and shows their commitment to their beliefs.

> I crossed the line at the Nevada Test Site and was arrested with nine other Utahns for trespassing on military lands. They are still conducting nuclear tests in the desert. Ours was an act of civil disobedience. But as I walked toward the town of Mercury, it was more than a gesture of peace. It was a gesture on behalf of the Clan of One-Breasted Women. (Williams 1990:11)

Another protester writes:

> We all lit our candles and the procession began in ones and twos down the lonely road. … the procession arrived at the entrance to the Test Site, now guarded by 20 or more police officers … the police informed the people that those who entered would be cited for trespassing and held in a fenced area … Over three hundred of us decided to cross the line ... Upon release from the holding area and being cited, we line-crossers were welcomed back. … The welcome I received was from an elderly Japanese man who was a nuclear survivor from Hiroshima. (Peach and O'Brien 2000)

Test Site workers drive daily by the camp but do not stop. There is curiosity but a reluctance to enter the space of those opposed to their activities; while the protesters seek to enter the Test Site to demonstrate their commitment to their cause, to draw attention to their goals, and in some cases to disrupt activities there.

A retired engineer summarised the Test Site workers' viewpoint well when he said:

> You have these people that go out there and sit outside and protest. I always said, and will say it until the day I die, the very thing that they were protesting against is the very thing that allowed them to protest. It gave them the freedom in this country to do anything that they want to do including protest. (Beck and Green 2004:15)

While the protesters seek an end to the activities at the Nevada Test Site, at times this outcome often seems unattainable to them. Yet, writing about the Nevada Test Site, Terry Tempest Williams is optimistic when she talks about 'A Rock of Resistance, Stones of Compassion'.

> When … a poet from Kazakhstan … came to visit the Nevada Test Site in … 1995, he initiated an old … custom: Each person takes a stone and places it in a pile. 'It starts small', [he said] 'But one day this mountain of stone will close this test site down'. … In 1995 … on the fiftieth anniversary of the bombing of Hiroshima, [I] visited the Test Site to pay respects with many citizens from around the world … the rock pile started in 1991 had grown to eight feet in height. … stone by stone ... this is a gesture of hope [for peace and the end of war]. (Williams 2002)

Looking back at the end of the Cold War and the role of antinuclear protesters, some involved have asserted that the Nevada Desert Experience and its vigils at the Nevada Test Site were critical in expanding the antinuclear testing movement, creating a social climate that allowed society to accept the nuclear testing moratorium in 1992 (Butigan 2003).

CONCLUSION

The Nevada Test Site is significant in the history of the Cold War as a testing ground for nuclear weapons, and the world's nuclear testing locations were the only places nuclear weapons were used during the Cold War. The Peace Camp was created in response to the existence of the Test Site. In opposing the work at the Nevada Test Site, the camp is interrelated and directly connected to the facility. The material remains at the Peace Camp tell the story of those who objected to government policy and the world political situation. Together, the Nevada Test Site and the Peace Camp represent a duality of Cold War views.

In recent times and primarily because of the 1992 nuclear testing moratorium, the frequency of protests and the number of protesters have declined. This somewhat subdued turnout may be viewed as a reflection of the social and political milieu of the times. For instance, according to the *Bulletin of the Atomic Scientists*, the Doomsday Clock is currently set to seven minutes before midnight, a number that is not of great concern and near average since the inception of the clock in 1947. The furthest time from midnight occurred during the 1990s when there was a significant reduction in the stockpiles of nuclear weapons for both the United States and the former Soviet Union with the minutes ranging between nine and 17. During the previous decade in the 1980s, however, the minutes were much closer to midnight, varying from three to six. The 1980s was a time when there was an increase in nuclear weapons due to an accelerated arms race between the two superpowers. Perhaps in response, it was also during the 1980s when the protests at the Peace Camp were the most frequent and intense. From 1986 to 1994, over 500 demonstrations took place involving more than 37,000 participants, 15,740 of whom were arrested. In 1988 it was estimated that 8,800 participants were involved in a single protest event, with 2,067 arrested. Although the number of participants has dwindled since the 1992 moratorium on nuclear weapons testing, some continue to come and regularly protest at the Test Site with larger groups participating in annual demonstrations, such as those at Easter time and on Mothers Day weekend.

The archaeology of the Peace Camp is an opportunity to understand the material remains of a 20th-century minority political movement. The antinuclear activists want to be rid of all nuclear weapons to gain world peace and harmony, end pollution of the earth, and honor all living things including Mother Earth; while the Test Site, as representative of the government, seeks to gain stability and peace, albeit an uneasy one, through the strength of the nuclear weapon. Each side has its monuments and symbols. The ones at the Peace Camp are made mostly of stone, are relatively small and simple, and individualistic. On the Test

Site are various industrial complexes scattered across the facility, built of concrete and metal. Remnants of past nuclear tests dot the landscape, with a few towers, remaining as symbols of testing.

The Peace Camp was and continues to be active concurrently with the government power structure that is the focus of the dissent. Instead of engaging in acts of destruction to express their desires, the people at the Peace Camp have put their efforts into creating symbols in the desert as testimony to their intent and hopes, establishing their own separate, permanent cultural legacy.

ACKNOWLEDGMENTS

The authors would like to thank Wayne Cocroft for assisting us with the field work; Corbin Harney, the Western Shoshone spiritual leader, for his time and knowledge; the protesters from the Peace Camp who shared their views with us; and the Las Vegas Office of the U.S. Bureau of Land Management who worked with us on the permitting policy for access to the Peace Camp. Financial support for this project was provided by the Desert Research Institute. All photos in this chapter are by the authors.

REFERENCES

Angelo, JA Jr and Buden D (1985) *Space Nuclear Power*, Malabar, Florida: Orbit Book Company, Inc.

Baker, D (1996) *Spaceflight and Rocketry: A Chronology*, New York: Facts On File, Inc.

Beck, CM (2002) 'The archaeology of scientific experiments at a nuclear testing ground', *Matériel Culture: The Archaeology of Twentieth Century Conflict*, edited by Schofield J, Johnson WG and Beck CM, 65–79, London: Routledge

Beck, CM and Green HL, editors (2004) *Al O'Donnell: Oral History*, Las Vegas, Nevada: Desert Research Institute

Butigan, K (2003) *Pilgrimage through a Burning World: Spiritual Practice and Nonviolent Protest at the Nevada Test Site*, Albany: State University of New York Press

Cocroft, WD (2003) *Atomic Weapons Research Establishment, Foulness, Essex*. Archaeological Investigation Report Series AI/21/2004, Cambridge: English Heritage

Cohen-Joppa, J and Cohen-Joppa, F (1990) *Nuclear Resister*, January 19 (www.uq.net.au/%7Ezzdkeena/NvT/16/16.9.txt)

Halle, LJ (1967) *The Cold War as History*, New York: Harper and Row

Johnson, WG (2002) 'Archaeological examination of Cold War architecture: A reactionary cultural response to the threat of nuclear war', *Matériel Culture: The Archaeology of Twentieth Century Conflict*, edited by Schofield J, Johnson WG and Beck CM, 227–235, London: Routledge

Kruckewitt, J (2001) *The Death of Ben Linder: The Story of a North American in Sandinista Nicaragua*, New York: Seven Stories Press

Loeber, CR (2002) *Building the Bombs: A History of the Nuclear Weapons Complex*, Albuquerque, New Mexico: Sandia National Laboratories

Marceau, TE, Harvey, DW, Stapp, DC, Cannon, SD, Conway, CA, Deford, DH, Freer, BJ, Gerber, MS, Keating, JK, Noonan, CF, and Weisskopf, G (2003) *Hanford Site Historic District History of the Plutonium Production Facilities 1943–1990*, Columbus, Ohio: Batelle Press

Peach, P and O'Brien, M (2000) 'Nevada Test Site peacemakers ring in new millennium', *Salt Online*, www.bvmcong.org/salt/salt/spring2000/peachobrien.htm (last accessed September 10, 2002)

Schofield, J and Anderton, M (2000) 'The queer archaeology of Green Gate: interpreting contested space at Greenham Common Airbase', *World Archaeology* 32(2): 236–51

Vanderbilt, T (2002) *Survival City: Adventures among the Ruins of Atomic America*, New York: Princeton Architectural Press

Whorton, M (2002) 'Evaluating and managing Cold War era historic properties: The cultural significance of US Air Force defensive radar systems', *Matériel Culture: The Archaeology of Twentieth Century Conflict*, edited by Schofield, J , Johnson, WG and Beck, CM, 216–226, London: Routledge

Williams, TT (1990) 'The clan of one-breasted women', *Northern Lights* 6(1): 9–11

Williams, TT (2002) 'A Rock of Resistance', at www.arockofresistance.org (last accessed 23 September 2002)

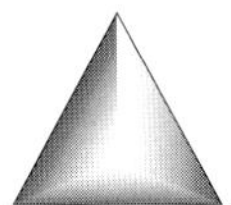

Index

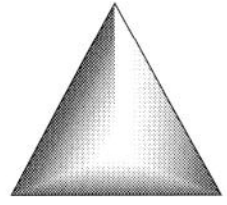

About the Contributors

Olwen Beazley is a PhD researcher at the Australian National University, Centre for Cross Cultural Research. Her research considers the history of ideas in relation to intangible cultural heritage values, and how these values have been included on UNESCO's World Heritage List since 1978. Before moving to Australia, Olwen worked for a number of years as field archaeologist and heritage manager in the United Kingdom. She currently works for the Australian Commonwealth Department of the Environment and Heritage.

Colleen M Beck is a research professor at the University of Nevada's Desert Research Institute. Since 1991, she has been involved in research related to Cold War archaeology, in particular the nuclear testing remains at the Nevada Test Site and the protesters' legacy at the Nevada Peace Camp. She is interested in the ways these types of remains embody the perceptions and views of their makers. She also works with the Western Shoshone, documenting their traditional cultural properties, and regularly conducts prehistoric and historic archaeological projects in the southern Great Basin.

Angus Boulton began investigating the European legacy of the Soviet Military at the end of the 1990s. The DG Bank Kunststipendium of 1998/99, and subsequent residency in Berlin, allowed an initial opportunity to turn his attention towards this aspect of the Cold War. The films and photographic series arising from this and earlier projects have been exhibited internationally. He is currently an AHRC research fellow at Manchester Metropolitan University, attached to the Location, Memory and Visual Research Group.

Victor Buchli is Reader in Material Culture at the Department of Anthropology, University College London. His previous books have been *An Archaeology of Socialism* (Berg 1999) and, with Gavin Lucas, *Archaeologies of the Contemporary Past* (Routledge 2001). He has edited *The Material Culture Reader* (Berg 2002) and *Material Culture: Critical Concepts* (Routledge 2004). He is also a founding editor of the interdisciplinary journal of the domestic sphere *Home Cultures*.

Wayne Cocroft is a senior archaeological investigator with English Heritage, and since the early 1990s has been involved in research into the archaeological legacy of modern defence sites. Recent publications include *Dangerous Energy: The Archaeology of Gunpowder and Military Explosives Manufacture* (2000) and *Cold War Building for Nuclear Confrontation 1946–1989* (2003) with Roger Thomas.

Harold Drollinger is a research archaeologist at the Desert Research Institute in Las Vegas, Nevada. He has over 25 years experience on prehistoric and historic sites in the Midwest, Southwest, and southern Great Basin regions of the United States. Currently his work includes Peace Camp outside the Nevada Test Site, and research on spatial analyses and religious and symbolic expressions in archaeological and natural landscapes.

Graham Fairclough, an archaeologist, has worked with several periods of archaeology but mainly in historic periods and mainly in the applied field of resource management. He has written and published on archaeological resource management, notably with regard to sustainability, landscape, perception and the interplay of significance and context. He works in the UK but also with European networks as well. He has been a detached observer at the edge of the growth of Cold War studies in archaeology, as he was a detached observer during the Cold War itself, and at the edge of Greenham.

Polly Feversham lives in Helmsley, North Yorkshire. She studied history of art and philosophy in Paris and London, and took a postgraduate degree in conservation at York University. She has extensive practical experience in restoration and site management, particularly of country houses. In 1999 she published a book entitled *The Berlin Wall Today* jointly with Leo Schmidt.

Veronica Fiorato currently works for English Heritage. She has a particular interest in military archaeology, principally battlefield and 20th-century archaeology. She is involved with the Common Ground research project examining the archaeology of the former women's peace camps at Greenham. Publications include *Blood Red Roses: The Archaeology of a Mass Grave from the Battle of Towton AD 1461*.

Alice Gorman is a lecturer in archaeology at Flinders University, Adelaide, and a consultant on Indigenous and European heritage management. Her main research interest is the cultural heritage of space exploration, with a focus on satellites and terrestrial launch facilities. She is also Co-Chair of the World Archaeological Congress' Space Heritage Task Force.

Since 1998 **Barton C Hacker** has worked in the Smithsonian's Museum of American History, contributing to major exhibits on Cold War submarines and West Point's role in American military development. He has also continued to write history of technology and military history, especially 20th-century military technology, women's military history, and comparative history of military institutions. His and Margaret Vining's narrative history of American military technology appeared in 2006, and their edited collection of articles on military interactions with American science and technology is in press. He was the 2003 recipient of the Leonardo da Vinci medal for lifetime achievement from the Society for the History of Technology.

Yannis Kyriakides was born in Cyprus in 1969, emigrated to England in 1975, and has been living in The Netherlands since 1992. His musical language synthesises disparate sound sources and explores spatial and temporal experience. Recent large-scale works include an electronic opera on Spinoza *The Thing Like Us*; a music-text-video piece *Subliminal: the Lucretian Picnic*; a BBC commission *Lab Fly Dreams* for Big Noise; and a new opera for FNM der Staatsoper Stuttgart, *Escamotage*. Prizes have included the Gaudeamus Composition Prize (2000) and an Honorary Mention in the Prix Ars Electronica (2006). He is artistic director of Ensemble MAE and the electronic music label Unsounds, and teaches composition at the Royal Conservatoire in Den Haag.

Beth O'Leary is Assistant College Professor in Anthropology at New Mexico State University in Las Cruces, NM, USA. Along with two graduate students, she received a grant from the New Mexico Space Grant Consortium (through NASA) to investigate the archaeological site of Tranquility Base created by the *Apollo 11* astronauts on the moon. Her research interests are in US and international cultural resource management laws and their application to space sites, objects, features and structures. She recently co-chaired two international symposia on Space Heritage.

Leo Schmidt is an architectural historian and professor of conservation at Brandenburg University of Technology in Cottbus, Germany. He is the author of a book on the cultural significance of the Berlin Wall, written jointly with Polly Feversham in 1999, and of a detailed documentation of the Wall's extant remains, published jointly with Axel Klausmeier in 2004. He has just published the proceedings of a symposium on the conservation of sites of the Cold War era held in Potsdam in 2004.

John Schofield works for English Heritage, coordinating research programmes on military heritage. He also teaches heritage management at the University of Southampton. John's current research interests include work at the Nevada and Greenham Common Cold War peace camps, and amongst the abandoned bars and clubs of Valletta (Malta). Recent publications include *Modern Military Matters* (2004) and *Combat Archaeology: Material Culture and Modern Conflict* (2005).

Anita Smith, until recently a lecturer in the Cultural Heritage Centre for Asia and the Pacific at Deakin University, Australia, now works for Heritage Victoria. Her principal research interest is in Pacific Island cultural landscapes and heritage management. She is currently working in association with UNESCO in training Pacific Island heritage managers and with the Fijian government on their World Heritage nomination for the colonial capital of Levuka.

Reinhild Steingröver is Associate Professor of German at the Eastman School of Music, University of Rochester, where she teaches German and Film Studies. She is the author of a book on the Austrian writer Thomas Bernhard (Peter Lang, 2000) and co-editor with Patricia Mazon of an anthology on Afro-German history and culture (University of Rochester Press, 2005). She has published articles on German women's theatre, contemporary German women writers, Glenn Gould and East German cinema. She is currently writing a book on the last generation of East German filmmakers and co-editing with Randall Halle an anthology on contemporary German experimental film (Camden House, 2007)

Margaret Vining works at the Smithsonian Institution's National Museum of American History specializing in U.S. military and diplomatic history. She determines collecting priorities, curates exhibitions and researches and writes about the material culture of the armed forces. She has a special interest in the history of women in military institutions, the subject of a book in progress. She currently serves as Secretary General of the United States Commission on Military History.

Frank Watson is a practicing artist based in London. He is also a lecturer in photography at Westminster University and Croydon College of Art. In 2002 he curated the show 'Living in This Mess'. In 2004 he published a book of photographs, *The Hush House: Cold War Sites in England*. He is currently researching the relationship between photography, architecture and utopias.

Louise K Wilson is a visual artist who has exhibited widely in Europe and North America, most recently in International Film Festival Rotterdam (2006), A Record of Fear on Orford Ness (2005), Artists Airshow at RAE Farnborough (2004) and Arena at the Baltic, Gateshead (2003). Her work explores perceptual and social aspects of science and technology and frequently involves the participation of individuals from industry, museums and scientific research. She is a doctoral student at the University of Derby.